PRIESTLESS

PRIESTESS

Woman as Sacred Celebrant

PAMELA   EAKINS, PH.D.

SAMUEL WEISER, INC.

York Beach, Maine

First published in 1996 by
Samuel Weiser, Inc.
P.O. Box 612
York Beach, ME 03910-0612

Library of Congress Cataloging-in-Publication Data

Eakins, Pamela.
    Priestess : woman as sacred celebrant / Pamela Eakins.
      p.   cm.
    ISBN 0-87728-890-9 (alk. paper)
      1. Women—Religious life.   2. Spirituality.   3. Women priests.
4. Eakins, Pamela.   I. Title.
BL625.7.E35   1996
291.6'1'082–dc20   96-8716
                                         CIP

MV

Typeset in 10 point Book Antiqua

Printed in the United States of America

04   03   02   01   00   99   98   97   96
10 9   8   7   6   5   4   3   2   1

Thank you, Peter, for attending the Ordination, and for your invaluable support during the course of this writing. You are a dear man and I know we shall meet again and again across the boundaries of space and time.

ABOUT THE COVER

The cover art is the High Priestess from *The Tarot of the Spirit* painted by Joyce Eakins. The High Priestess is one of the seventy-eight traditional cards contained in a tarot deck. All classical tarot decks contain the High Priestess card although it sometimes goes by a different name. The High Priestess represents a personality type, a role in society and/or a state of consciousness.

As a traditional figure, the High Priestess of the tarot is said to integrate all knowledge of light and dark forces. She realizes that every experience contains a message for growth. "Listen" they say, "and you may hear the High Priestess whisper." She guides you in realms of secret knowledge, realms of hidden mystery, the exploration of the soul. She represents the power of remembrance, the memory of all that has been, all that is and all that ever shall be. "The power of remembrance," they say, "we hold inside ourselves." This is because the High Priestess is an aspect of our own consciousness.

When the High Priestess appears in a tarot reading, the reader lowers her voice and says, "The gift of insight is now at hand. Attune to your intuition, go deep within yourself to find the answer because you *know. . .*"

&

The High Priestess of the tarot is one of antiquity's great teachers. To learn more about her, please refer to *The Tarot of the Spirit* written by Pamela Eakins, Ph.D., painted by Joyce Eakins, M.F.A., and published by Samuel Weiser, Inc.

TABLE OF CONTENTS

Dear Reader,

This is a story of a woman's journey through time. It tells what happens during different eras as she attempts, life after life, to find and celebrate sacred spirit.

As I began the meditation I discuss throughout the book, a question which I had been asked to write about was churning in the back of my mind: *What was the single most important event in the early Christian Church that removed the goddess-oriented religious base and replaced the goddess-orientation with a father-orientation? I* had no idea how deep this question would take me.

The problem and the *magic* was not only that I could not answer the question succinctly—in a simple essay, for example—but that I found my own soul moving inside of the question. The *quest* is a "journey"; *-ion* means to "enter into." To ask a question implies that your mind will begin to travel. The more you ask, the farther you go.

I *became* the question, I *lived* the question, and one mystery led to another until the question itself began to change form. My imagination was activated, the massive bronze doors of past and future swung open and I stepped through. As a result of this process, the subject evolved from the history of women under Christianity to the freedom of *consciousness* itself. I began to wonder: *Are we bound by matter, time and space as we have been taught to believe, or are we limited merely by our own perceptions?*

With this new question in mind, I submit to you this work of autobiographical fiction which emerged from the deep field of imagination juxtaposed with actual historically-documented events. All events from the 20th century occurred exactly as I have reported them.

Now I invite you to journey with me. As together we slip through the doors of perception, perhaps you will notice, as have I, that young women and men are reaching toward us from the future. They are wide-eyed, confused, innocent, searching, skeptical and curious. They are looking for direction. They are seeking inspiration.

These are the grandchildren of the world yet to come.

It is to you, my great-great-grandchildren, I dedicate this book. I hear you calling and I am with you. I cross the mystery of death and birth to hold you in my loving embrace. Fear not, dear child, daily we learn that *every single thing is possible.*

Lovingly,

the Author

PART I

THE MOSQUE

THE MOSQUE

California, Late 20th Century.

This is the truth about what happened:

Cross-legged and barefoot, I sat in the mosque. I sat there with the Sufi master, highest of high, swaying in prayer. He with white turban, morocco-brown tunic and pants, gray beard, long and cascading like a scraggly waterfall down his chest, bare feet, chanting and breathing: "Aaaah-laaah...Aaaah-laaah...Aaaah-laaah," as if he had chanted this name from the moment of his birth. Facing each other, in mirrored image, cross-legged, eyes closed, chanting, chanting, praying, breath in and breath out.

Me, black blouse, long black skirt, feet which had borne street shoes within the last hour, white and gold hair falling loosely on my shoulders, cross-legged, swaying, swaying, chanting with the master. Floating on the ancient reds and blues of hand-woven rugs. Floating on a sea of magic carpets. We chanted and swayed, swayed and chanted, swayed and chanted in the dim, inner light in that inner sanctum with no windows.

Incense wafted lightly, setting off an altered state of consciousness, which, for me, was enhanced by the vision of the prostrate devotee, lying flat on his stomach, face to the ground on the master's right, my left.

The master chanted and swayed—"Allah, Allah, Allah"— and the word seemed to emanate from the depths of his soul. My eyes flicked open involuntarily. I was, in that mystical moment, so attuned through the pulsation of the rhythmic sound that I could discern every open pore of the sheikh's sallow cheeks, every differentiated hair in every shade of gray and white that poured from his chin down that undulating chest rising and falling with the taught softness of his effort.

His brown hands rested lightly on their sides upon his knees. I can see those hands now as clearly as I saw them then. Callused hands, brown hands that had worked fields, gripped the handles of wooden barrows, traded goods and coins in the market, dug in the dirt. Fingers relaxed but bent inward, telling a tale of seasoned usage.

"Allah. Allah. Allah." He chanted, and his soft and powerful practiced voice drifted through the mosque, resonating outward to the six directions, emanating upward to cathedral ceilings, dissipating in the corners like tendrils of smoke from a sacred fire.

I chanted with him, just he and I, chanting and chanting, chanting beyond boredom, until I felt the pores of my skin open and tingle, open and spark over every inch of my body—my fingers, my toes. Chanting and chanting until I opened my consciousness so wide that I became all emptiness. I became like a great chasm.

My body became like a great and black abyss. I became like a dark and open cave, a deep, black tunnel. The I of me disappeared and what remained was empty blackness spiralling infinitely into the earth, or the past, or the future, or another dimension. I spiralled in, in, in, past etchings in the deepest recesses, glyphs and symbols carved in ancient caverns, chipped out by spirits come and gone and yet to come.

Far, far away, as remote as the elusive past, as inaccessible as the ungraspable future, as endless as infinite planes of awareness, a figure stood, statuesque, in the circular portal at the end of the tunnel. It stood framed in the opening, silhouetted in blindingly radiant light. It stood there like an apparition in exile, beckoning me, calling me, moaning to me to follow or to lead. I was not sure which.

I discerned this being and, at once, I was back in my body and my whole self began to tingle and shake, pulsing endlessly with electric energy. Then—and this was unmistakable—I felt a presence enter my body. It was as if I recognized a feeling, opened a door onto a memory that sailed endlessly through time and space. This presence filled me. . .It felt like the undying presence of She Who Was Before Time Began. I felt like the Soul of the World had entered my form. . .The Soul of All entered my form and in my heart of hearts, I recognized the awesome and auspicious power of the moment.

I felt her enter my body through a central core of emptiness, then expand and expand, expanding until she filled my hips, my breasts, the base of my spine, my thighs, biceps and triceps, elbows, the back of my calves, forearms, wrists, hands, feet, fingers, toes, neck, cheeks, scalp, eyes. And I called out inwardly, "Guide me, Mother," for I felt this sacred Soul was like a mother or a long, lost, older sister, and she answered clearly, saying distinctly, "Call my name. Call my name."

And then she filled my vocal cords, mouth, teeth, tongue, with a sound that rose from the middle of the beginning of being. The sound rose, quiet at first, then louder and louder, emanating from my very depths, in and out with the tides of my lungs: "Maaah Maaah. . .Aaaah Maaah."

The master called "Aaaah laaah. . .Aaaah laaah. . ." The voice in me called "Aaaah Maaah. . .Maaah Maaah. . . ."

We floated above that ancient geometry of the abstracted tree of life, the beginning of existence, the point at which all things start, and we chanted and chanted, calling into the void and through ourselves the sacred name of the holy of holies.

I drifted into a great state of peace. Tranquil. Serene. Complete. Fulfilled. I felt an immense compassion flood my being—a deep love of all big and little, vast and miniscule—and I saw the web of all life interconnect and encompass all that is in a shining exuberance. I bore witness in that sacred space to the rarefied essence of pure and endless joy.

Glimmering threads of insight began to interweave within me. Empty spaces began to fill.

My heart thrilled! My soul delighted!

The tapestry of life began to unfurl within and outside me as if the warp and woof of creation stretched and quivered all through my physical form. My spirit, mind and body became like a thriving fabric quivering with the vibrant consciousness of universal life.

Imagine, if your mind allows, how, in that pure and radiant moment as I chanted with the master, electronic circuits seemed to form and interlace. Then, in radiating gold and silver, a voltaic charge began, weak at first, then infinitely stronger, until each and every filament of force and form, within and without, glittered with indescribable potency. The sacred life revealed itself like a dancing message board containing the codified structure of all that is. Patterns shimmered and danced, waking energies long ignored. Tendrils of energetic force raced to awaken muscles, bones, ideas and memories long neglected, given up for dead.

What a feeling of delight, terror and mysterious portent poured through my form as I began to chant the feminine name of god! Oh, holy, holy, holy. I cannot tell you how that felt. I wanted to laugh. I wanted to sob. I knew she was inside me! I knew that all life is divine! I felt my own divinity! I felt as if I had touched the sacred hem, heard with joy and fortitude the sacred admonition:

You must be willing to walk your own path.

Instantly, I awoke to mysteries long untold. Through the eye of my open mind, I witnessed initiations of old, was catapulted into ancient mystic rites. I transmigrated into scenes of rituals, sacraments, purifications, interments, weddings, funerals, and baptisms. In a matter of seconds, stories, like moving pictures with acts and scenes, sets and dialogues, began to reveal themselves in scores.

I saw all this in a matter of moments. Sacred time, they say, moves apart from ordinary time. I reached out in that sacred moment clipped from time, reached down and gently touched the sedimentary layers of the thin crust of earth beneath me.

Suddenly, and without warning, my ascended partner, as if in mid-sentence, stopped chanting. My eyes were closed; my belly, breasts, throat, and heart continued to throb with the Mother's essence, although I sensed his eyes had flashed open and that he now eyed me with suspicion.

I finished the phrase and dropped the song, opening my eyes to meet his gaze. His little ripe blackberry pupils sparked and glinted from their narrowed slits wrinkled with time's etching and the power of the sun.

I said nothing; met his eyes with serenity.

I opened my eyes wide so he could see, donned a childlike mask of innocence, yet I felt I could not quite hide the play and laughter that must be leaping from my own little blueberry orbs. I both knew and knew not what I was doing. Suddenly I started. What if he thought I was the devil? The devil in the shape of a woman?

The shift in his posture was barely apparent: the soles of his feet turned upward, exposing them to more air and light.

Quietly and with reverence, he said to me, "Allah is the first word out of a child's mouth." He said, "Allah is the very breath of life. With every breath in this life, we breathe in and out *Aaaah-laaah. Aaaah-laaah.*"

He stopped.

I waited for him to continue, but he said nothing. The silence extended infinitely and became uncomfortable.

Very quietly and with reverence, I whispered, "Maamaaa. Maaamaaa. The baby speaks Mama. I am a mother. I have seen this."

The devotee was alarmed. He pushed himself up into a seated position and said, "Master, this is a highly educated American woman, a doctor. She has something important to say."

Had those four eyes not been so intent upon me at that very moment, I might have pinched myself to make sure I was not dreaming, but then I was dreaming, was I not? Dreaming the dream of life on earth. How very strange. How very unpredictable and magnificent. Poetic. Synchronistic. It seemed funny, too. I wanted to laugh.

Clearly, keenly intelligent and sensitive, imagining I was making some kind of statement about women or the position of women, in his heavily accented English the master said, "Muhammed was the last prophet. He brought equal opportunity for women. Before Muhammed," he said, "women could not inherit property. They were bought and sold, possessed and raped as men desired. They could not walk in the country. They were not educated. They were for man's use, no more than animals. Under Islam," he said, "a man must fully support his wives. He cannot take a wife unless he can support her fully. And she must consent before there is marriage. It takes a long time for change," he said, "but Muhammed said over time women will achieve full equality. That time is coming."

I sat very straight, my back and head aligned. Looking deeply into his eyes, I said, "Yes, Muhammed was the last prophet and what he did was very great, very great. Moses also. And Jesus. Moses was brought out of the water into freedom and received the message from the burning bush. Yes, he was great. 'Son, Son,' called the bush, 'the place you are standing is sacred ground. Take the suffering sons of Israel out of Egypt and build for them a holy nation.' Moses was great. His eyes never dimmed, nor his vision abated. Then came Jesus, the Son of God. Christ. The Sun. He conveyed illumination through his words, his hands, his image. He called to his people, 'Heal the sick, raise the dead, cleanse lepers, cast out demons. Freely you received, freely give. . .The kingdom of light,' he said, 'is like a mustard seed, smaller than all other seeds, but when it is grown, it is larger than all the plants of the garden, so big that the birds of the air nest in its branches. . .Love, my sons. . . And you will be sons of the Most High.' He rose from the dead, then; and he, too, was very great.

"Then came Muhammed, the 'Highly Praised.' The angels of God, they say, opened his heart, opened it up and poured in light. 'Cry out,' the Lord called to him on the famous Night of Power and Excellence. 'What shall I cry?' Muhammed called. And the Lord called to his son, 'Cry—Cry in the name of thy Lord! Cry! Thy Lord is wondrous kind!' And the Lord sent to Muhammed rules for the details of daily living and charged the prophet to bring his message to the people through the Koran.

"Yes," I said, "God is revealed through the prophets. Abraham. Moses. Jesus and Muhammed. Through Abraham, the truth of monotheism. Through Moses, the Ten Commandments. Through Jesus, the Golden Rule. Through Muhammed, the holy gift of administration.

"Yes, Muhammed," I said, "was the last prophet and he was great, very great. . ." And here I felt my hands move into prayer position in front of my heart, my body leaned dramatically forward, my eyes closed. I sat there in my black dress with bare feet, carrying a volume of women's erotica which I shall later explain, and I began to whisper:

"There is a new prophet coming and through her, man and woman will rise up as one. Muhammed was the last prophet, but there is a new prophet coming. And she is a *woman*. . ."

A sidelong glance was exchanged between the master and the devotee. I knew I had spoken blasphemy. I was amused at their horrified expressions and also at the fact that I saw they heard me and were taking me seriously. I was also afraid all of a sudden for reasons I could not explain. I was sorry I had given the devotee my business card. At this moment, I would have greatly preferred to remain anonymous.

Who was I to sit there chanting and swaying with this master of masters from across the ocean anyway?

How I came to be there and how deeply they listened to me was something that left me nothing short of dumbfounded.

I was having my car serviced at a dealership in the San Francisco Bay area near where I live. I was just waiting, when I remembered that there was a bookstore on the corner and that one of my students had just published a couple of chapters under a penname in a book of erotic stories by women. These were the first two stories she had ever written and all of a sudden this book—and more particularly her work—was being acclaimed in the book review section of the *New York Times*. Amazing.

I bought the book at the corner bookstore:

"Bag?"

"No thanks."

I was walking down College Avenue looking at this book reading an occasional passage—". . .What does an orgasm look like? Like fish shooting out in all different directions from a pebble dropped in their pond. . ."—and pretty soon I was wishing I had asked for a sack. Brown paper.

I had no coat, no purse, no car, no place at all to hide this explosive volume.

I tucked the book under my arm and strolled. Halfway up the block, I came upon a movie theater where years earlier I had seen a film about Mahatma Gandhi. I leaned in the open doorway—*isn't this how it always happens?*—and saw that the seats were gone. There was no popcorn, no soda, only a huge, empty theater filled with piles and piles and piles of gorgeous Persian rugs.

"May I help you?"

"Oh, no thanks, I was just remembering when this was a movie theater."

"Oh?" The man was genial and smiled at me. "What did you see here?"

"Gandhi."

"Oh? Where did you sit?"

"Well," I said, laughing, both of us making a joke out of his line of questioning since the movie theater had obviously been gone a long time, "I always sat in the middle of the middle."

"Feel free to go back and sit there. Sit in your usual spot. Sit on the rugs. Please. Sit on the rugs. Please. Sit."

I walked down toward the front of the theater. He followed me. Right about the middle of the middle, I had a strange feeling.

"You know," I said to him, "this doesn't feel like a *movie* theater... It feels like a *sacred place*."

He narrowed his eyes and beckoned, saying, "Come with me."

I do not need to tell you that this man turned out to be the devotee, that we took off our shoes and went upstairs, that we were really in a mosque, that he laid a feast of tea and rice and vegetables before me, that we shared this bounty with a man who had just escaped from Bosnia and another who had fled out of Egypt, that we discussed Islam and the position of women in Islamic countries, that I gave him my business card, that it turned out that the master of masters had just arrived from far-off lands, that the devotee learned I was a doctor, that I was just about to be ordained as a minister, that I said a new prophet was coming and she was a woman, that the men raised their eyebrows, that the devotee took me to the master, that he prostrated himself upon the floor, that he entreated the master to listen to me, that the master and I chanted, and that all the time the book with the naked woman on the cover was sitting at my side on top of the antique red handwoven carpet.

CHAPTER 2

THE TEACHER

Two Weeks Later.

To all events there is a sacred interior.

On the surface, events move within the confines of time and space in an ongoing context of circumstances, one event leading into the other, each in its proper time and sequence, each in alignment with what has been and what is to come.

On a deeper level, events happen out of time, out of place. Events are parallel and synchronous. Events happen as endless metaphors for layers and layers and layers of knowing.

The event in the mosque, which happened only a month prior to my ordination, was a metaphor that stretched itself deeper and deeper and deeper within me until it touched the deepest folds of my being, until it reached my soul and burst out on the other side with wakened tendrils racing toward the deepest codes of sacred knowledge.

I telephoned my teacher on the East Coast, the archbishop of the church in which I had studied for four years—interfaith, nondenominational and international—and was scheduled to be ordained at Summer Solstice, and I told her what had happened: how I wound up in the mosque, how strange it felt, how timeless, how mythical.

I asked her if she had any mystical interpretations as to what the experience was all about.

She said, "Why, Pamela Dear. It is entirely clear. You have walked this Earth for many lifetimes. Do you remember Atlantis? Do you mind my saying this? I know it may sound strange to you. I don't know if you want to hear it."

She laughed.

"Oh, no, please tell," I responded. I was skeptical, but definitely curious.She said, "You were a teacher in the Temple of Wisdom. Do you remember? You were paid by the State at Poseidenus to teach philosophy, mathematics, and ethics. Atlantis had a technological legacy of thousands of years. You were bridging the gap between the technical and the spiritual. You are doing that today, bridging technology and spirit."

Inwardly, I smiled at the irony. The archbishop did not know that I have frequently lectured on the subject of ethics in Western medicine.

"Do you remember your students?" she asked. "They were all ages. Anyone could come to your classes as long as they could understand the subject matter and were motivated. Even children could come, but you refused to talk down to them. They had to be capable of following the information as you presented it."

Then her story became even more outlandish. The archbishop said, "Before you came to the planet Earth, you were already adept at teaching and healing—do you remember?—but there came a time when the people on those planets became so advanced in healing themselves they no longer needed your skills. You thought, what's the use of staying here just to set a broken leg every now and then. You chose to come to Earth, the most difficult of all the planets, where you believed you could serve. You wanted to serve.

"Yes, my dear, you came and offered your heart, but in so many lifetimes your heart has been thwarted. You wanted to give, but so many times, your desire to serve has been thrown back in your face. Do you recognize that feeling?"

I had to admit I did.

"Also, Pamela, there were many times you desired spiritual initiation and something went wrong. Usually because you were female. As a woman, you certainly had your go-arounds with the Roman Catholic Church!"

The archbishop laughed.

"You have had many, many incarnations on Earth and beyond, and in each you have learned something about service and something about the path of your soul.

"The focus of your soul, Pamela Dear, is freedom.

"In this century you have rebelled in order to know freedom. You have pushed away from authority, from institutions that would control your thoughts and your destiny, from patriarchal gods. You have pushed away from authority just as you did in the mosque.

"The focus of your soul is freedom. This planet is not a giver of that concept. So you have rebelled."

The archbishop was right about that. My nature is entirely rebellious and always has been. I have never been able to respond well to anyone's orders. Perhaps that is conditioned by my family history: My father left the Church in a strong Irish Catholic family. My mother's family, who settled Utah with Brigham Young, walked away from the Mormons.

My teacher said, "Now, my dear, you will remember everything. You will gather together your ancient family and they will surround you and teach you. All memories will awaken.

"At your ordination," she continued, "you will receive the spark. I will lay my hands on your head. My teacher on the astral plane will lay hands on my head and his teacher will be there doing the same thing, and on and on and on, and back and back and back, until the spark is flowing through all the hands from the source of all being. Your teachers on the astral plane will bear witness to this event. The cosmic fire will be transferred to you and it is up to you, my dear, to receive it and to direct it into all areas of your life.

"It is now time to remember the lessons you have learned through the course of your incarnations. For now, meditate. Call into yourself the highest, most loving and instructive powers in the universe, and the path of your soul will be revealed. You will soon know why you said, *There is a new prophet coming. And she is a woman.* Then, at Summer Solstice, let the wings of angels fly you across the country to our humble ceremony where the spark of your ministry will be ignited."

CHAPTER 3

THE MEDITATION

The Next Day.

O n the cliffs over the Pacific Ocean, glittering in the sun like a moving field of diamonds, I sat in silence—without judgment—contemplating the path of my soul.

Day after day as I prepared for ordination, I fasted, waited and thought. I blocked external stimulation—turned off the television and radio—and taught myself to go into a trance. I taught myself to slow down, to concentrate on the flame of a burning candle.

What sound is heard at the center of fire? What color is seen at the center of flame? I asked myself these questions and contemplated the source of being. I contemplated the meaning of "the spark," the nature of "cosmic fire."

I meditated deeply on the flame of the candle, contemplating the heart of fire, sinking down, down, down in meditation. At first my thoughts came fast and furiously—it was hard to slow down, hard to let go—but after a while, thoughts came further and further apart. It seemed as if each idea, one by one, like moths in darkness, became attracted to the flame. Ideas began to drift into fire, were singed and burned, transformed into smoke, wafted away. One by one, thoughts expired. Ideas became drifting smoke.

My mind opened up and emptied. My heart emptied. My spirit emptied. Gradually, I became cleansed and purified by fire, burned and turned to ashes, emptied of preconceived notions until I began to see that, at the core of everything was nothing at all. Nothing. No thing.

In nothingness exists capacity. Potential requires space to grow.

The deeper I went, the more I awakened.

I felt a surge of spiritual force: like heat, light or electricity. I felt this force begin to expand within me. It was like a small flame that grew and grew and grew into a large fire. It grew like the fire of truth expanding into infinity.

I opened completely to anything that might occur.

I called into my consciousness all the positive, loving and instructive powers of the universe.

It was then, when I was deep in trancelike meditation above the sparkling sea—deep in emptiness, engulfed at the center of flame—my Guide appeared. He appeared before me, not like a man, but more like a vision of love and beauty in the center of the empty diamond field of my open consciousness. He appeared as a shimmering entity I could not quite discern.

It was not as if he were actually standing there, but as if I saw him internally, a moving picture behind my eyes.

I could not make out the setting from which he spoke, but I knew he was speaking to me from a particular place. It felt like a white and gold enclosure, a round temple filled with knowledge. It felt like another dimension or another planet.

He spoke, but his lips did not move. Nor did he speak English, yet I understood everything he said. He spoke to me telepathically and showed me pictures, telling me:

"This is the Time. This is the Place."

He said it was time to awaken, time to remember, time to recall the reason for my existence, the vow I had entered into. He said it was time for me to remember why I had come to Earth; time to awaken to the calling of my mission.

"I am your contact," he said, "your Brother, your twin. I stayed behind when you and the others emanated so all of you would have a contact point. You selected difficult tasks. You are on your own, but we are still here to help and guide you. And now the window is open, the lines of communication are activated."

This experience was very strange to me; completely unlike my usual meditations. I felt this Guide could read my thoughts.

He said, "The reason the memories of your place of origin did not surface earlier in your life, Dear Sister, is because it was critically important for you to live the experience of Earth so that you could understand the Earth World from the inside. Only when you are on the inside can you be effective. You knew this from the beginning. You knew how important it was for you to temporarily forget your source. All of you knew this."

Then he named several of my acquaintances and told me they had emanated in the same wave. He described to me their missions. He showed me moving pictures of each taking his or her vow to serve. He told me about my children, how, even though they were born to me on Earth, they, too, radiated from the same emanation. As did my mother.

Then he showed me a memory of me taking my own vow of service just prior to crossing the River of Forgetfulness on the passage to Earth.

I saw myself vowing solemnly to "Affect the Philosophy and Values of the People."

I witnessed these entities taking their vows. They stood in a circle and spoke telepathically. Clearly they were not male or female at all, but androgynous: tall, thin, hairless and golden. They were not wearing clothing as we know it on Earth.

Then their bodies changed into the bodies of men and women. As they became human, they were dressed in white clothing: cross-cultural, cross-temporal ceremonial vestments that might belong to any period or place in Earth's history.

I became a brown-haired, brown-eyed, dark-skinned woman of indeterminable race or ethnicity. I was wearing a long, white dress. Then I programmed my thoughts to emanate to Earth.

The way we came to Earth was not in a metal spaceship with flashing lights or in any other material contraption. We came through a Channel of Consciousness. This Channel was activated by the power of intention alone.

Many of us left in the same emanation, at the same time, but we arrived on Earth in different time periods and different generations.

Riavek—that seemed to be the Guide's name as closely as I can translate it—said, "I will show you lifetimes that have affected you. You will remember through viewing these lives what you have been and what the world on Earth has been, and then you will remember who you are. You will be able to do what your heart of hearts says is right.

"When you know how you came to be as you are, you will be able to build a firm base of clear knowledge from which to work. You will have clear insight and presence of mind. You will realize what aspects of the Earth World can and cannot be controlled. Your success will be based on your ability to change that which is changeable and to detach from that which cannot be moved. You will attain the power of initiative through knowing what has been. Through understanding what has been, the nature, depth and mutability of what is will be made perfectly clear. When you understand the nature of the present, you will also know the nature of the future. The present results from what has been. The future is born from what is. When you come into the full realization of this, you will be able to fulfill your mission."

Riavek told me that Earth is viewed as one of the most visually entrancing dimensions in the system. The Garden Planet. Small, but full of majesty. Exquisitely sensual. An olfactory feast. Vibrant, verdant. Mysteriously alive. That is partly why I chose to come. I chose to defend the ancient mountains, shifting deserts, rolling plains, tropical and icy seas, skies of the most astonishing pink, lavendar, orange, baby blue, cobalt and turquoise, aurora borealis. Glaciers. Volcanoes. Winds that uproot trees. Creatures with wings and fins, fur. Flowers that unfold by day and night, giving off fragrances that entice the heart to love. A planet of dualities elsewhere unknown. Hundreds of nations with plans, hopes, and dreams. The quintessential experiment.

He said throughout the system, all beings realize that the Earth World's existence is threatened. That anger, greed, recklessness, technological excess, and production-oriented intervention in natural processes threaten to destroy the sphere. Technical intervention and war. The battle for resources. Values clashing values. That is why critical philosophical reflection is so important at this time.

"Now you," Riavek said, "like the Sisters and Brothers with whom you left here, must awaken. One by one, stationed all over the Earth, you will remember your origins and begin to pursue your missions.

"Your mission is to affect the philosophy and values of the Earth World, Dear Sister. You chose this mission yourself, of your own free will.

"Do not focus on the outcome of this work, but attend to the process of creation.

"Be with the process. Enact the drama of your current life as if it matters.

"Seek peace, balance, and considered action.

"Begin to rise to the task before you by observing the lives you have lived, which I will begin to reflect back to you in your next meditation. Observe these lives with detachment. Learn from them, then let any negative effects they have created within you leave your Earthly body. In this way, you will attain wisdom and be freed from the constraints of the past. You will gain the wisdom and understanding of nearly six thousand years of Earth's history. You will begin to understand aspects of the formation of Earth's thought patterns.

"When you begin to understand these ideas, you will begin to understand the nature of the soul of life.

"Tomorrow we begin."

As I sat in meditation—the candle still aflame—my soul screamed with the agony and the ecstasy of whole-body recognition. Then, in one passing heartbeat, my whole self flooded with possibility. The old adage came to me:

Knowledge is power.

I was incredibly excited.

Suddenly, the phone rang and my feeling of expansive consciousness disappeared.

Remaining somewhat in a dreamlike state, I stood up and shook my head, wondering at the appearance of the Guide who seemed to disappear as suddenly as he had appeared. I put out the candle. I did not answer the phone.

❧

I called my big white Labrador retriever to go out for a walk.

Skipper bounded over the high bluffs, leaping through the blooming yellow lupin and sage, chasing rabbits deep into the thickets. Big black bumble bees buzzed in and out of hives formed in the mud. Along the way, I sang and thought, occasionally sitting on a clifftop to observe the reefs below, serenading sea lions who barked at mates and dove in the currents. Skipper and I scaled the steep path down to Hidden Beach where surfers bobbed offshore in the big waves beyond the point at Mavericks, the place they say has the best surf on the California coast. I carressed the warm sands with the bare soles of my feet and daringly walked the edge of the cool lapping water. I squinted my eyes to cut down the diamond brightness. Yes, it was sensual: hot and electric: a *very* sensual experience.

I thought about my great good fortune to be in this place at this time. Enough food. A peaceful period. Then I immediately felt guilty—thinking of destitution everywhere. At that very moment, I distinctly heard the Guide's voice say:

"You are exactly where you need to be.
This is your place. This is your time."

❧

What a strange day!

Pamela Dear, I laughed to myself, *Welcome to the realm of The Mysteries.* I wondered what would happen next.

CHAPTER 4

THE EXPLANATION

The Possibilities.

Riavek attended me diligently.

Over the course of the next interlude, he showed me many lives, all incarnations of what I would call holy women.

These lives spanned thousands of years of Western history; ancient Sumeria, ancient Egypt, Old Testament times, ancient Greece, the early Christian period, the Dark Ages, the Reformation. . . . I witnessed all these lives and I felt that I was part of them. I felt I was contained by them even as I contained them.

Witnessing the revelation of this information was intensely emotional. I laughed and cried, made love, ate, danced, and entered sacred initiation through the eyes of all the characters. I was in them; they were in me. We were one, inseparable. I felt I was witnessing the journey of my own soul on the path to self-expression. Each life took me closer to the ultimate destination.

My rational mind, however, not as impressionable as my heart or as emotionally reactive, sought explanation for what I observed. Four possibilities occurred to me: The experience of past lives could be attributed to imagination, genetic memory, or tapping a pool of telepathically-received information. I also could not discount the possibility that I was experiencing actual past life incarnations.

1. Imagination

I have long believed that the human imagination is extraordinarily creative. If I ask you to close your eyes and imagine a tree, there are very few who will not be able to do it. You will know the type of tree, whether it is a pine or an oak, how lush it is, whether it stands alone or in a forest. You will know whether it is a tree you have seen before or a new and different tree. Close your eyes and experiment. Imagine a tree. Or a past life. What do you see?

In part, the ability to imagine opens up as a conscious or subconscious attempt to explain that which seems inexplicable. This is what happens when people create myths to explain the beginning of existence. It also happens when we are seeking to fill gaps in scientific knowledge or even gaps in the continuity or cohesion of our own lives.

I like to think imagination opens up, too, for the sheer sake of celebrating its own creativity.

It is a thrilling thing when the bounds of thought are pushed ever-outward, when the parameters of knowledge are shaken loose, when everyday life is lived as if it is art immersed in its own creation. How refreshing, revealing and awe-inspiring to see life through an artist's eyes, to witness things of the common world as if one has never seen them before! The artist comes to view the world as a pliable reality, as a fabulously malleable medium of which superb sculpture can be made.

2. Genetic Memory

According to geneticists, I am a "walking encyclopedia." When I was the egg, they say, and the tiny fish enfolded by it, two sets of chromosomes bonded, twenty-three from each parent. Each chromosome contained two hundred genes. A simple mathematical calculation tells me that almost ten thousand genes lived in my embryonic self, and, according to geneticists, each gene contains a thousand symbols. Each symbol is a bit memory, a fragment of what we know. In a single human cell, there are ten thousand to a hundred thousand symbolic coded messages. If all the symbolic messages in the forty-six chromosomes were written out in words, each of us, they say, could fill a thousand three-hundred-page volumes.

Just think. My parents contain the genes of their parents. I contain the genes of my parents and theirs. What does this mean with regard to memory? If I think back a hundred years, can I activate fragments of the lives of my great-great grandparents? Might their experiences have been encoded in the chromosomes they passed on; become instinctive symbolic information lodged at the cellular level of descendants?

Could I access thousand-year-old encoded memories by somehow attuning to the very cells of my body?

What if I really contain, within every cell, skeletal memories of ancient lands, of daily life, of initiations, of executions? What if this is enhanced by my mind's ability—conscious or unconscious—to *imagine* connective tissue—muscle, sinew—tissue that gives form, sense, and proportion to vague symbolic recollections? Could I explain why my leg aches when doctors can find no known cause?

3. Tapping the Flow of Collective Information

Ancient schools of mysticism taught that there is a pool of exhaustless information generated from all that is, all that ever has been, and all that ever shall be. It was said that adepts could tap this information and thereby come into "sympathy" with all existence. With practice, "psychic powers" would open up, and the seeker would attain the limitless knowledge of past, present, and future.

Tapping this information flow, they say, is like a tapping a Unified Field of Mind, a Mind that exists within and outside of things as well as before, during, and after their existence.

Perhaps I unwittingly stumbled into this arena, the timeless sphere of the Universal Mind or the Soul of All. This idea raises many questions:

What constitutes mind; how extensive is it?

What is thought? Does it emanate from mind? Can it be transferred telepathically from one being to another? Is thought vibrational? Might it travel like waves of sound or light? Could I pick up ideas from someone across the world? From a being in another universe? Another dimension? Could I pick up vibrations from a tree? A rock? A river?

Could I tap a vibration of what no longer exists or of what is yet to come?

As my visionary quest began to open, I felt that all these things and more were not only possible—they were *likely*.

So open did my consciousness become, I began to feel my mind—as well as my creative imagination—was bounded only by whatever I imagined to be a limitation.

4. Reincarnation

A large proportion of the world's population believes that a mind or spirit inhabits a body, but is not the body. The body is viewed as a temporary house. When the body is no longer functioning, the spirit departs, only to return in a new body. The spirit passes through life on the material plane, incarnating again and again in body after body. Each incarnation is dedicated to the growth of the soul. Each soul grows steadily, learning lesson after lesson on the path to achieving oneness with "Universal Life."

When a soul first enters a human body, according to Eastern doctrine, it wants nothing more than to taste the delights of Earth. The soul progresses through ascending strata of human desires, eventually—with repeated stimulation—becoming disenchanted or bored with one desire after another, until the only remaining desire is union with the essence of life itself. Some call this essence god or goddess. I prefer to think of it as the Creative Principle. When the individual soul attains union with the Soul of the World, there is no more incarnation because there is no more desire, no more striving, only eternal bliss.

Through meditation I detached my thoughts from everything I had been taught to think and all possibility opened. I ended up with a multitude of questions. Every question became like a finger pointing to an answer.

I felt my imagination open up and flow freely. I felt that the essence of the visions of past lives were contained in the very cells of my body. I felt the images were also contained in my mind. I felt I could enhance these visions through the mysterious workings of creative imagination.

The visions also seemed to come from outside my body and mind, as if I were being directed. It was as if I were not only meditating, but *being meditated.* I was within and outside myself all at once. I witnessed my self, waking my self up. I was teacher, guide, student, and subject.

The stories that came to me seemed progressive in some ways—and linear—even though they seemed to zigzag through time and space; some of the lessons learned at later dates seemed less advanced than lessons learned earlier. Still, there was a true feeling of purposeful and successive incarnation.

There seemed to be seeds of truth in every rational explanation my mind was creative enough to invent or explore.

Now, I share these stories with you, exactly as the scenes unfolded. Judge the process for yourself. Then I will give you tools, point the way and invite you to embark upon your own expansive journey, a journey into past, present, and future, a journey that will take you beyond everything you have ever known.

PART II

THE SISTERS

CHAPTER 5

LAI-ILA
ANCIENT MESOPOTAMIA

Ur, 3000 B.C.E.

I gaze into the candle.

My body energizes. Hands and feet grow hot. Mind shifts. Rushing. Rushing. I open to possibility and this frees my spirit. I follow my heart and my spirit grows light. I abandon the comfortable; risk the fear of losing the firm foundation of science.

"You are safe." I hear the voice of Riavek.

I clench my eyes, hold my breath, step to the edge of what I know. I try to remember what it means to start at the beginning. Baby steps. I recall that to learn to walk, I had to learn to fall. I dip my toe in the cosmic fire. It is inviting. . .I must trust.

I ask for visions and visions come. Pounding. Receiving. Receiving.

Riavek says, "Take your pen and use it like a paintbrush. Record the images you are given. These are the gifts of imagination and they have the power to free your caged soul. These visions have the power to free the caged hearts of your people."

My mind shifts, shimmers, sifting through layers of time and place and strange dimensions. Riavek opens a window and I travel through time, past scenes, faces, old and young, spinning through known and unknown spaces.

I find myself in Ur on the Euphrates River above the Persian Gulf, in the Cradle of Civilization, ancient Mesopotamia. I am in the Ancient City, ancient even in the ancient time four thousand years before the archaeologists would name it "ancient." I know this is Ur because I—who am no longer the "I" I was, but a woman dressed in the robes of an ancient priestess—am in a small walled area adjacent to the terraced pyramid with the holy shrine to the Moon on top. This is the ziggurat, the hill to the goddess, the tower that has been built higher and higher for a hundred generations, ever-upward to honor our place of origin in the stars. I recognize the place where I am kneeling. I know it well from a lifetime of devotion. It is the sanctuary in the temple of the Great Goddess, the Queen of Heaven and Earth, Inanna. I am in the walled sanctuary open to the sky. Everywhere the seal of the Queen is etched on stone plates all around the perimeter. Her signature is vertical, long and chainlike with a loop at the top. It looks like something containing the genetic code, something capable of transmitting genetic pattern. They call this seal, simply, the Tree of Life. It is her sign.

Inanna means Ancient Grandmother. The word Nana—meaning grandmother—descended from her worship.

Queen Inanna is the Great Goddess, She Who Gives Birth to the World, She who is the life inside and behind each succeeding generation of people, each succeeding generation of the lush yield from the garden beyond the walls of the sanctuary, each succeeding generation of the lazy and beautiful cats that stretch and yawn and groom themselves in patches of sunlight all about the temple grounds.

Queen Inanna is like a woman you might know, only more so than any woman you could possibly know. You can call on her personally when you need something, when you want to pray. She is easy to picture in your mind just like any other woman. She has emotions like a real person. She is contented, angry, jealous, cruel, joyous, indifferent, engaged, enraged, caustic, and loving, depending on the time of day, the time of her cycle, the season of growth, and many other factors.

Sometimes I call on Her when I need the comfort of a human face in my meditations.

I am in the sanctuary of Inanna now. This is the same sanctuary where I first entered as Novitiate Priestess of the Sisters of Nun when the seventeen women kissed my forehead and passed on their blessings.

I am a priestess, anointed, dressed in the flowing robes of Initiation. My consciousness floods fully into the memory of my apprenticeship.

I am in the sanctuary to review, to take stock of what I have learned. I am in silence. In three days time, I will undergo the Initiation of Interment in the sealed clay-brick room from which there is no exit in the heart of the labyrinth of the temple at the ziggurat. They call this place of initiation "the cell." In this place between worlds, I will enter the heart of darkness seeking an answer to that which lies beyond the abyss that separates this world from the next. I believe I am ready for this initiation although there are rumors that, even after seven notches of preparation, some will die.

Inanna, the Great Goddess, went through Interment. She was locked, without escape, in the cell inside the temple and there she gave up everything she had, including her life. They do not leave priestesses so long now.

Originally, Inanna was a priestess like I am now. She was the Queen of Uruk, a nearby city on the Holy Waters. After many years of study, the High Priestess of Nun interred Inanna in the temple for her last Initiation. In isolation, it is said, Queen Inanna experienced nightmarish visions of the Underworld. She felt herself descend, descend, descend, through seven gates of the seven concentric circles of brick walls, one circle for each of the seven worlds, into a hellish place where someone she thought was her sister, who went by the name of Erishkegal—as did her real sister—was in the throes of labor giving birth to a child.

Queen Inanna went dressed for a wedding. Oh, but she was beautiful! Can you imagine the sublime draping of her blood-red dress slipping gently over curving breasts and flowing to the floor? Can you see the train dragging regally, rippling over the stones? Imagine transparent veils wafting mysteriously across the Queen's rich, brown eyes, the richly crafted headdress dangling with sparkling gold representations of suns, moons and swirling stars. Can you see the soft shoes, the glinting bracelets, the fine worked breastplate etched with the symbols for "Come, Man, Come"?

But then, as she passed through each gate, Queen Inanna was forced by its guardians to give up a part of her queenly attire. She relinquished her guilded bracelets, her hammered gold breastplate, her gold and copper crown, her crimson gown of fine cotton, her silken shoes, everything that identified her as Queen. When she got to the last gate, she was naked and defenseless. All her possessions had been tortured from her. She was forced to enter the Underworld crawling.

Poor Inanna!

She bowed down and entered, her regal head dangling like old fruit between her arms, giving her tears lastly which she thought was all she had left.

Erishkegal, however, knew there was one more thing Inanna could relinquish: that was her life.

This cruel sister, deep in the morass of her own pain, screamed out and beat Inanna's naked body with a post. She beat her mercilessly until Inanna was knocked senseless. Then she beat her empty shell out of sheer fury alone. She beat her and beat her until dear Inanna was pulpy dead meat, and then she hung the bloody battered corpse, repugnant and untouchable, on a peg to rot.

In the Initiation of Interment inside that cell at the end of the labyrinth, inside the deepest bowels of the temple, Queen Inanna had this dream.

She believed she had died, shut up in that stark baked brick tomb. She believed all was ended. No light. No air. No warmth. Only the deathly cold of the vegetable cellar, the cool grip of death. She realized that, in death, there are no queens. And with that vision, she relinquished her life.

Her uncle, Enki, had a dream then. He dreamed that Inanna was dying, and one day before Inanna was to be released from the Initiation of Interment, he convinced the Reverend High Priestess of Uruk to open the passages to the inner labyrinth of the temple to let Inanna out. The High Priestess, as was her bent, went alone with her chosen to help her lift the bars that locked the entries. When the priestess arrived in the inner chamber, she found Queen Inanna dead. There was no breath, no pulse, nor could she feel a beating heart beneath the indigo-violet robes of High Initiation.

As the story goes, the High Priestess would not believe her beloved Queen had perished. She had been her best student. She leaned down and breathed her own breath into Queen Inanna's mouth. She placed her hands on Queen Inanna's heart and ran wavelets of radiating rainbow energy into her soul. She kissed Inanna's brow in the place where she could see, in the wavering light of the torch, the stain of fish oil she herself had administered, now six days faded.

The chosen held their breath as one entity, praying, praying, praying that Inanna would awake.

Suddenly, she came to life. She rose up from the Land of the Dead. All the witnesses gasped because she was dead and then she was not. She stood and pointed northward numbly. Her only words were the following: "There are no queens in the Land of the Dead."

She walked like a dead person out of the temple.

Queen Inanna spoke to no one for an entire cycle of the Moon. When she did speak, the teachers told us, she was changed. She was full with compassion for all that lives.

Thirteen thousand cycles of the moon passed and Queen Inanna became a legend. The people no longer remember that she was a goddess who walked on Earth. Erishkegal became known as the Goddess of the Underworld and Enki as the God of the Waters. Only we who are initiates of the Order of the Sisters of Nun know to what extent this story is true, that we are directly descended from Queen Inanna, that she lived in Uruk, that she is our grandmother. Some have seen her real signature; it is still etched at the center of the labyrinth.

I am here to review. I will undergo interment—enclosure in that dark and empty space, that liminal world between all worlds—and I will go there in three days time.

In the middle of this yard, this sanctuary to Queen Inanna, this place which bears her seal upon the walls, is a stone slab raised up upon a stone cube. This altar is the only thing here to occupy my attention, along with the alabaster goblet brought to Ur in the ancient days and the rectangular cistern of water in the corner, filled with runoff from the gutter descending down the side of the ziggurat.

I fill the alabaster goblet with fresh waters from the spring rain and place it upon that stone altar in the middle of the sanctuary.

I kneel in front of the slab and bow, stretching my hands out across the fire-baked paving tiles before me. I face east, my forehead touches the ground. I touch my forehead to the ground in the place where my teacher has anointed me with the orb of the dark blueish-purple secretion that comes from the Murex, the spiral purple shellfish with the magical powers. My teacher boiled the yellow substance until it turned violet, folded it into olive oil and consecrated this mixture especially for my Interment. I have worn this orb for four days since the beginning of isolation. I have seen no one but my teacher, Rilkah Ramih, the High Priestess to Inanna, the Queen of Heaven who stands in front of Aisha. Aisha is really the Nameless One, Nameless and Formless, but that idea is difficult for most people to grasp. It is easier to think of Aisha in the form of a Great Goddess like Queen Inanna. Queen Inanna is comforting. Aisha is unknown. Aisha is the energy behind the Goddess personified. She is the beginning and the continuation of all things, the spark of life within all that lives, the connecting link that fills the air with possibility.

The high priestess Rilkah Ramih has guided my studies for twelve-and-a-half notches on my mother's door. I have learned from Rilkah Ramih the paths of moon and sun, the positions of stars in the seasons and the geometry of the sacred spiral at the center of death. I have learned the spiral geometry of that sacred being, the Murex, the guardian of the seas who produces the oil of the violet-blue veil, the light at the end of the dollmaking.

Rilkah Ramih, this day, took that oil upon her thumb from the tiny vial she carries on a cord around her neck and anointed my forehead between my eyebrows that I might better see with my inner eye. I believe my eyes are becoming single, seeing as one.

This point on my head touches the blue paving stones laid in sacred spiral alignment upon the beautiful earth of Ur.

I stretch my hands before me, fingers pointing like stars toward the heart of the universe. I feel the sun bearing down inside the walls of this sacred place, welcoming me, warming me, warming the paving stones, warming my heart as the walls of Queen Inanna with their Tree of Life design block the harsh entry of the wind.

I clear all thoughts from my mind, relax my face, the lines around my eyes, and I drift into a harmonious state of liminal nothingness. I have nowhere to be but here, in this sanctuary to Queen Inanna.

The ancient chant enters my consciousness and silently repeats itself across the endless field of mind: *Shanti. Shanti. Shanti.* It lengthens and encircles a vast consciousness becoming *Shan—ti.—Ah—ee—ee—sha—ah. Shan—ti.—Ah—ee—ee—shah—ah. Shan—ti. Om.*

These phrases repeat and repeat. This pattern of sounds emerges from the ancient language of the holy ones who, in the time of Queen Inanna, crossed the desert on camels, came up the sea in reed boats. *Peace be to the Holy Mother. Peace be in the soul. Peace be to Holy Aisha. Peace be in your own soul. Peace. Peace. Peace.* And then the sacred sound of the Universe turning, *Om.*

I chant and I chant until the silent chant becomes a song releasing itself from a holy sea within, but beyond, myself.

The energy raises me up until I kneel and face the stone altar. I sing praises to the Mother of All That Is. *Om Shanti Om Aisha.* How beautiful feels this day, this time, this place. How glorious to be alive. How glorious to give birth, to be part of the exquisite chain of being.

Om Shanti Om Aisha Shanti Om Om Aisha.

Through my closed eyelids I can see and feel the rich, warm, golden red cast of the sun gleaming.

My heart dances. My happiness seems unbounded. From head to toe I resound with love.

With sudden impact, then, an unexpected outside noise crashes my eardrums, causes my heart to stop, my voice to freeze. Peace leaps a million miles away. Time slows, all stills. There is scuffling. Out of place. Something wrong. Then I am shoved. I cannot see. . .Unused to feeling fear, I scream before I can stop myself or think. I catch my balance then, spin around, startled, ready to run or face my enemy.

Behind me stands little Ramil. He bursts with laughter, covers his mouth with his fist.

"You little *griffin!* You startled me! Where's Nana? You're not supposed to be here!" I am yelling at him.

He cannot stop laughing. Ramil, not even five notches on the door jamb. He points to the gate. It is disconcerting that my own son can scare me to this degree.

My mother comes in view, steps in the gate and stands there apologetically, shaking her head saying "Rami! Come here! You are old enough to know better than to disturb Mami."

"Go on," I say, "Go with Nani and I'll see you in a few days." I pull Ramil to me, hug him and kiss him and out of the corner of my eye, I see my mother pull a rare green apple from her satchel. Ramil sees the apple, too. Children miss nothing. Like a little dog with passion and hunger, he trails her out the gate.

My rhythm is broken, but I would not change it.

I sit down on the spiral stones and began to think about my first-born, Katah. Katah was born to be a healer; Ramil to perform the dance. My middleborn, Lida, was born to fill the temple, the palace, and the fields with song. Before each was born, these things were known by the high priestess Rilkah Ramih who, all these years, has been my teacher.

Rilkah Ramih can see into the past and the future. She knows the mind of Aisha. She opened herself up this way through unleashing her imagination and intuition and traveling on the wind. Her teacher, TuTu from Nuba in the Farsouth, taught her much, but not how to fly through the seven veils of knowing. This, Rilkah Ramih taught herself. She was already old when I came to her, thirty-five notches. Now I suppose she must have almost forty-eight. There are few that old in all of Ur.

When I came to Rilkah Ramih I had fifteen sun-cycles notched in my mother's door jamb, and Katah had only one but nearly two. Two weeks ago, Nani chiseled Katah's thirteenth notch. One week ago, that notch was stained with Katah's first blood, and we welcomed her to apprenticeship with the Sisters of Nun, right here in Queen Inanna's sanctuary.

I sit on the blue tiles now, having worked toward this moment for one hundred and fifty-four moons. This is a very auspicious time. All of the omens point to joy, happiness, and healing. I have not suffered miscarriage, nor have my children died. Now, my darling Katah is ready to take a lover and I shall become as Inanna, "Nana," a grand-mother of Ur.

When I first came to Rilkah Ramih, she taught me to heal with clay. With the other young priestesses, I chanted and formed with my hands images of Queen Inanna, she who represents the life of Aisha. This was how we came to understand energy behind form.

Some of the priestesses carved images from stone, carving and chipping with horns from the Fareast. Others molded images in metal.

My hands loved the clay. I dug a mudhole in the side of the irriga-tion stream that ran through the garden to the south of the ziggurat. Other sisters, though, got their clay at the great bubbling river saying their clay came from sacred waters and had more power.

I believe now, as I did then, that all waters are sacred. Too, I loved my little clayhole in the garden.

I asked all my mothers to bring me their broken dolls and the cracked grandmothers' watercups from the altars. These sacred objects I would break and crush, pulverize with stones and water from the stream, mash to a pulpy dough and mix with clay from my mudhole in the temple garden. This was my own idea. Others seemed not to under-stand it, but to me it brought a continuation of the energy of the sacred objects of the grandmothers. I contained this energy in new form in the dolls that would be placed upon the altars and in the graves of the daughters living now and the daughters to come. Rilkah Ramih under-stood.

I felt this process made my own clay stronger, too. Some of my pieces cracked in the fire because of the added "impurities" (in the words of one of the Sisters) but, in this case, I felt the impurities were the purest of pure and I worshipped each crack knowing the crack contained the wisdom of the priestesses who had occupied the doll-making table for more moons than I could even imagine. It contained, too, the devotional energy of every grandmother who had held it in her hands or placed it on her altar. Sometimes "impurities" sanctify further that which is holy to begin with.

My hands knew the mind of the clay before they touched it. My designs were fine. My fingers were nimble. I made the same figure over and over. I knew from the start, no matter what shell her outer form took, whether it was black or brown, gray or red, depending on the mix, that her essence was the same. Her essence was Aisha, the one I called up in the sanctuary of Inanna on the side of the ziggurat, the grandmother and granddaughter who energizes us all.

I was taught by Rilkah Ramih that we were making the little god-desses to remind the people of Ur that life is infinite, that Inanna is eter-nal, that Aisha springs forever.

Each goddess was imprinted with the sound of sacred life coursing through the Universe. I chanted with the priestesses as the figures came through my hands. Each doll received the sacred vibration of life: devotion to the sacred law of cause and effect through sound vibration. This was my endless mantra, *Aa—ee—shah. Aa—ee—shah.*

For seventy-seven moons I made the dolls at the long table with the young Sisters of Nun. My hands were so fast. I made thousands of fig-ures: beautiful little faces, etched collars of gold plates, pubic hair swirled into tiny rows of connecting spirals. They were so precious. At the end of each day, my baked clay shelves were covered with little women.

The clay goddesses healed.

As we worked the clay, illness passed out of our bodies through our hands. The clay drew out all that was sick. If I thought a bad thought, the goddess would take it. All negativity would be drawn into the little woman. Then she would be put in the fire of the kiln and the fire would burn away these bad things, and she would be purified. She would come out completely pure, burned clean, and I would be burned clean as well.

This is how I apprenticed. I learned, in this manner, the art of healing. I learned that to heal means to make whole, and that becoming whole involves learning many levels of purification, balance, and reformation.

Each time my blood came, one of the dolls received my blood blessing so there were, in this time, seventy-seven images bearing the fertility of Aisha and hundreds of others that bore the energy of her lifeforce.

I never kept these dolls, because after they came through me, my work was done. Young apprentices, like Teri and Mai, would take them from the ashes, in their purified state, and place them on the Great Altar to the Moon and Stars on top of the ziggurat at Ur.

The Nanas would come and take the dolls, leaving valuables and food in their places. The dolls would be presented to a child at its birth, to a birthing mother, to a young woman experiencing her first blood, to a young man who had first come inside a woman, to a young woman who had first held a man inside her, to a priestess upon her emergence from the Initiation of Interment, and at other critically important times in Queen Inanna's chain.

In the first eleven moons I worked with Rilkah Ramih, she instructed me to make dolls of red light. This did not mean that the dolls themselves were red, but that I was to meditate upon the red field of consciousness known as the red veil as I worked. I called into the redness silently. I learned that the red veil involved matter inside the bones. The red field was about marrow, and to work a doll of red light drew impurities from the center of being. These impurities were transformed in the firing, and by intention alone, anyone touching a doll of red light would be purified from the inside out.

When I understood the red veil, I moved into orange. The orange dolls were blood dolls, the ones that brought fertility to earth and opened the cradling wombs of women. In orange light, all problems of the blood were alleviated. While I was in orange, I conceived Lida, a daughter of the goddess and god, the one who plays music, the one whose hands and feet and face glow with the purified blood of song and laughter.

In the third cycle, I made dolls of yellow, the light of breath. I gave birth in yellow light and in the thirty-third moon with Rilkah Ramih, when my mother was near to carving my eighteenth notch on her door jamb, when my firstborn Katah had nearly five—almost the same as Ramil now—and Lida had one, I began to call the name of Aisha to a different tune and rhythm in the sanctuary of Queen Inanna. So it was that my song began to heal my thoughts through regulating my breath; this began to free my ability to see as Rilkah Ramih could see.

Then I made the dolls of green. These were dolls of love. In the green cycle, I began to write. I wrote my love. I wrote the songs of sacred life that came through my mind and heart and lungs. I wrote these songs using the symbols of my people and the symbols given to me by Ankar Ali, the oarsman who had lain with me as the god when Lida, child of god and goddess, grew wings in my womb.

The green light was so fertile, all verdant, all receiving, reception of Aisha, the idea of Life, the energy before or beneath the beginning of all that is. I received that essence: essential word, symbol, story, rhythm, humanity, divinity, love. These things came to me and I began to write them, impressing them first on the wall at my mudhole, and later on flat pieces of clay that I rolled out with a breadmaker and put into the fire with the dolls, bricks, and paving stones.

In the next cycle, I came to blue: blue sky, the heavens, pale to indigo. Here my voice deepened, and in the seventh dark moon of the fourth round of eleven, as my new voice matured, I received the Initiation of Temple Leadership. Two young girls were assigned to me to begin to learn the red light, the cycle of bones.

At first I was intimidated by my new role and responsibility in service to Rilkah Ramih and the temple, but by the completion of seven moons, I had built my confidence. Teri and Mai were in the red veil and already getting excited about entering the round of orange blood.

Then I went to the violet light. I chanted, sang, wrote, prayed, and dedicated every doll to the violet field of Aisha, She Who Is The Structure Behind All Form and The Light of Life Itself. For eleven moons, I chanted and prayed in violet light. I chanted and prayed and chanted and prayed until the spirit of Aisha entered my form and I became her life. Every doll that flowed from my hands contained the energy and lifeforce of Aisha, and this power could not be washed away by water nor burned by fire.

Teri and Mai could see the change in me and they followed me closely, touching me often, as if they were dolls of clay and could draw out of me the force of Aisha.

Then I discovered the secret of *giving* the energy of Aisha so they would not have to take it from me. This energy began to flow through my hands. The energy of Aisha seemed to travel through red light, then orange, then yellow, green, blue, violet, then explode into white rays

that shot through my hands and feet. My whole body shook with cascading energies. I passed light through my hands, and this light healed
the people.

The people began to come to me, and with Rilkah Ramih present
and guiding, I placed my hands on their hearts, their hips, their feet,
their heads, throats, and hands, and they closed their eyes, receiving
and healing, feeling their minds relax, their bodies made whole again,
the lines around their eyes and across their foreheads fade and disappear. After my seventh healing, Rilkah Ramih took the consecrated
purple oil from her vial, put it on her thumb and anointed my forehead
between my eyes. In that moment, I felt the energy of all those who had
ever healed enter my head, flow through every atom of my being, and
my whole body shook with the power and awe of wholeness.

I was in the last cycle of lights as my mother made my twenty-first
notch on her door. This was the cycle of white light, the light that contains and combines all lights. The dolls seemed to jump out of the clay
and sing. From my hands flew rainbows. Rainbows jumped into the
dolls. And I felt light everywhere streaming, radiating from the dolls. I
felt myself pulsate like a tumbling star in the sky.

Rilkah Ramih said I had come of age.

The dark of the seventy-seventh moon came and with Katah, Lida,
Teri, Mai, my mother, her sisters and grandmothers and their mothers
all in attendance, Rilkah Ramih wrapped about my shoulders the midnight blue shawl of Novitiate Priestess of the Sisters of Nun. The seventeen of us stood together chanting the name of Inanna and the ancient
sacred syllables from the silken sisters of the Fareast. Each woman delivered to me the kiss of peace and laid her hands with rainbows
streaming upon my head.

We passed the sacred alabaster goblet and drank to indicate that
we all shared the womb of Aisha's holy waters. And we cried together
as each one spoke her words for me and blessed me in my studies.

For the next seventy-seven moons I studied the skies, numerical
formulae, the life cycle of plants, all the stories known by the priestesses before me and all that was revealed in my own illuminated field of
consciousness. With each moon I saw and knew more and more, until
the field of my mind was expanded into infinity, like the mind of Rilkah Ramih.

∽

Now I sit on the paving stones in my third day of isolation, only
seeing Rilkah Ramih once each morning, who, in silence, anoints my

invisible eye, the sacred eye with mystical vision, with the oil of the Murex. I am to spend my time in the sanctuary of Inanna with nothing to distract my hands, my feet, my heart, or my mind except the alabaster goblet, the stone cistern of spring waters, and the holy altar at the heart of the spiral.

I have to laugh. Amid the serious intention of all this, only three days before the Great Interment, after one hundred and fifty-four moons of preparation and twelve notches in apprenticeship to Rilkah Ramih chiseled like leaves on a vine upon my mother's door, here comes that little griffin Ramil, sneaking up on me, laughing and pushing me like it is the greatest joke the world has ever seen. His Mami. The Great Priestess of Ur.

I have to laugh. Not a thing would I change. Not a single thing would I change as I give myself over to life or death, to whatever will come as I enter the Initiation of Interment of High Priestess of the Sisters of Nun that serve in the wake of Queen Inanna in the sacred city of Ur.

The mind of Aisha is my mind. I am in the mind of Aisha.

The young priestess, Teri, stood on the temple steps. Teri was a Dream Knower. She knew the symbols of house, tree, lion, snake, palace, temple, monster, flight, desert, and sea, and told the people the meaning of the past and the future by these symbols. The people came to her in the Dream Chamber at the temple and she helped them. She was young, but her fame was spreading quickly through the Land of Ur. Word spread fast when it was discovered someone had tapped the mind of Aisha and knew the sacred codes. Teri stood on the temple steps. She had a long, black stick that looked like a snake. It was curved just so, perfectly. One end was larger and shaped like a head. There were even knots that looked like eyes on either side. The tail end curved and tapered just like a snake. She held this stick before a small crowd of people and waved it in a certain way that produced the optical illusion of bending motion so it looked like the stick had come alive and become a real snake. Some of the people were afraid.

The young woman had the ability to convince the people that she had changed a stick into a snake because she was able to move into the mind of Aisha, the field where all minds converge. She put the idea in the mind of Aisha that she had created a real living serpent out of a stick and because the people were in the mind of Aisha, too—even though they did not realize this—they believed her.

Only priestesses studied the mind of Aisha, even though others sometimes stumbled upon the knowledge. Sometimes a person of Ur would fall into the mind of Aisha and believe that she or he had lost touch with the moment-by-moment reality of everyday life. People who had not studied did not realize the power they were tapping and felt, too, that it set them apart from others. They did not want to be set apart or cast out. This, for some, would have been a fate worse than death—even though the set-apartness was only in the mind of the "afflicted" individual. The truth is that other people aren't as concerned as we believe them to be. Each one goes about her own business.

The young priestess with the stick drew ever-bigger crowds over the passage of a few days time until some of the children—most notably a rambunctuous nine notcher—insisted on trying to replicate the Sister's famous miracle.

Within two days, the little urchins were all over the temple steps, waving sticks like snakes. It looked like they had all caught serpents in the river. And the spell of Aisha was broken.

The young priestess came upon the children with their snakes. She thought it so amusing and began to laugh incessantly until all of them were bent over in a great paroxysm of laughter. Teri had a good nature. The kids were enthralled with themselves, in awe of their own adepthood. They were proud and Teri was proud, too, proud of their persistance.

Over the next few moons, almost everyone in Ur adopted their own pet snakestick and entertained friends and family until everyone in the fields was quite bored with the whole thing.

It seemed like every oarswoman and man coming up the river were introduced to the trick as well, and I imagined news of this trick being spread all over the world.

Eventually the trick was forgotten. A trick like that lasts only so long. Funny how I remember it just now.

Truth told, it was that same oarsman who I laid down with, Ankar Ali, who showed her that trick. He learned this illusion in the Land of Egypt, a place about which he shared many stories. He said they had pyramids built to resemble our ziggurats, modeled after our towers, in fact, but that these pyramids had hollow passages—as the Egyptians were enamored of "void" and "emptiness"—and deep inside these hollow passages was where the High Initiation took place. This was the same initiation we underwent in the temple, he said, except that in Egypt the initiate was led into the chamber by a lionness and placed inside a sarcophagas, a "flesh-eating box" of a kind of stone called lime that caused the body to rapidly disintegrate. The reason Ankar Ali knew this information was because everyone trusted him. I had told him what I knew about Queen Inanna even though I was sworn to secrecy. I believe being sworn to secrecy means that you use your judgment about what to say and how much of it. That is how learning takes place; I know many of the things I know because I am trusted by my teacher, the High Priestess to Queen Inanna, Rilkah Ramih.

Ankar Ali was not a priest himself, but it was a priest by the holy waters of the Great Nile River who taught him about the magic held in the stick. He also knew of magic in stones and bones. What Ankar Ali called magic was what we Sisters of Nun called the Mind of Aisha.

Ankar Ali said the priest told him the magic came from the Waters of Nun. *Nun.* This must have been the name for the Mind of Aisha in Egypt because this was the name of our order.

I laid down with the oarsman Ankar Ali and I had never been with such a god. I remember his arms. They were so thick at the top that my two hands put together could not encircle them. He wore a thin red band of dyed wool around one of these arms. I could not take my eyes from that armband, or from his gold-tipped curls, sun-dipped in reflections off the sea. His skin glowed red-golden-brown and it rippled supplely over his sinews.

I saw him in the temple garden. I donned my most exquisite attire, put the gold ring on my wrist, twisted my hair upon my head. I walked into the garden and sweetly sang a wedding song in the image of Queen Inanna:

> *My vulva, my open horn,*
> *the crescent moon boat of glorious heaven*
> *awaits to ferry my beloved across the night*
>
> *Behold, I am the earth mother*
> *wet ground on the high plain*
> *river flooding the field lying fallow*
>
> *Beloved, will you come?*
> *Will you till my wet ground?*
> *Will you ride in my moon boat on the currents of night?*

And he had answered me tenderly, singing in his own tongue:

> *I will ride in your moon boat*
> *my Sister, my Bride,*
> *I will sail your deep seas*
> *through the river of night.*

And, there in the temple garden, we entered the union that rejoices the heart. He held my breasts in his hands and I could feel his reverence:

> *Your breasts, my Bride, my Sister*
> *are like young does, high brown hills*
> *milking and sprouting like fountains in the sand*
>
> *Your belly is round, my Sister, my Bride*
> *swollen and fertile*
> *round and hidden, safe*
> *like a burrow where young foxes lie*
>
> *Your deep eyes are a clear reflective oracle*
> *of what has been and is*
>
> *And your mouth is a river's song*
> *Sing, my sweet love, my Sister, my Bride*
> *Sing and my soul shall waken.*

I sang to him the sweet songs of Inanna:

> *Come in me, my Brother, my Love*
> *grow, wide and tall, like a tree*
> *by the rivers of the water*
> *that brings forth fruit in his season*
>
> *Spout, deep and lush, like a lily in the valley*
>
> *Your eyes are the eyes of doves*
> *by the rivers of the waters*
> *washed white with milk,*
> *cooing,*
> *and overlaid with gold.*

We spoke with our hands and feet. We shared syllables and words; understood our juxtaposed meanings. Our eyes spoke and understood. Our mouths and tongues spoke and understood.

Ankar Ali and I laid down in the garden of the temple. God and goddess moved through us and we were drawn toward each other as if we were pulled by ropes. Never had god and goddess danced so well. We could not have stopped our union. It must have been arranged by Queen Inanna and King Dumuzi. Too, it must have been a critical union in the mind of Aisha, because Lida grew from it. I cannot forget. As goddess and god, we rolled in soft green grasses in the soft heat of day, we rolled in the heat of night, renewing the fertility of Ur. Oh, Love! Oh, bed that rejoices! I could not breathe enough of his breath, smell enough of his skin, taste enough of his juices, see enough of that red band.

He wore a stone ring on a leather cord around his neck. This ring was to remind him of the womb-ring from which he came. It was a parting gift when he first took up the oar, designed and carved for him by his mother, a stone mason who worked by the edge of a great sea in the place of Ankar Ali's birth called Antalya.

As we rolled in the garden, carrying out our duty of ensuring on-going fertility for the people and the land, he wore only that red band and that stone ring. I drank in his body, the body of the god. He breathed and tasted and drank me, too, drank me, the goddess, consumed my essence like a dolphin taking air and diving, and he was upon me this way until my mind and body exploded in rainbow lights. That was when I first saw the rainbow veil. Almost fifty moons before I would know it in apprenticeship.

Al Ali, my beautiful god.

I knew that very day that I carried the pod of Lida. Ankar Ali knew this also.

He had lain with many priestesses during the time he was in Ur, but only the young girl Teri with the sticksnake and I were in the mind of Aisha to grow a child.

Later, Al Ali looked deep into my eyes, deeper than anyone had ever looked, as deep as the mind of Aisha, as deep as the Sea of Nun, and he spoke to me through this sea, saying, "I have a lyre for which I traded a great deal up the river. Tomorrow I will be gone, but you will find this lyre upon the Great Altar to the Moon and Stars in the place of a doll of yellow light, and you must take it for the child in your womb. To her, I give the endless voice, the one that goes beyond words and symbols, the universal voice that sings from the Sea of Nun. This is the voice you and I, as goddess and god, shared that day in your temple garden at the ziggurat of Ur. Remember this always my beautiful sister. Remember this always, my Sister, my Bride."

I did not cry that night—it is not fitting for a priestess to Inanna to cry about a consort; we are taught to view them only as representatives of the god who ensures continued procreation—but rather I stayed in the orange veil as was my place in my studies. In the morning I climbed the ziggurat. As I ascended the staircases, following the squared spiral path, I lightly brushed my fingers upon the glimmering blue tiles inlaid along the side. In the still dark of early morning, I dreamily thought of Ankar Ali and the goddess child who grew in my womb. She would be a priestess in the palace. I climbed slowly to re-tain my breath and as I climbed I chanted softly, singing a hundred by a hundred sacred syllables in honor of the Moon. When I reached the top, I kneeled and bowed. Then I rose and reverentially walked to the Great Altar to the Moon and Stars. There, upon the altar, stood the most beautiful stringed instrument I have ever seen. It was fashioned from a sun-bleached breastbone smoothed by moon after moon of rolling in soft waters and strung with animal sinews. In the breaking light of dawn I could see that carved into the top were two of the symbols I had learned from Ankar Ali. He must have carved them himself. One was Li. The other was Da. Ankar Ali had called me Li. It meant Grace or Beauty in his mother's tongue. Da, he had spoken, meant Prayer. As the pale moon of morning was my witness, I lifted the lyre from the altar, cradled it against my breast, and with trembling fingers, plucked each string.

So, my daughter's name, too, was a gift of the mind of Aisha through the god Ankar Ali, my beloved Al Ali. Lida, Beautiful Prayer.

Sometimes people need fond memories more than soup or barley cakes to keep them alive or to help them heal.

I have never seen Ankar Ali since that day in the temple garden—I know he left our shore by moon—but I have carried his touch in my heart and my dreams all through these long years. I send him warmth and comfort through the Sea of Nun, and I imagine he receives it whether he is above or under the sea at the river's mouth.

Sometimes I wonder, though. Did Ankar Ali and I really share to the depths of our soul as I remember, or was this the fantasy of a young lover, seeing only in her lover that which she wishes to see? I suppose it is well that Ankar Ali of Antalya should never return to Ur, that I should never hold his strong form or again cast my eye upon that mysterious armband from Egypt or the maternal ring of stone. He floats in the mind of Aisha eternally with big arms, sun-tipped hair, tasting like the sweet honeyed nectar that drips from the passion flower in spring.

This morning I waited in the sanctuary, my head bowed to the ground.

Rilkah Ramih anointed me in her chamber earlier this day, the same as on each preceding day. Today though, in silence, through the mind of Aisha, she asked that I turn my palms upward. I did so, holding my fingers out, and she anointed each palm with the consecated oil of the purple fish. As she did this, she made a spiraling motion with her thumb. This was the symbol for the center of the labyrinth.

Then I waited, alone, wondering if fear would enter. "Do not fear," an older sister had said to me. "It is fear that kills, not immediate experience. Replace fear with awe. Open up for all that will flow through the mind of Aisha and you will be blessed with the power to know your true name."

I heard the bare feet as soft as cat paws on the paving stones. Chanting as soft as the sound of breath itself, the five women entered the sanctuary of Inanna. Each was wrapped in a simple white cloth of linen, rich but simple clothes, for which two reed vessels had been traded to the Wood Boat People. The cloths were tied with purple strips dyed in Murex oil.

Rilkah Ramih motioned me to stand. I stood.

The eldest priestess took my robe from my body while another Sister filled a large earthen bowl with water from the cistern. With big soft sponges from the sea, the Sisters washed my hair and body as I stood naked, facing eastward in the sanctuary of Inanna.

It was warm, but I felt a strange chill as the sponge touched the small of my back. I could feel my face flush and a weakness grow in me, even though my nipples were erect.

I went inward, deep inside myself and said to my inner ear: *This is not the time to weaken. You are facing the biggest challenge of your life.*

I told myself this again and again, and then I had the odd sensation that I wanted to lie down and sleep. Right there. Right on the paving stones.

No, I called inwardly, *to sleep is to die.* I do not know why I thought of this. *Be strong. Be strong. Awake. Aware. Awake. Aware.*

The Sisters chanted, calling the name of Inanna again and again. "Inanna protect her journey. Inanna keep her safe. Inanna protect this priestess. Bring her strong vision. Bring power to her name."

They seemed to sway all around me as I stood naked in the walled yard.

The younger of the elder Sisters approached me with an obsidian awl.

I felt my teeth clench and my hands become moist. *Relax. Relax. Bring down the heart beat. Open your hands. Relax your jaw. Relax. Relax. Relax. Slow your heart. Give thanks.* The messages I sent my inner being were endless.

She pointed the sharp tool to the center of my breastbone between my breasts that hung out to either side. Then the tip touched my skin and with a spiraling motion she gently twisted a small round hole in the top layers. She made a fine, small, bloody hole. She opened thirteen holes in my chest in the form of a spiral, the insignia of the Initiation of Interment of the Sisters of Nun. Another Sister took ground dust from altar dolls that broke in the kiln and rubbed the dust into the thirteen open wounds as droplets of blood crept over my belly and into my mound of dark curls.

I tried not to hold my breath, but I could not help myself.

"Sing!" demanded Rilkah Ramih, and I began to chant softly with the Sisters, then louder as I felt the one Sister cut skin over my heart and the other rub in dust.

One of the priestesses tenderly sponged the blood, taking care not to rub out the dust that was supposed to lodge itself inside the open wounds. If it healed properly, it would create the raised spiral pattern worn by the elder priestesses since the teacher of Rilkah Ramih, TuTu, had brought the technique from Nuba.

This was my time, my place, my world. I felt, at that moment, pride in the discipline that had taken me through one hundred and fifty-four moons of study with the great teacher Rilkah Ramih. I prayed for guidance from the mind of Aisha.

As I prayed for guidance, the Sisters began to chant "Ah—ee—ee—shah. Ah—ee—ee—shah." They were in the mind of Aisha and had heard my prayer.

Then a Sister brought forth a cloth that looked like the cloths worn by all the Sisters. She carried it regally across her arms and presented it to Rilkah Ramih who came to stand before me bearing the cloth.

Rilkah Ramih opened the cloth and inside was another cloth dyed rich purple with the consecrated oil of the Murex. I had never seen anything so beautiful.

She wrapped this purple cloth around me and caught it at the shoulder with a stone circle held by a pin.

I shuddered when I saw that stone circle. It looked like the circular womb-ring of the stone mason from Antalya that I had seen so long ago. But it held my wrap and this was not the time to imagine things that could not be.

A Sister took the hair that fell down my back and twisted it until she had bundled it neatly at the top of my head, and this she tied in place with a strip of skin from a waterdeer.

Then the priestess with the waterbowl came forward with red and blue pigments, and painted small dots representing the moons of the journey on my cheeks and the back of my hands.

They put the white cloth over my shoulders and Rilkah Ramih signaled for me to follow her.

We walked ever so slowly out of the sanctuary chanting the name of the Great Goddess, the Queen of Heaven and Earth, Inanna.

We ascended narrow steps at the side of the temple and entered through a doorway that only priestesses knew. The passageway was dark, but there were torches at the entrance. One of the Sisters lit a torch from an oil fire that burned just inside the door. Someone had already been here preparing the way for my Interment.

The Sisters motioned for me to sit upon a baked clay slab by the door. I sat. They gave me a tiny sip of water they said contained knowledge for my journey—I had eaten nothing for two days—and then the four Sisters knelt before me and began to wash my feet. They washed my feet with their hands and big sponges from the sea, ladling water from the earthen bowl. Then they dried my feet with the tresses of their own beautiful black hair that hung to the floor and fell across the stones.

Then Rilkah Ramih came forward, opening the little vial she carried on her chest. She tenderly stained the soles of my feet with spirals from the oil of the Murex. These were the only words she spoke: "Walk to the center of all that is."

She led me down a narrow and uneven passageway. The others stayed behind. We seemed to spiral in, in, in to the secret areas of the temple. Sometimes passageways would open up to the sides, but Rilkah Ramih knew the way to the heart of the labyrinth. She carried the light and I, walking behind her, could discern very little. The walls seemed to be etched with shapes or textures that the mind of Aisha told me told a story.

We went deeper and deeper, and it seemed Rilkah Ramih walked faster and faster and I walked slower and slower, like I was in a trance and could not keep up. I felt my way in the darkness, groping along the sides of the narrow passage.

There was a time when my hand, sliding along the wall, felt something long and thin and smooth hanging on the wall, and I knew it was a bone. This frightened me and I tried to move faster, barely discerning that there were bones everywhere now, and I must be in the Passageway of the Dead.

I clipped my little toe on a brick or stone that jutted unexpectedly from the wall—I do now know why it was there, because the walls seemed mostly smooth—and felt a sudden searing jolt of pain. I knew my toe was broken but I had to keep on.

Now, something came to me: I was drugged. This was why the labyrinth seemed endless. Something was in the water they gave me to drink and I was having trouble gripping my senses.

Now it was pitch black. I had lost sight of the torch of Rilkah Ramih and I was afraid. I stopped. I could go forward or I could go back. *Don't forget*, I thought, *which way is which.*

My whole being seemed to shudder from inside to outside, beginning in the fluttering region of my heart just beneath the bone of my breast. I had trouble catching my breath. My hands were damp and trembling.

Go on, the mind of Aisha spoke, *Go on.*

I felt for the walls and moved forward, going deeper and deeper into the temple, my feet taking me down, down, down, as if to the edge of some great chasm.

My hands led me to a plastered brick corner, and when I went around it, I ran straight into a wall. Smack! It was dizzying, but worse was the revelation that I was closed in! I gasped. Then I heard the words, *Push the door.*

I pushed the wall in front of me and it swung open, revealing a tiny cell lit all around with torches. Rilkah Ramih stood at the far end.

Now I knew I had come to the heart of the labyrinth.

I stood facing her. She did not look at me. She had already taught me all she knew.

Rilkah Ramih systematically went to each direction, picked up each torch from its holder on the wall, and turned it upside down into a container of water that stood at its base. This act symbolized the Mystery of Fire in Water in Fire. In this way she extinguished all the torches, one by one, all but the one she carried for herself.

She stepped right past me and through the door as if she didn't even see me, as if she were blind to me, closed it behind her, and I stood in abject darkness in that empty, forsaken room. Alone.

I heard heavy bars bang down across the outside of the door. I knew I was locked in. This may have been for my own safety. I had seen the passageways. One would be so lost if one escaped. . .Could die in the dark of the endless maze. . .

I cautiously felt my way to the wall and sank down, pulling the white cloth tight around my shoulders. It was so cold encased in that brick and mortar and clammy mud plaster. I felt down for my broken toe, felt heat, swelling, and a fierce but dull pain that flared up in a spasm.

Oh, my Goddess, my Queen Inanna, help me.

Tears leapt into my eyes. I felt so sorry for myself. I began to whimper like a forlorn child. All of this, I could finally see, was, in the end, nonsensical. I was locked inside the temple. To what end? Why? There was no redeeming value in this frigid experience, no value at all, especially after one hundred and fifty-four moons of preparation. It was terrible and primitive. It was meanhearted. Meanspirited. It was not a fitting act on the part of the Sisters of Nun. What had possessed Rilkah Ramih? What did they think they would gain by locking me in this place? By torturing my mind with drugs? By leaving me without a blanket or a light? By locking *anyone* in here? I understood Queen Inanna's madness.

I never heard Rilkah Ramih move away, but I knew she was no longer there.

I had the realization that I had never truly been alone in my life. I had never been truly lonely. I felt a deep loneliness creep out of my solar plexus. I felt the sadness increase and envelop me. My emptiness was pervasive. The life of a priestess was cruel. I felt trapped in my own mind, my bony shell, my weakness and insecurity, my fear, my lack of purpose, by everything in my life as I leaned against the wall of this damp tomb. Everything within me fought. I longed so for the dry heat of the sun.

I wanted the Sun. I imagined the Sun. I built up its image in my heart, hot, burning, searing and fringing brown grasses. Sun, brilliant, blinding, reflecting off Holy Waters. Heat. Rays. Warmth. Light. Vision. I built up the image of the Sun, built it up stronger and stronger until I actually felt the bright rays. I felt the bright rays pour down over me, pervade my form, engulf me in their shining yellow-white energy. Then I felt all right. I felt peaceful. I felt calm. Like the Moon. Like a clear, soft reflection. I felt as calm, as if I sat in the shrine to the Moon atop the ziggurat. I felt tranquil then, and lapsed serenely and without pain or fear into a deep and peaceful slumber. Oh, great peace of sleep. Great peace of sleep.

I know not how long I slept, only that during that time I held in my mind an image like a dream of a curve that seemed to rotate around a straight line going down, down, down like a spiral, revolving down like the inside of the Murex. This shape seemed to curve down through many planes and layers of knowing, pointing directly to the center of the world. I saw the way my mind must follow.

I am in the tomb. I tell this to myself. *I am in the tomb. This is how my people are buried in death. They are laid beneath the brick floors of the temple, of the palace, of the houses. Quarters of the City have been given to the Dead. Quarters have been abandoned by the Living for use by the Dead. I am under the floor, but I am alive. I am alive. I am live meat in the shell.*

I travel down, down, down the winding slide; I feel myself slide through levels. Suddenly there is brightness and pictures begin to open to me like windows to admit light and air.

In the first picture, I see a woman and I know she is a priestess. Although I do not recognize her strange black clothing, or the sparkling ornaments that dangle from her earlobes, I can tell she is a priestess by the way she sits. She sits with a priest, who seems somehow familiar, inside a temple with ceilings higher than I have ever seen. They are as high as the sky. The priestess and the priest face each other chanting, even as I have chanted.

They chant "Allah. . .Allah. . ."

They are not of this Land. They sit on carpets of the Desert People. The woman holds a set of writings on flat sheets. On the top is painted a picture of a naked woman who floats on a pink veil. The naked woman may be her goddess.

The priestess changes her chant, begins to chant one of the names of Aisha. She chants, "Maah Maah. Aaah Maah. Aaah Maaah."

The priest stops chanting. He shifts his body and I can see the priestess stiffen. Her body is suddenly charged with fear. I cannot see what she is afraid of. There are two other priests nearby, but they do not threaten. The priestess speaks words I understand but do not understand the meaning of. She speaks the names of gods I have not knowledge of.

Then I feel I am this priestess. She calls me from another place and I am her. What does this mean? I am in her body; I see through her eyes. Her mind does not realize how visibly her body has tensed with fear. I am fearful inside her body. I am her and me at once, and I fear for her as I sit in this tomb.

The picture changes. I see a woman. The gold symbol of a high priestess of Egypt hangs around her neck. I know this symbol. It has come to us from the Wood Boat People. It is the sign of the womb of goddess.

The woman is lecturing in a large hall about geometry. I recognize the formula she is teaching. I have learned it in my studies with Rilkah Ramih.

Then she is laughing in the street, laughing with disdain, about the trick of turning a stick into a snake. "They call this a miracle," she says. She is disgusted.

Then I feel I am her, too. I am inside of her, looking through her eyes. I can feel her white linen tunic fall over my breasts and hips. I can feel her golden necklace against my chest.

I am in a chariot, driving near the lecture hall. Men block my way, force me to stop. They pull me violently from my car, throw me in the street and begin to bang my head.

I am paralyzed. What is this terror? I shake my head. Trying to shake off the potion of Rilkah Ramih.

Then I see a woman in a dark and dirty room. She is in chains. She is in tatters. She is ill. She is crying; then she is staring off into nothing;

she is praying. She is speaking like a mother to a handsome young man. She is absently singing a strange chant: "Loving angel, you are a bird with wings. . ."

All the visions have the same eyes. I realize this now. Different colors. Different shapes. But the same eyes. I see through her eyes. They are my eyes. They are the eyes of every woman in every vision. I look in, I look out.

I see her forced to stand, but it is me standing, with my hands tied behind me around a stake in the middle of a city. My hair is cut off. Then men are lighting a fire all around me. Many, many people—women, men, and children—are throwing on fuel. I shall be burned! I scream and scream for help. I scream the names "Jesus! Mary! Joseph!" but I am not screaming from my body.

I do not understand these visions, but I feel an intense fear. A pulsing fear. I am so cold, so cold, so afraid. I think I cannot endure the mad phantoms of Initiation.

Lida. Lida! I cry into the mind of Aisha, *My beautiful Lida. Play your sweet song for me.* And I hear strains of music. She has heard me through the mind of Aisha! *My beautiful Lida, play your sweet song for Mami.* I hear the bone lyre. I hear her soft song. *Oh, comfort me, Sweet Lida!* She comes to me. She comes through the mind of Aisha with her music; then I know I am not alone.

I fly to the end of the spiral and another window opens. I close my eyes, but the vision is the same whether they are open or closed. *Please, no more violence,* I cry inwardly. *No more.* I am shivering.

I am in a round white room. This room is in the stars. I know this place, I know this time, and yet I have never been here. It is a stone room, part of Aisha's mind. The stone is stone like I have never seen. It is polished brilliant white, and it sparkles beyond any stone ever worked in Ur. The center of the circular floor is inlaid with a circle of gold that shines like the Sun. Inside the circle are seven symbols, like those given to me by Al Ali. I try to make them out. They seem to be a crook or a staff, a goblet, a sword or feather, a tree, a seedpod, a shell from the sea, and a crystal. In the very middle is a stone ring, the stone womb I wear upon my shoulder. I am sure.

Suddenly the white room is full of people. They are people of this place, women and men, and others I cannot discern. They are so tall, so thin. They are dressed in gold, or perhaps the gold is their skin. They seem to ripple, change, and then change into a vision so they look like the people of Ur. They look like the people of Ur wearing white robes.

Standing in a circle, I hear them talking or communicating through the mind of Aisha. It all seems the same. I seem to understand them. I believe they are taking vows. It seems I am standing in the circle with them. One at a time, each vows to carry out some kind of task in the world. One says he will guard the seas. Another says she will heal with herbs. Another says she will teach the people to build strong shelters. Another will feed the hungry. One says he will make paintings to delight the people's eyes. Then they all look at me.

They wait. Clearly, I am one of them. I look at them, but I cannot see them clearly. I am too anxious. Am I to make a vow?

I wake up then and open my eyes. But I am still in the white room. All at the same time, I am in my dream and outside it.

"What is your vow, Lai-ila?" They are speaking to me.

Lai-ila. Lai-ila. I know this name. It means She Who Is Born in Darkness. She Who Is Black.

"What is your vow," they are asking, "before you cross the River?"

"My vow"—was this me talking?—"My vow is to help the priestesses who are afraid. My vow is to tell a story. A tale that helps them recall the mind of Aisha. The mind of Aisha," I said—and I spoke with an authority far beyond my station, I do not know where the words came from; they just seemed to come through me—"The mind of Aisha is free."

A voice spoke and I saw that Al Ali stood across from me in the circle. He stepped toward me, took the stone ring from my shoulder, clasped my wrap with the metal pin, and placed the stone in my hands. He spoke softly and tenderly, his lips moving near my ear: "Sister Lai-ila, people must have stories to give their lives meaning. Sometimes the story told becomes more important for survival than barley cakes or beer. Sometimes a story surrounds people so completely, it becomes as common as the air they breathe. They do not even know they are breathing a story unless the story becomes tainted, unless it becomes rancid, polluted, like sour air, air that can no longer be taken in. Air that is no good for life. I have seen people shackled in many lands over the River. These, dear Lai-ila, must have a new dream. I have seen those, my love, who would put all women or men in slavery. They have, my sister, no reverence for life. Make for these souls, Lai-ila Li, a way to Aisha. Make for these souls, my Bride, a path of stories to the sacred. I will help you, my Sister. I will carry your stories on the Sea of Nun. I will hear you through the mind of Aisha. Call and I will hear your cry through space as I row upon the Waters of Time."

Part of me was stunned. Part of me was fully knowing.

Al Ali spoke again, "The pattern of all, Sister Lai-ila, Born of Dark, is endless, sometimes painful, but not without hope. Possibility is endless. With the limitless substance of Aisha and limitless freedom, we create the world like a mirror reflection. Creation reflects our internal imaging. Let our souls, my Sister, fill with reverence. Let us share stories that celebrate life."

I looked around the circle. I saw the faces of many I knew. Lida stepped forward and began to sing

> *I lift the heart of love through song*
> *My mother's dream springs eternal*
> *Ah ee ee shah*
> *Ah ee ee shah*
> *Shan—ti Shan—ti*
> *Peace—Peace*
> *Om—Shan—ti—Om.*

All was black then, and I did not know if I was awake or asleep. I did not know if my eyes were open or closed. I was numb. Cold froze my bones. I felt dead, frozen dead, like the corpses beneath the temple floor.

The young priestess Teri stood before me waving the black snakestick and laughing. "Is it alive?" she asked. And it wound up her arm. I heard Ramil squeal with delight in the distance.

Just then the door opened behind me and I was blinded by torchlight, as the priestesses entered the chamber and wrapped me up in warm woolen blankets. I clamped my eyes shut and clutched the stone ring to my heart as they lifted the alabaster goblet filled with warm red wine to my lips.

✐

The candle was burning low; the night growing dark.

I emerged from the meditation feeling like I was Lai-ila and Pamela all at once.

I felt how life might be for a free heart, a heart that chooses, wilfully, love and initiation, each in its own time and course.

The voice of Riavek spoke to me through my reverie. He was still with me. He had never left.

"What did you learn in your life as Sister Lai-ila?" he asked.

At first I was startled, then it came to me abruptly. I said, "I learned that life is sacred."

He said, "Etch that on your heart."

All screens suddenly closed. I was alone. And I knew the day's lessons had come to an end.

CHAPTER 6

MERITATON
ANCIENT EGYPT

Thebes Restored to Amon, 1345 B.C.E.

Oh, bliss!

Oh, the magnificence of what is revealed!

Spiritual force, bubbling up like a geyser, punctures the surface, and that which was unknown is illumined at last!

To be fully in the present, awake, aware and free from past conditioning, is the greatest miracle of all, controlled as we are by subconscious impulses and residue from bygone eras.

How empowering it is to know why and how a thing came to be, how and why it lodges in the body of the child, in the soul of the world.

Remembering why and how unravels the mesh of entrapment, frees the spirit to journey, unfettered, into new and limitless dimensions of potential.

I lit the candle. "Open your mind," called Riavek, "Be courageous. Open yourself to the journey to remember who you are. Memory. Conscientious action. Detachment from outcome. Let these be your guides as you enter the spiraling realm of endless possibility."

Instantly, I was in another life.

I see a woman lying on a pallet against the wall in a small sparsely furnished room secluded in the top of a large public-looking edifice. The inside walls are finely worked stone that has been plastered or painted with a thick sallow substance, now chipping. She lies there on her back, looking withered beyond her years. I see traces of beauty and fire in her wizened face. Long, slim hands with delicate fingers arch expressively over the once fine linen coverlet. These hands feel strangely like *my* hands. It is something in the shape, something in the expression, as if they have danced the divine story, as if I *know* the story, as if I can *feel* it.

Her thin musculature is graceful, retaining the curvature of a once-powerful form.

Fair is she. Fair is she whose golden light penetrates this dim-lit room. These cold walls. This prison. I want to touch her. I want to warm her. I want to reach out and hold this prophetess of my dreams.

Softly, I sing to her across the chasm between us:

> *Your hands are like lilies*
> *unfolding in the morning*
> *Your eyes are the windows*
> *of the temple beyond*
> *Creatures of sea and star*
> *dance at your bidding*
> *Prophetess of Golden Light*
> *Seer of Forever*
> *dancer in the sacred dream*
> *of silence and song.*

I close my eyes, but see her still. I see a vision of her as a young woman. She places a small alabaster bowl filled with consecrated water before a faience image of Isis nursing a baby at her breast.

I am aware then, that the prophetess speaks. Her voice is low and shaking: "You are not one of the forty-two I expected to see at this time. Although you are a goddess, you are not the goddess Ma'at who would stand with scales to weigh my heart."

The old woman turns her head away from me and sighs. She looks toward the windowless wall—there is a vent near the ceiling—a dirty yellowish ivory that has not been painted for a very long time. She addresses the crumbling plaster, murmuring so quietly I can barely hear, "How does a heart weigh," she asks, "who has abandoned its priest-hood?"

She moves her face back toward me, slowly turning her head, and I can see that her thin gray hair is matted. She locks onto my presence and for a moment her listless gray eyes brighten in the weary sockets.

"You are not Isis—" she drawls with effort, "who wrapped me in loving wings as I rocked on the cold stones of the Queen's chamber." Her attention drifts and she whispers, "Isis, did your heart say I had left you?"

Perceiving me again, her eyes narrow and her voice grows firmer.

"You are not Sekhmet, for whom I was named," she says, "for your head is not the head of a lioness. I would like to know who you are, what you are doing here, why you have come. You do not speak, yet you ask questions with your eyes. Must I tell you my story?"

Raising her arm, she motions for me to sit. I seem to stand at the room's center, towering above her like a black pillar. I do not sit. I cannot move. I cannot speak or explain myself. I have appeared. That is all. I lean toward her bed as she rambles, half to me, half to herself, relating her tale as if she is wandering between memories and layers of consciousness.

"They say I am dying. This I know. They say I am mad, Priestess of the Future—if that is your name—but I am not mad. Unless madness is the time and place when one body, one temple, is torn limb from limb from internal conflict, as the incompatible values of past and future lodge side by side under the same awning. I am not mad, unless one becomes mad when past and future begin to switch places, so that in one lifetime the priestess jumps forward and back, and forward and back again, and becomes confused.

"Daughter, you stand before me as I lie in death upon this little mat. You are a strange vision. You wear black like the radiant darkness of all that is. You glow with the strange newness of an old soul, the childlikeness of an Ancient One. You are a goddess and yet you are not. What ornaments dangle from your ears? Like fine silver crosses worked in Nubia. But you do not look like a Queen of the South. No, your skin is not so light-darkened. You are like one from the northern tribes. I see in your eyes, the eyes I once had. Your eyes, the windows of your soul, sparkle with hope, like pools of deep sacred water reflecting memories you have not yet had. I know what it is to be like you. Old enough to have power. Young enough to have faith. I know how it is now, when old eyes hold tears that will not roll out.

"You open your eyes wide, with wonder, asking of me—with your strange singing—*how much sorrow can one heart hold?* Oh, My Heart, do not rise up against me as a foe!

"Do you stand in judgment, Priestess? Do you know the life I have led? The names I have lived by?"

I smile sadly, softly aware of her scrutiny. I cannot answer.

A small beetle ambles across the dusty floor, moving this way and that, searching.

The beetle rolls before it a ball of its own dung, they say. That is why it is mythically known as He Who Pushes the Sun Across the Sky. I have always found this curious, that a ball of dung can be transformed into a god simply by telling a story.

"For a moment," she says, interrupting my thought, "I fancied I saw you sitting and chanting, chanting with a bearded priest under a ceiling as high as any I have ever seen. No, but this was not in the Two

Lands. Asia? You sat upon carpets of the Desert People. I saw the Tree of Life woven in deep, rich, red wool. As deep as blood. As red as the dyes made from crushed beetles. As red as fresh woman-blood smeared on the doorjambs.

"Your eyes glow like bronze mirrors, then burn like a brazier. As sure as I see you standing there, I see my soul reflected: Oh, my Soul: Lioness of the Death Pit. I remember the smothering tension in the Death Pit under the Great Pyramid and I know what makes cats stalk. I know, too, why caged ones roar.

"I am not mad, Sister. Do you find me mad? No, I am not mad. It is just that I have had more than one name and cannot remember which one will save my life. My legs are crumpled, but the fire has not gone out of my blood. Not completely. I remember the flame. Shall my soul dance before you?

"Why do you not sit? With what substance do you paint your toenails? The most concentrated henna could never make such redness. Judge of All, Oh, my Heart—are you here to judge me? I will tell you what I remember. Then will I be released? Then will I know Paradise? My heart beats still. I will try to share my truth. I am not yet beyond the River. They have not yet crossed my hands, placed in them the ostrich feathers, nor sprinkled my corpse with rosemary and myrrh."

I cannot help but think her end is near. I can almost see her wrinkled arms crossed upon her breast, her lifeless hands holding the ostrich feather, her empty form sprinkled from head to toe with aromatic herbs. She shifts, as if trying to get comfortable, moving up on her elbows, sliding her hips and torso over, grimmacing slightly. She is in pain. Pain spasms in her legs.

Eyes closed, neck muscles taut, she must relax before she is able to go on.

"Listen Sister, I am Sekhmet—" She speaks haltingly, choosing her words carefully.

"I am Sekhmet, Violent Heat of the Sun. I am priestess to the goddess Isis. Or at least I was Sekhmet, then I was Meritaton, then Sekhmet again. This is the part that is not so clear. At the last initiation when Queen Tiy and I were young women trained for the priesthood in the temple, I officiated as Sekhmet the Lioness at the Great Pyramid on the sacred waters. I will tell you of that if you will listen. Look at you there, golden hair wild upon your head. Indigo waters in the pools of your eyes. Where are your ostrich feathers? Your sistra? Your bracelets? Where is your cobra headdress? Your priestess collar? What is that language that comes through your heart?

"No matter, I will tell you. This is how it was. High Initiation was mandatory for Queen and King, Highest Priestess and Priest of all the world, so we went by funeral boat with the priests and priestesses of Amon-Re to the Pyramid of High Initiation. Only a few were allowed in, and I was among them.

"I was a young priestess then, so full of adventure. I had never been away from Thebes in all my life, having been born in high estate in the seat of the Empire, and having been given into service at the age of 9.

"Because my blood was filled with fire, I was allowed to wear the mask of the Lioness in Darkness. I was chosen as mask-bearer because they said my heart contained the Sun's passion. The fire in all of life blazed in my soul. The Great Goddess danced through my arms and legs. Isis danced like heat in my blood."

Her nostrils flare, her old body floods with coursing passion, and she begins to chant, chant-singing like a temple cantor. As the volume rises, chills burst from my core. I am frightened by the sharp echo as the sound in the room crescendoes:

Isis, Mistress of Gods!
Bearer of Wings!
Mistress of Scarlet Garments!
Queen of the Crowns of South and North!
Queen of the Holy Waters!
Queen of Lightning and Sands!
Mistress of Words of Power!
Mistress of Cradle and Grave!
Mother in the Horizon of Heaven!
Queen Isis, praise be to Thee!
Mightier than all the gods!
Praise be to the mystery of my Lady!

"I shook the sistrum in the name of Queen Isis and my lungs roared in great claps like thunder.

"I shook the sistrum," she implores, calling for me to hear, as if I have the power to free her, "and kept the cycle of life in continued agitation, continual movement. Movement that never ceases! With the sound of my rattle, I drove away the clogging beast of corruption, he who would enter the empire if movement stopped. I cried, Open to the power of nature! Open to the generation of life!

"I sang and screamed and roared at Temple until my hair stood on end. I was Goddess of the Dance. I was she, Sekhmet, and I could dance with lions. I knew their hearts. I could lie with them. The hungry mother purred at my touch, licked my cheeks and hair. I was inside of her, and she in me. We danced paw to paw. We danced like flames and our claws struck sparks upon the earth. We danced at Temple. The mighty Lioness jumped through fire before me and laid down at my feet, purring the sacred sound at the center of the world! I was Sekhmet, Goddess of Lions. Bells jingled on my ankles. Flames shot from my hoop. Crystals in my glass collar sparked and clinked rhythms like water over stones at the edge of a flood. The sistra in my hands clanked louder and louder as I shook and shook and shook until my screaming roar pealed through the palace causing Queen and King to rise to their feet, gasping in awestruck ecstasy."

She exhales and closes her eyes. The room light dims as if clouds are passing overhead. Very distinctly, I smell the scent of lavendar. Eyelids fluttering, she continues with painful effort.

"In those times, before King Amenhotep crossed the Great River to the Land of the Dead and before the son of the Queen changed his name to Akenaton, left Thebes and built the temple city to Aton, all the gods and goddesses were honored. I was a young woman. I stood like you, with the fire of passion blazing. I was priestess in the Temple of Isis in Thebes, but Sekhmet the Lioness danced in my body and soul, and this was well. Isis was not a jealous teacher. She understood the Sun's fire. I served my goddess well but, as I remember, no goddess or god was so greatly honored as Amon-Re, the Theban god of Wind and Sun. The Theban priests ruled the Empire. Amon-Re belonged to Thebes and Thebes to Amon-Re. The royal family—of which I was a daughter—accrued enormous power."

As if parting a veil, she moves her hands before her. Her voice thins, becomes hollow.

"My vision grows clearer just now as I remember the darkness. How my eyes adjusted. It was I, priestess to Isis in Thebes, called Sekhmet for She Who Holds the Fire of the Lion, who wore the mask of Lioness in the passageway to the Chamber of Chaos, passage to the Underworld of Zero Degree Initiation.

"We had journeyed down the Great River, the two way road beneath the River of Sky Above over which sail the Sun, Moon, and stars each night, and the River Beneath the Ground upon which the Sun and Moon return. As priestesses and priests of Thebes, most powerful city in the world, we traveled the waters safely and with many slaves.

"We began our initiation between the lion's two paws," she whispers.

A sudden shudder ripples her bones, visibly jolting her thin shoulders beneath the worn gown. "Yes—I remember the feeling of those stone cold paws," she says. "Cold as the Underworld."

She shivers.

"One by one, as part of the priestly entourage, I guided them—the initiates—through the deep inner passages of the pyramid. I put one paw down in front of the other. My feet knew how to step. I trusted. I had the keen sense of a cat, and cat-like, I led them crawling when it was too low to stand.

"One by one I took the highest initiates of the Two Lands into the Death Pit of the Great Pyramid, the Chamber of Chaos. There they began the journey through the Place of Crossing the Water of Life to the Hall of Darkness, to the Hall of Truth in Light, and then to the Queen's Chamber—the place where Queen Tiy met her soul.

"Oh, My Heart! To meet one's Soul!

"The Queen's Chamber was the Womb of the Second Birth, high up in the pyramid.

"In the Queen's Chamber, some crossed into the Land of the Dead and did not return.

"It was in the Queen's Chamber that my Queen, Queen Tiy, stayed still, locked in the body case, semi-lifeless, on her inner journey for seven days and nights. As her mind traveled she met her soul's vision: All of Life is Light! All of Life is Light!

"This vision was a gift of power. In opening to receive it, my dear Queen became a goddess!

"To become a goddess again! To feel the blood of divinity coursing through your body! To feel the eyes of the goddess seeing the world through eyes in the world! To feel your hands and feet doing the work of the goddess, dancing the goddess's own dance!

"Oh, bless my soul, I *remember*.

"I remember when we removed the top of the casket. Our beautiful Queen was deathly purple. She remained unconscious, nursed by the Queen Mother of the King and a hundred slaves. Entranced as she was, she did not know Sekhmet had led her in and led her out again, but I was Sekhmet and I had stayed with her there in the Queen's Chamber for seven days and nights. I had stayed there, shivering, at first. The memory, though dark, is stark and clear. I can feel each moment as if I am there now.

"Time seemed to stretch interminably. Even the Cosmic Fire could not keep my body warm. I was there to guard my Queen, but I felt myself go cold like a cobra under ground and I could not move. I came to know how the snake feels deep below. The spine goes cold until movement ceases and consciousness abandons itself to trust in the natural cycles, surrenders itself to its own nature. I resigned there into the cobra state. I sank against the floor like a stone-cold serpent and I waited.

"The heat from the torch barely kept my heart beating or I would not have returned from the Land of the Dead.

"I sank into the cobra nature. No thought but stillness in the snake pit. Then I saw water. It was as if water glinted under a gray sky. I stood by the River. The boat was coming for me and it was her boat. The Queen's boat. Her yellow boat comes. Her yellow lake boat comes. Aton Gleams comes. It moves across the waters. I see the waters now. They are gray, like molten iron from Asia. The waters roll, the surface ripples, sparking with lights that seem to generate beneath the surface. The leader calls. His voice is pure and clear. And the slaves' oars dip through the surface at once, cutting the dripless pattern of endless ripples. They are singing:

> *The barques sail the Rivers*
> *the Rivers stream with Light*
> *the Light teems with fish*
> *whales leap in gladness*
> *and Thy rays are the joy of the churning sea*

> *Men move the barques*
> *the oars drip with life*
> *life floods with Light*
> *brilliant is the Sun*
> *and Thy rays are the joy of the churning sea.*

"The boat seems to come from what has been or what is to come. The song is a song I have never heard before, but I later heard it come from the mouth of Pharoah at the Temple of Aton. He sang this song and I recognized it. That is why I left the Temple of Isis to serve the Temple of Aton. Is this a crime?"

She stops. She opens her eyes.
"I love Isis, but the song called me in a vision and then I heard it in the world."

The woman closes her eyes and smiles, as if smiling in her sleep.
"I see the slaves. They are laughing. They are happy. No cracking whip pains them.
"Painted on the yellow boat's side is the turquoise Sun with lapis rays streaming down like arms with hands. I can see this Sun now as if I am there. Each hand holds a golden ankh, the symbol for the womb of the goddess, generating essence of all that lives. I feel her arms, the arms of the Sun, reach out to embrace me. She calls me to the water's edge. I stand upon the shore and the boat drifts in upon the sand. The men place a stairway before me. A priestess leads me onto the boat, to a dais in the middle. I sit upon the dais like the queen of my own funeral.

I no longer wear the mask of Sekhmet. The Light is so bright, even the power of Sekhmet cannot contain it.

"The rowers row—one, two, one, two—can you feel the rhythm?—and I am carried on silver waters. Fish jump before our bow, flying into the sky and back into the water. Glowing rainbows appear in all directions, everywhere the enchanted eye turns. The priestess kneels before me and places a golden ankh in my hand. She says, 'This is the key to the temple. It unlocks every door. With it you will open the stores of loving kindness.' She stands up, bows and moves away. Unmoving, I hold the key.

"Then we are on the other side. The Land of the Dead. The Dead come to meet me. They sparkle like gold. They glow, golden with silver light, with everlasting beauty. They take me among them and a young girl steps forward.

"I ask her, 'Where is the Temple of Loving Kindness?'

"I ask her this question as I hold the key to the stores in my hand.

"She answers: 'It is above the people that walk on the ground. It is above the people, above, below, and all around them. It is not a solid place, but misty, like a pyramid of mist. It is shiny gold and on a sad day it makes you happy to go there. To get there, go into a deep trance until you can see your soul float outside of you. It floats into a bright gold and shining light. And when you look around you will see what you imagine in your heart to be Paradise. Look around and you will see your Paradise. You will realize you are in Paradise, you have always been, and love and light and happiness will mix in your soul until your soul bursts with golden beauty.'

"She began to sing:

> *Rise up, my love, my fair one*
> *Come away,*
> *Lo, the rain is gone, the winter past*
> *Lilies abound*
> *The singing of birds is come*
> *The voice of the turtle is heard in our land*
> *The fig tree bursts with green fruits*
> *and the vines with tender grapes ripen*
> *Arise my fair one, come away,*
> *come away to the Temple of Love ."*

The old woman stops, mid-song, remembering my presence, the Silent Observer. "Wait, I know you now," she says. Her eyes flash open. "That was your voice singing. You are She! *Pamela.* The messenger from the Land of the Dead! You come from across the River. Do you not come for me?"

I, the Observer, am astonished and cannot respond. The old woman continues: "I felt your words, Priestess. I felt them in that time across the River. I felt as if I had followed you into the temple. You spoke to me again, saying, 'Then when you feel the love, you can take it back into your body, the temple of your soul. Your soul will float back into the heart of body. You will see, and you will know, that the temple is the heart of your own heart. There is no room for sadness to reside where love has taken residence. Love will fill you, then will you waken and then will your heart find its wings.'

"My goddess Isis came then—you disappeared; the River was gone—she came and wrapped her wings about me. She wrapped me and rocked me like a mother rocks an infant. She said, 'I will never leave you. Never. Never.' I felt secure and aglow in her arms. Secure and aglow with that Light of Love inside me. Light and comfort. Like a child in a mother's arms."

"I do not remember riding back across the River, but I woke inside the Queen's Chamber. The torch was still lit.

"I was with her then. I was with my Queen. I guarded her. When they came to get her, they roused her, and placed the gold cobra headdress of Highest Initiation upon her head. Then the High Priestess of Isis turned to me, looked into my eyes saying, 'Guardian of our Queen, you, too, have seen.' And she placed a cobra crown upon my brow.

"Are you still here? Are you still here, Priestess of the Future? I remember you now. You were there. You were the young girl in the Land of the Dead. You were the one called the White Mourning Dove in the Tree of Life. It was you who led me to the Temple. It was you who led me to my own heart. I see you, and then I see you not. My eyes are dim now. It does not matter. I must remember. I must remember for myself. I must remember for the weight of my heart is heavy and my own dear heart stands in judgment. I must remember now because I know the funeral boat comes. I can feel it coming closer. *Aton Gleams! Aton Gleams!*

"I can see the massive limestone stelas towering over the valley of the temple city of Akhetaton, the Horizon of Aton." The old woman rolls her eyes from side to side as if she is scanning a landscape. Her hand grips the edge of her cover. "Their beauty tells of Pharoah's rise, just as the vandalism tells of his fall. Not Pharoah's fall from grace with Aton, for that could never be, but his fall from grace with the priesthood."

"Akenaton was the little child born to my Queen after her Initiation. He was born to Thebes as Amenhotep IV after his father Amenhotep III, Rests in Amon. Akenaton was not well.

"My Queen was a physician, a master healer, but she could not magically heal the baby inside her. As she gave birth, I stood by with all my charms and medicines.

"The baby came out of the womb of Queen Tiy and was laid on the pillow, small and flacid. He did not move, nor did he breathe. I had seen births, but not one like this. He seemed unformed and his little legs were twisted.

"His eyes were open, but glazed. The nurse, who was standing by, breathed breath into him, and he coughed a little. His cry was not a normal cry.

"I felt he departed the womb too soon, for he was not yet formed. Yet, his parents said, he will be King, and Mai, the head of the military, proclaimed him to the people as Amenhotep IV.

"All the priesthood were informed of the birth through the empire's couriers who carried the news throughout Thebes, to South and North along the Great River and to all of Asia and Nubia.

"We did not know then that he would become our Pharoah, that he would build the Temple City, that he would transfer the seat of power out of Thebes. We never expected him to live!"

"The Horizon of Aton! I can see the city he built as clear as day in the eye of my heart.

"In the memory of my heart, the light of Akhetaton is white and radiant. Heat waves rise and curl about the elegant columns. I can see the city teeming with Pharoah's spiritual community, the women and men, beautiful artists, creating faience sculptures and multi-colored glassworks for export. I can see the gleaming radiance in their eyes as the light of Aton, the Cosmic Fire, shines.

"This was the first time ever a King had attempted to shift the flow of money away from war and into art. Oh, but the art was glorious! I will die soon, and just now I wish to remember it.

"Pharoah, himself, was the Spirit of Aton. His body was a temple that housed the Sun. He said all the people could share his Light, his Love, his Winged Heart, that they did not need priests and priestesses to find it, that the old gods and goddesses need no longer serve the Empire. We lovingly called him Pharoah, Great House, Temple. He said, 'You, too, are the Great House. Touch your hearts and you will remember.'

"All of this he learned from his mother. All of life is Light at the center. This Light is the Light of Love.

"Never mind that invasions were crushing the empire. Never mind that Pharoah was a poet and an artist and a seer and believed, truly, with all his heart, that the way he saw was the way of the future."

"I will die soon and just now I want to remember the beauty—not the terror. Nevertheless, terror there was."

"The baby's father, Rests in Amon, had *rested in the politics* of the priests of Amon-Re. The king was wise, but absolutely controlled.

"His love, Queen Tiy, a brilliant healer imbued with the healing eye, the Eye of Providence, the Eye of Wisdom, was surrounded by the golden glory of mystical vision. She alone instructed her son. I remember him playing in the gateway to her chambers, building pyramids with little blocks of stone. No one could have known how great he would become. "

The old woman raises up her eyes and gazes about the ceiling as if searching her memory for something. Quietly I sit down, cross-legged, beside her—I find I can move now—but it is as if she does not see me at all. She begins to call out to the Queen.

"You have crossed the Great River now, my Queen, and in my mind, since I cannot now stand, I bow before your spirit. May your spirit be cared for always! May you have plates of bread, vegetables, fruits, sweet delicacies from Asia, the best wines in the Empire! May your cask be full! May you drink the finest! May thirty-three thousand scarabs always bear your name!"

She shifts her concentration to the beetle now crossing her bed. Her bony old hand trembles.

"I am old and I must remember. I must remember so my own heart will not betray me."

Her mind wanders. Her eyes roll back. Her jaw quivers.

"I remember just now the warmth of Akenaton," she says. "On a beautiful, brave, and rare day in Thebes, Amenhotep became Akenaton, the Living Spirit of Cosmic Flame. How striking was the ceremony. How much I knew he spoke the truth that day for I, too, had learned that loving kindness is contained in the temple of the soul, not just in the temples of priestess and priest. I became his follower. I followed him. Me! I, who had served as Sekhmet in the Temple of Isis. I followed him, my beautiful Queen's son. I knelt before him in the glorious city to the Cosmic Fire of the Sun, and he named me Meritaton, Beloved of Light. As he touched my bowed head with the ostrich feather, the seeing eye of my heart opened as it had never opened before. By the truth of Aton, my vision was made whole.

"I truly held the key to the Inner Temple of Loving Kindness and, at this temple, I worshiped daily.

"You must know, though, how the infrastructure of the Empire began to collapse, how the priests—who no longer received silver from the people—plotted against him in every alcove. They would tear out his heart and feed it to the jackals so his soul would never enter the Land of the Dead. "

She pauses, clenches her eyes, coughs, inhales, then relaxes.

"I can feel the warmth of his hand now as he takes hold of my own cool hand." She is looking up, reaching out her hand. So convincing are her actions, she seems to be touching him.

"We stood by the lotus pool at the palace," she says, "The day was warm, the sun bright. He said to me, 'Dearest Meritaton, you must carry on my teachings for they come not from me, but from the innermost reaches of life itself.' *Oh, I remember, my Pharoah.'* They come, not from me, but from the glory of Aton. You must tell them, Meritaton, tell the people they are free. They need not tithe to the temples nor feed the spirits of the dead.

"'Dearest Meritaton, help the people see that they can live simply and beautifully, in peace and harmony, that truth sings in their hearts, that their own hearts have wings, that they can fly to the heart of the sacred, that their own heart is the Great Temple.

"'Meritaton, invite them to witness the dawn. Open your lungs and let divine song flow through you. Place your hands upon your spiritual heart. Cross your breastbone with your fingers extended like wings. Place your hands like the winged heart of Aton, as you have seen me do everyday before the people, as the glory of Aton rises in the east. Sing songs of love to them and their hearts shall be glad, and they will know they no longer need to fear the wrath of the dead, the gods, and the priests.

"'Such fears have been created out of greed. The priests of Amon have controlled the empire in His name, controlled trade and war and peace and manipulated the people of the Lands. Let us change the world, Meritaton. Let us see with our inner vision and build a new land, a land of justice, righteousness and truth.'"

"Truth was the most important thing to Pharoah. He ended every song he sang with the phrase *Living in Truth.* Truth is conscience, he said. It does not come from what we are taught. It does not involve being clever. Truth is the original mind which resides in the heart. It is the balance of light and dark forces within the self. It is divine inspiration, the soul that is free. With Pharoah, we lived in Truth. The spirit of the spiritual community was Truth. And all were honored."

"They said he was a dreamer. The priests and priestesses said he was insane and strove to discredit him in the eyes of the people. They ridiculed him. They said I was a traitor to the Temple of Isis. He was not insane—I will tell you that much, Pamela, White Mourning Dove Woman," *I am surprised she has remembered me,* "but no one like him had ever existed and no one else ever would. He was an avatar. I could see this. He was a messenger from the Land of the Dead."

She looked straight into my eyes, her own eyes brimming with life.
"And I was no traitor, for Isis never left me. She was with me and in me, expanded into Light, all the time I dwelt in Akhetaton."

"'Meritaton,' he said to me that day by the pool, 'Meritaton, there is life itself. And life itself is holy. I know this thought is radical, that it is different from the teachings of all who teach. I know I am misunderstood by the people outside the spiritual community of Aton, and that the priestesses fear me, that the priests perpetrate the misunder- standing. If only I could touch everyone in the Empire. If I could only sing to them. Show them another way of being. If only I could show them that all the gods and goddesses are contained in one sacred energy, and that all the gods and goddesses contain a spark of this energy. Aton is everywhere, in everything!

"'The gods of the territories need not go warring. In the name of Aton, we could stop the wars.

"'But I shall never move beyond this city. In my inner ear I hear the priests saying that Aton is just a new Sun God, created to usurp the power of Amon-Re.

"'They call to the people to rise against me, accusing me of casting out the peoples' gods.

"'But Meritaton, you, as priestess of Isis, know that Aton is no personal god. Aton is life, itself, and the people must know this. You must go to them, Meritaton. And this revelation you must carry.'"

The old woman begins to cry. Soft tears, like rivers of rain, fill small crevices in her withered cheek. I sit on the floor beside her and my heart contracts with pain.

My voice will not rise to aid me, so I pray for her in silence. *Blessed Meritaton, Blessed Sister, May the end be near that you may suffer no more.*

Presently, the old priestess quiets. Her breathing evens. *Sleep, my frail Sister, sleep.*

I close my eyes and pray, *May Aton be with you and with your spirit.*
May Aton be with you and with your spirit. May Aton be—

I hear her stirring. Her weak voice intones, "I cried, Priestess of the
Future, as I stood beside the lotus pool with this crippled child, now
grown, now the father of four young women. I could not fight my tears.
Pharoah also wept. Even then I felt doom like a black pall smothering
the temple grounds.

"I remember that day so well, how green the papyrus stood along
the path, how the lilies bloomed, how the lotus opened in the pool. I
remember the turtle at the pool's edge, happily extending its neck as if
in greeting to Aton. The turtle stands in my mind now as if the moment
is forever etched on the wall of Time.

"I did not know the pool would soon be cracked and dry, the turtle
made into soup, the papyrus drooping or dead, fallen on the royal
walkway. Did you know this, Presence Who Stands Before Me? Do you
know of the tragedies, of all that would befall us?

"'Akenaton,' I had said to him that day as he held my hand by the
pool, 'Dear Pharoah, beloved son of my Queen, she for whom I was Lioness of Initiation, Sekhmet, She Who Holds the Violent Heat of the
Sun, Dear Akenaton, Son of Tiy, Goddess of Nubia, flee! In her name, in
the name of Queen Tiy, I beg you to flee! There is time. There still is a
chance. We can help you. We can take you down the sacred waters in
Aton Rises. The boat remains untouched at the harbor. I have heard this
from my youngest brother who loves you as do I. We can take you to the
sea, across the waters to safety, to the land where the spiral trees grow.'

"And this is how he answered: 'No, dearest Meritaton, no,' he said
to me. 'Even in my mother's name, I cannot go. To leave this place, Glory Be to Aton, would be the death of my soul. This is my spiritual
home. The city I built to Aton. To live anyplace else would be to live as
dead. I will stay. I must stay. Let them come. Let them take me, for the
eternal life of Aton is mine. Mother and Father of all. Fire of Life Everlasting. Remember my song, Meritaton. Remember as you walk the
Two Lands and call the people to witness the Light.'

"And he began to sing:

> *Bright is the earth*
> *When Thou risest in the distance*
> *when Thou risest as Aton by day*
>
> *Bright is the heart*
> *when the darkness is banished*
> *when Thou sendest forth Thy bright rays*

Awaken all children
all children of Aton
innocent and loving and trusting as babes
arms uplifted adoring Thy dawning
singing with beauty
Thy glory be praised.

"I remember the song. How often had I heard it sung? How often had I heard his beautiful clear voice rise, divinely inspired, sailing to the sky?

"I can see him now. He walks, limping, as he has from childhood, from the palace in the soft yellow light of morning that comes just before the glory of Aton. He walks the path with Nefertiti—Nefru Aton—the Beauty of Aton. The royal couple walk with their daughters and Queen Tiy. The people have gathered all about the palace, all about the Temple of Aton, inside and out. Spiritual seekers gather all about the steps, waiting for the glorious burst of Aton over the limestone cliffs. We wait for the day to begin, for the praises to be sung, for the divine to fill our spirits, to carry us through another day of loving.

"Akenaton ascends the steps, passing with his family under the transom of the temple. He passes between the two columns, and beneath the gateway to the Sun adorned with the blue and yellow solar disk, the winged Sun that reaches down to comfort all who pass asunder.

"I can see him now. He smiles and bows to the people who smile and bow in turn. They are energized with the radiant energy of Aton.

"Nefru Aton softly shakes her sistra.

"The four girls gleam with the radiance of Aton.

"Akenaton, the Great Seer, moves between the people to the stone altar in the center of the temple. He bows, prostrates himself before the altar—can you see him?—then rises to his feet and faces the back wall, the eastern light, the rising Aton.

"Akenaton raises his arms, reaches to the heavens, instantaneously as the rays of Aton reach over the limestone cliff, brilliantly painting the red walls of the temple. All the world is illumined. All the world shines. He raises his arms and begins to sing,

'Oh, Glory of Aton
Bring Truth to my heart
May Thy beauty remind me
That life begins anew each day
That I recognize the errors I have made in the dark
That the heart of my heart is made new with Thy birth

That I am born again each day
That I fill my path with Truth.'

"I remember how the son of my beloved Queen Tiy took my hand in the garden by the lotus pool to the east of Aton's temple, the lotus pool whose waters reflected the glory of Aton at midday, and I remember how he refused to leave.

"Dear Akenaton, the sickly crippled boy, the one at whose birth I stood by, the one who would not breathe, the one with twisted legs, he who seemed too delicate to rule, he whom none expected to live through boyhood. Dear Akenaton. He released my hand and took the gold ankh on the golden chain from around his neck and placed it over my head.

"I cannot take this," I said.

"'You must, dear Meritaton, you *must*. It will be destroyed even as this body is destroyed. The priests of Amon will come. Take it, Meritaton. It is enough that the High Priestess to Aton, Nefru Aton, has fled with her daughters to safety, and that my mother is protected. I am resigned, Meritaton. I must never leave the gleaming Horizon of Aton again. Take this ankh, beloved Priestess. Take it in the name of Queen Tiy, she who wore it with humility, she who taught me the love of Aton. Take her ankh. Wear it in pure spirit, pure truth. Take it out at dawn. At dawn, expose it to Aton. Feel it gleam when you sing the praises of Aton before the people of our Lands.'

"Akenaton bent and kissed the golden ankh that hung between my breasts. He turned away from me then and walked with his limping gait toward the palace. I bowed to his shadow but he saw me not. He never looked back. I never saw him again."

"I am 60 years old. I have seen what has transpired and I shall speak. The priests of Amon-Re took me to the temple quarter, the place Akenaton had named the Brightness of Aton the Great in the City of the Brightness of Aton, and as they restored the Theban temple, they restored me to Sekhmet, Priestess to Isis. They forced me to change back my name.

"They took his daughters also—the girls he thought were safe—and caused them, through threat of damage to their bodies and loss of life, through threat of loss of their own children, to publicly embrace Amon-Re, the power behind the priesthood.

"Like me, they were forced to change their names.

"Queen Tiy and Nefru Aton, disappeared. I know not what became of them. This pains me deeply.

"Akenaton, too, disappeared and was rarely spoken of.

"The temple city of the Horizon of Aton was forcibly abandoned. The name of Aton was chipped off the stelas. The spiritual community was scattered apart. Colored glass was smashed in the desert. Songs to Aton ceased.

"It was as if Akenaton had never lived, and those who did remember him began to call him the Criminal of the Ages. Oh, my heart is heavy. My heart is so heavy, Strange Daughter. I tried to carry his teachings, but I feared my own death.

"The priests took me, tried to crush my soul, made me live crippled—as he was. My own older brother, High Priest of Amon-Re, laughed when they twisted my legs until they broke my knees. He laughed and said, 'Now you are just as he was. Just as he said you could be. Your body is a Temple. Just like his. The fool. Twisted and smashed.' He laughed that I had danced the Cosmic Dance, laughed that I would never dance again.

"They killed Akenaton. I know they did. Little Akenaton with twisted legs: he who could not run away and would not if he could. They killed Akenaton and placed Sakere, the Puppet, upon his throne. Sakere was unequal. He could not placate the people. They found that the only one with an image powerful enough to revitalize the military was Akenaton's own son-in-law, Tutenkhaton, the Living Image of Aton.

"Poor Tutenkhaton.

"Naturally, this beautiful boy, the living spirit of his father-in-law, was physically threatened. Naturally, they threatened to torture his wife, Pharoah's own daughter. Naturally, the priests of Amon-Re went to great extremes to assure that he appeared as they wanted him to appear.

"At first King Tutenkhaton planned to do the bidding of the priests of Amon while he strove to devise a plan to restore the universal teachings. But over time, his idealism fell to ruin. With his soul under seige, he changed back everything in the Empire, and they rewarded him amply: they showered him with gold. He lived a golden death. They changed his name from Tutenkhaton, Living Image of Aton, to Tutenkhamon, Living Image of Amon. He was forced to restore the name of Amon-Re to the stelas. He was forced to strike the Aton from the records.

"The City of the Brightness of Aton was restored to Thebes, under the power of Amon-Re and the self-interested priesthood, once again."

"Oh, I am dying! My name is Sekhmet. I must remember. I have worn the robes of lioness. I have danced Light into dark passages. I am dying. I see the funeral boat coming. Yes it is coming. I see it sailing upon the floor. I see the boat named Aton Gleams, Queen Tiy's lake boat. It comes for me."

"Oh, my heart is heavy.

"I see you, Strange Observer, standing there as witness of what is and I am telling you: the peaceful ways of the royal family sent the priests of Amon into fits of anxiety as they watched invasions into the Empire. The Hittites came, laughing at our peaceful Queen. And her King, Pharoah's father, stepped not to stop them. They said he should dispatch the entire army. He dispatched no one. And Pharoah, after him, dispatched only a small company. The priests were livid. The Hittites pushed the boundary and the boundary fell away.

"I am trying to remember—

"The Hittites were amused by our weakness. They laughed at Pharoah's twisted legs. They said he was no god. That he was not even a man. But he was a man and a god. This I remember clearly."

"My name is Sekhmet, but Meritaton is in me, too. I must not speak the name he gave me. I must not let it slip through my lips before them—the priests—for they will hurt me more. In my mind, I cross my hands over my breastbone. I cross my hands over my mouth. Keep quiet."

"What is life, my Judge, when it is living death?"

"I would like to gladden my heart again, to leap from this bed and dance as the people of the spiritual community of Aton would dance. I would like to dance the voice of Truth. I would like to peer through multi-colored glass at the beauty of Aton's rays. I would like my heart to fly. But when I think of Queen Tiy now and her baby boy born with twisted legs, my heart wads up like a twisted rag.

"When this body ends, and this soul crosses the Great River and comes before the court of Osiris at the Great Transition in the Land of the Dead, the forty-two gods and goddesses will ask me: 'Have you killed? Have you stolen? Have you stolen from a child? Have you lied? Were you deceitful? Have you borne false witness? Have you slandered? Have you eavesdropped? Have you committed adultery? Have you committed reviling deeds? Have you committed crimes against the gods and goddesses? Have you blasphemed? Have you stolen mor- tuary offerings?' And to all these questions, I shall answer *No*.

"Then, they say, my heart shall be light as a feather, light as the os-trich feather of She-Who-Holds-Justice, Ma'at, light as the ostrich feather he held in his beautiful hand when he named me Meritaton.

They say my heart will be light as a feather and that, as I prepare to enter Paradise beyond, I will be judged by no god, not Ma'at, not Osiris. I will be judged by the weight of my heart alone. What is the penalty for witnessing cruelty in the name of the sacred? What will the tariff be?"

I move closer then, me, the Observer. I sit on that cold plastered floor and pray. I pray to Osiris. I pray to Isis. I pray to Ma'at. *Oh, goddesses, gods. Oh, Aton. Aton. Aton. Oh, all-seeing Eye of Providence. Oh, all-knowing Eye of Healing. Oh, power of the ankh. Oh, holy sistrum, purveyer of the energies of all that has been, is, and shall become. Let her soul pass into Paradise. Let her heart be a kind and loving witness. Let my own small heart be apprenticed.*

I look up then and I know the boatman has come. I know she is embarking. I lean toward her, place the kiss of peace upon her forehead. Be well, Beautiful Dancer.

In that moment, a wave of Light moves through her wilted form. The Priestess Sekhmet shines in guilded-silver radiance.

"Sleep, Meritaton. Sleep, beautiful Priestess," I whisper. "Sleep in the sacred dream of silence and song. And, very soon, dear teacher, I shall meet you over the River where we shall serve forever in the Temple of Love."

Everything faded then and I was back in my room where the candle flame flickered before me.

My kitten, the one my son calls Foolie, was meowing in the next room, calling out for a bowl of milk.

I shifted my weight on my cushion. My leg was asleep.

"Just a minute, Kitty-Kitty," I called.

"Wait." said Riavek, "Be still. What have you learned from Sister Meritaton?"

I returned my thought to the meditation, my mind merged instantly with the flame. "The body is a temple," I whispered, "It holds Cosmic Flame, endless, the fire behind all life. All of life is Light at the center. All of Light is Love."

I laughed out loud. Oh, my soul, what a marvelous gift I had received! I bowed in gratitude and that felt right.

Riavek said, "Go now and feed little Foolie." He laughed. Then I fed Kitty-Kitty—and I did give her a little milk—even though I know—have known since the lions—that milk is not good for a cat's digestion.

CHAPTER 7

ALILAT
THE OLD TESTAMENT

The Red Sea, 967 B.C.E.

Throughout the revelations of lifetimes in which I felt personally involved—lifetimes that took place millenia before the 20th century—I began to see history in a new way, to experience it in my soul. I began to see myself as a member and a product of the great, long pilgrimage of humanity through time. Along the way, it felt as if triumph and pain had found a home in my spirit; created the nature of the woman I am today.

Upon viewing the life of Meritaton, I felt compelled to ask: Was Akenaton's monotheism the ruin of women? I had indeed espoused this perspective—the contemporary feminist viewpoint—before the visions were revealed to me. After meditating, I cannot say I believe Pharoah intended to desecrate the sacred feminine. It seems to me he was a lofty idealist who espoused the philosophical principle that the many gods and goddesses are all aspects of one sacred life, a life neither male nor female; a life that each of us contains just as we are contained by it. His formula might be viewed as one that heals, a formula for tolerance, a formula that opens the omniscient Eye of Wisdom to new dimensions of seeing.

I do not believe Akenaton intended to ruin women, but his idea of one overarching spiritual entity may have laid the groundwork for woman's fall from the inner sanctum as, over time, the idea of one "god" became associated with a male "god-head."

A few hundred years after Akenaton's reign, the desert people, competing for scarce resources, began bloody battles in the name of tribal gods. These were holy wars. Gods and goddesses stood in command of armies, and it was said, the strongest god or goddess would prevail. It was felt that only when one god reigned, would peace come to the land.

In my next meditation, Riavek took me into the legacy of Kings David and Solomon of the Old Testament, a period that took place about a thousand years before the birth of Jesus.

King David—David means "Commander"—was a powerful warrior who brutally conquered the tribes of Israel and Judah. He defeated the Philistines, Moab, Aram, Amalek, Zobah, Ammon, the Arameans of Damascus and the Valley of Salt, Betah, Berothai, and Hamath. He fought in the name of his god: a jealous, omnipotent male. He claimed territory for this god and believed that all competing gods and their representatives must be cast asunder, "burned, as in a fiery oven."

His son Solomon, whose name means "Sun" and "Peace," inherited the throne of Israel. It came to pass that, unlike his father, the son of David loved and exalted women and women loved him. He exalted local tribal goddesses. He exalted the sacred feminine. The large temple he built was filled with sensual imagery, celebrating the sexual union of women and men. In the hills he built shrines for the goddesses of the women of the tribes his father had conquered, the Moabites, Ammonites, Edomites, Zidonians, and Hittites. He made a "high holy place" for Ashtoreth, Hebrew for Astarte, the Mesopotamian descendent of Queen Inanna.

He wrote the *Song of Songs*, the best known love poem of all time.

Chroniclers say that King Solomon's attention to feminine divinity angered the god for whom his father, the great Commander, had shed so much blood. According to the Bible, the jealous deity said unto Solomon: "Because you have done this, and you have not kept my statutes, which I have commanded you, I will surely tear the kingdom from you."

From the time of that edict on, the Great and Ancient Mother Goddess, with all her names and representations, was officially banished. Yet, it took a thousand years, and the solidification of Western Civilization, to break her resilient spirit and force her underground.

On the third day of my visionary quest above the ocean, I lit a new white candle, breathed deeply to clear my mind, and called out silently for Riavek to come and guide my meditation. Riavek came gently in the midst of golden rays and opened the velvet veil onto a scene by the side of the Red Sea.

I saw a young woman—wealthy, powerful and beautiful—and I knew she was from the rich spice gardens of Sheba. Her tribe traded with the north, and when she came of age, she went with the caravan—willingly—to meet the legendary king who controlled the passages of the northern routes.

I moved into the story as if I were the young woman herself. Herein is the tale as I transcribed it:

Sensuous night. Sultry. Sandy. The land's rolling breasts slope down to the lapping sea, foaming in cool warmth at the edges as I sway side to side feeling the rhythmic pulse of the loping camel against my thighs. We move as one; I am hypnotized by the swaying rhythm. It moves my hips like the swaying dance I have learned since I was a baby, the dance that tells the story of my tribe for ten generations.

Pounded silver bells tinkle across my belly, around my ankles, about the neck, ears, and forehead of the camel, and all across the exquisitely patterned blanket, bells sewn like stars in the lapis sky, tell the story of the soul as it passes from birth to death in the seasonal cycle of Allat, the Great Mother.

Sensuous and sultry rhythms. The body moves. The hands and arms want to dance. The fingers want to form flowers, burst open like spring blossoms popping on the vines.

Oh, my goddess Allat. How beautiful is Thine glory as Thou danceth Thy rhythms upon Thy lands!

Sensuous night. Sultry night. New moon, blood moon, golden-orange crescent-horned silver, rich as the copper on the east bank, tilts sideways and floats like a chalice dipping into the Sea of Reeds. Sister Moon, Mother Moon, Goddess Moon, you are a chalice filled with essence of night and love, the sweet perfume of jasmine, dripping frankincense, honey in the stamen of the scarlet lily.

Oooh, the night. The night sings a chant, veiled in translucent blackness, sheer as the breeze. Oh, loose weave of evening, I feel the camel's form. I feel the moon sizzle, touching the top of the waters. I feel the sea's wetness. My bare foot brushes the bristles of the beast. I feel my womb's blood flow out on the camel cushion. I feel clots flow from the sea of this body. The same clots that made woman and man and the world, and I am thankful, Allat, for this paradise that is now. I am thankful that I am now a woman.

I reach beneath my loose dressings, flowing veils of red and green and purple draping over the camel's back lifting in the winds. I reach in the sacred gate, coating my fingers with blood, and I taste this blood with my tongue and with blood I smear my face and hands, feeling primal and beautiful on the east shore Incense Trail of the Red Sea.

I draw the sticks from the bag at the back of my blanket, smear them, too, with the blood of life, the blessing of womanhood, and begin to clack out a rhythm that matches the camel's gait.

The moon is a chalice
setting on the sea
The moon is a chalice
setting on the sea
Brother Sun, my Love,
calls to me
through the Moon, a golden chalice
setting on the sea.

Zuleika, woman of wisdom, I hear you calling. I hear you calling from my childhood and from the lands of the north!

Zuleika, Daughter of our tribe, called Bath-Sheba by your new people, how the camel sways beneath me. How the caravan's drummers pick up the rhythm, singing and playing to the camel's gait on the road to Jerusalem!

Zuleika, Mother of Jerusalem, how I have waited, lo, these long many years, until I would reach the fourteenth year beyond my birth and I could come to you Zuleika, Daughter of my tribe, celebrated Priestess of the crescent-horned chalice Moon, goddess woman of my mother. Oh, Zuleika, this is my time!

Alilat, they call me, and I sing to myself: sing and sob and sigh. You ride the camel to Jerusalem. You are a woman. Your blood flows on the camel's back. You are a priestess and a songstress and an heiress from a tribe of wealth and fame and generosity.

Alilat, living image of Allat, you are in your power with twenty camels carrying thirteen talents of silver formed into cups and plates and diadems to please the Egyptians, forty-four talents of frankincense rolled into sticks and balls for the priestess-women of Sinai, thirty-seven talents of qat leaves fresh, pressed flat in bags of sackcloth and riding on seven camels for the men of Beersheba. Lucky camels, eight hundred fifty miles, three and thirty days, of a light load you bear. Oh, but the last three hundred miles will be strenuous. We shall trade silver and spices and precious stones for gold at Elath. We shall carry one hundred and twenty talents of gold into Jerusalem where silver is abundant! Beyond that, strung together one hundred camels will be given for breeding. Oh, but my tribe is shrewd. And the qat is practically weightless. How they love to chew it in the Delta.

Alilat, they call you a lucky girl and so I am. Bound for the north-lands at the bidding of Zuleika, she who has placed her son, the one called Rising Sun, Ishraq, Prince of Peace, Man of Rest, King Solomon, upon the throne of Jerusalem.

And I, the "woman of Sheba," whom the Hebrews call "queen," woman among women, ride by night to meet this magical lover of women. Prince of Peace, I am ready.

Bless the beauty of man and woman, carrying the magical song of love. Solomon, will you love me? Solomon, will I please you? Will I teach you the secrets of fecundity that have been taught to me in the rich tents of my land?

You said, "Join me in my seat, Queen of Sheba," and I sent to you a graven ivory throne painted with winged deities making love beneath the very pillars you drew as the gateway to your temple, pillars topped with pomegranates and rings of lilies and lotus flowers that could only mean the gate of Allat is open; that could only mean you invite me to share the Red Love Mystery with you.

Man and woman need only one language, King Solomon, and that is the language of love. Oh, great blessings of the goddess.

You sent me these pictures and your sweet song of love by way of Zuleika's messenger and I sent you acceptance, the throne painted in ox-blood and ochre dripping with the feast of the senses and the cele-bration of life. Zuleika has blessed me. My mother has blessed me. Al-lat has blessed me.

Oh, night of nights! Oh, animals and plants! The Dog Star shines and moves from east to west. Shine bright, burning one. Shine bright as my heart shines. Burn bright as my heart beats, pulsing with love.

I drink wine from the bladder packed by my goddess-mother, gladdened to ride alone. Glad to be old enough to have my own camel. Glad to be young enough to be protected, surrounded by a caravan of men and women who honor and respect me and leave me to my dreams.

I find a new rhythm and clack again the sticks: My song is deep and earthy, from the bottom of my throat. I sing so no one can hear:

> *Kiss me with your mouth*
> *Your kiss is better than wine*
> *Your oils are rich*
> *Your name flows like light*
> *Rejoice and be glad*

The maidens love you more than wine
Your Queen of Sheba comes
Alilat comes
And rightly does she love you
I am dark as winter night
and comely and lovely
My veils flow like wine
honey, honey wine
My blood flows like wine
honey, honey wine
I am light-darkened
beauty of my tribe
beauty of my tribe.

Oh, Zuleika, I trust that you have not lied to me; that he is handsome as the gods of springtime! Handsome as the night is long!

It is dawn. The morning feels warm. Baba, the head driver, halts the caravan and instructs the younger ones to gather; shows them how to tie the camels carefully, securing each one. Unruly beasts they are. They will run for half a day to get to a scrawny thorn bush they remember somewhere in the desert. They have no feelings, maybe anger. They whine like babies. They spit in your face if they don't like your look. And they'll bite you even while you are riding them.

It is interesting that, in the language of those beyond the northern crossroads of the caravan routes, the word for priestess and the word for camel is the same word. Do priestesses have no feelings? Am I not alive with love? Would I spit in the face of my beloved? Would I whine like an infant?

I am full with love and yet it does seem to me that love is like water and that I have gone a lifetime without it.

Oh, Moon over the Sea, will my longing for love be sated? Allat, rush me to love!

A boy runs forth and takes my reins.

My camel kneels down among a great ado of tinkling bells and clanking. I get down and, for a moment, my legs are so stiff they will not move, the muscles having been molded like clay to the shape of the camel's body, but then I gain myself again and run as fast as I can, rushing to the sea. I run into the sea in my veils and robes, splash in the cool water of the inlet, dive down among the fishes and feel my clothes and my braids like a trail behind a shooting star, streaming out behind me as I twirl weightless off the shore.

Beneath the water are many rocks hiding strange creatures. I dive down to look, but fear I might tear my veils or I might catch on the reef. So I stand among the gentle waves, close to shore, peel off each wet layer, wash it gently in the sea and place it on rocks to dry beneath the rising sun. I stand naked, then, in the water—naked save for the ten strands of gleaming white pearls I wear about my neck. The water laps all about my waist and I dive deep and swim among the fishes.

Oh, beauteous life!

I tumble under water. I sing under water and bubbles and funny sounds come out of my mouth. It sounds so funny I laugh. I laugh as loud as I can in the sea. So amused am I at myself and all that is. I tumble and twirl beneath the surface poking through the blue-gray layers, looking up to see the sun in the sky, the flat disk widening in concentric circles of light on the rippling plane at the top of the pool.

Great bounty. My people collect oysters and fish. Down the beach, they are stirring grain in a pot of sea water. Pouring spices in another pot where they will steam open shells.

This is the most beautiful place I have ever seen.

The foothills slope gently down to the sea. All along there are trees and shrubs and bushes for the camels to eat. The cove rocks gently, enclosed by a coral reef that breaks the power of open water. My heart dances. My heart sings. Cliffs rise out of the water at the far end. The sand is as white as I have ever seen. The water, gray-red-violet when we came, becomes lapis, then malachite blue, as the sun moves higher. Then it is clear aqua and you can see animals through the reflective stillness.

On the beach, my woman wraps me in warm red linen and bids me sit on a menstrual cloth she has prepared. She loosens my braids and brushes my hair as she has brushed it a thousand times, rebraids it in countless strands, weaving in ribbons of red silk from across the desert as she has done a thousand times.

I do not speak. She sings a little, humming and making up words, singing of when I was young, of when my mother bore me, my first camel ride, of the birth of my brothers, of our trip to Jerusalem.

She does not sing the song of the generations. Her songs are not serious, but light-hearted memories. She laughs as she sings.

She, too, is happy. Ano, too, has waited fourteen years to make this journey.

She finishes my hair and gives me the sacred cloth to pin between my legs. I am so proud of my womanhood, so recently has the mystery come upon me. She, too, is so proud.

I ask to do her hair. No, she says. And, lithe and youthful, she jumps up and runs down the beach. I chase her for a bit, then we both stop, laughing. We have no more breath in our lungs. We pant like lions and fall on the ground laughing.

Beautiful Ano. Your soft, round face is a vision of peace and beauty. Your loving eyes, lined with black kohl and powdered lapis, are hypnotic and enveloping. The lines around your mouth tell of years of song and good humor.

Ano says, we must thank the spirit of this land and the goddess at the edge of the world who guides and protects us.

We build an altar in the sand, making a circle of tumbled seastones and filling it with offerings of shells and feathers.

She says we must leave something of ourselves, make sacrifice to the spirit of this land, she who feeds us and keeps us in such harmonious beauty.

Ano unties the thong of her necklace of amulets. She removes an amulet for the goddess of this cove and places it upon a rock in the midst of our altar. Then she leaves me alone, going away to the place of eating.

I find a sharp shell recently broken, and saw off a lock of my hair, so moved am I by the luxury of living. I place the braid beside the amulet of Ano and in my mind I hear the voice of the Cove Spirit speaking. She says, "Alilat, is there no more you would give to me?"

I am exalted and frightened on hearing this voice. I am startled and wondering, *who calls?*

I fall to my knees in the sand, bow my head and raise my arms in supplication. I bow to the ground in reverence for the terror and beauty of life.

The spirit asks: "Would you not sacrifice to me your fear, Alilat? Your doubt? Your terror of the northern tribes? Would you not leave your worry and your longing for your mother here upon my beach? Would you not open your hands and pour these things out to me that I may carry them away at high tide and purify their essence? Would you not let me turn your fear to courage? Doubt to will? Worry to strength? Longing to faith?"

Such thoughts had never occurred to me, but I felt the wisdom of this place. I felt tension flow out of me—tension for fear of the riches we carried and the supplication we may have to give to the gods of the northern tribes in order to preserve our lives. I felt the tension flow out of my form and I felt a new kind of strength enter. Faith filled my soul, poured in through open channels.

At that moment I stopped bleeding. I actually felt my bloodflow cease.

She said, "Sacrifice to me your fear and, as a gift, I will stop your bloodflow, for it is not time for you to conceive a child, but it is time for you to know the Mystery of Love. Feel your freedom, Alilat. Love. Love. Pay homage to me, and I shall guide your loving. Listen to this, Alilat, when you wish to conceive, you need only petition me. I shall start your bloodflow and thirteen days later, you will be ripe as an open hibiscus flower. So may you control the miracle of life. This is in your power, Alilat, as a woman of wisdom."

I felt the power of her words sink into my heart.

I answered, "What is your name, Spirit of this Cove? Goddess of this Sea? What is your name, Powerful One, and I shall pay homage to you as the Goddess of Love and Mistress of the Miracle of Life forever."

She said, "I am your own Allat. I have been with you from the beginning and shall be with you for all time. You have found my secret name. Love. My secret name is Love. My name is Beneficence. My name is Charity. And Faith. And Hope. All these are Love. And now that you travel, you see that I am not of the tribe of the south alone. There is one goddess, one Lady of Life, and her name is Love. They call me by a thousand names, by Al-Uzza and Menat, but my one true name is Love. Essense of the beating heart—of sea and shore and sky, of all creatures, even camels. Alilat, go now, they call you to eat. Open your oyster and you will see, hidden beneath her flesh, a great and shining black pearl. This is like the pearl you carry in the velvet pouch of your body. The pearl by the sacred gate. You will remember me when you think of this pearl. Now, go and eat for they call you and the food is ready."

When I opened my oyster, I found beneath her flesh a black pearl, shining with such luminescence as I have never seen. I slipped it into the little pouch that hangs at my side, and from that moment on, my life was changed.

Of the two thousand initiations of the sacred path, my people activate four. The first is the Red Love Mystery. This is where the priestess loves a man and experiences the opening of the sacred gate. The sacred gate is the gate of life and everyone knows that while the body of the priestess is a holy vessel, it takes the sacred act of Red Love to enliven the starseed of the plane of Creation Completed. The second mystery is called Transformation. It is where the priestess learns to change Blood into Light. This initiation takes place over months or years and during the rites of teaching, the priestess learns to transform her woman-blood.

Turning woman-blood into white light signifies that a sacred child will be born. The child will be called enlightened, full with light. It is said that the two eyes of the child will see as one, seeing only divinity in all directions. The enlightened child is full with reverence, full with gratitude, and marked sacred in the eyes of the people. The enlightened child has an aura of gold and silver flames and is filled with the passion of love and life and ecstatic being.

The third mystery is the Initiation of Water. I have wondered much about this mystery—I have been in the water and floated, but I have never felt more than flotation. Do they really walk on water? I have a vague memory, perhaps of a dream, of seeing an old man—a man not of my people, I think—walk across the top of the sea during the red tide. I remember him in white robes tied with red cords. I remember him in dark leather sandals laced up his calves and he walked on the sea's surface. This seems a strange mystery. They say it has to do with belief. They say it is not walking on water itself that is the mystery. They say walking on water proves nothing, signifies nothing. The important thing is understanding the mystery of possibility and believing in possibility. I believe in possibility, but I cannot walk on water.

The last mystery is called the Initiation of Saving the Hopeless. Ano told me that this is the highest of all initiations. It is as if you have seen a person buried alive and there is so much sand on top of this person that you feel no matter how fast you dig, you will never be able to save her, that she will be dead from fear, confinement, and asphyxiation. And it is as if you hope and believe she has a small pocket of air and you pray to her to know you are coming, even though you believe she cannot hear you, and you dig and dig and dig. It is as if, she says, the sand is light and dry and loose like the sands by the sea, and it falls away quickly, but there is so much of it, you feel you will never get through. Ano says you dig and dig and dig. You dig past your own fear, past your anger at having to do it all yourself, past your anxiety of not knowing whether the person is alive. You dig past your feelings of wanting to give up, until the only thing left to do is to accomplish the task as fast as you can, with no thought for yourself, only thinking of the other, while all the time your heart is calling, *Don't give up! Don't give up! I'm coming! I'm coming!*

This is what it means to Save the Hopeless. They call this also the Initiation of Fire because the person does not even know you are trying to save her life. Her life is the spark. Your will is fire. Fire is the will to life, itself. The trapped one is caught by loneliness, fear, resignation, and despair. You must escape your own fear of failing. So, in the end, the one who helps and the one who is helped, both cross the threshold of the Mystery of Fire.

Ano says this is the highest of the initiations she knows about. It is deeper than the Mystery of Water.

Ano says there are two thousand initiations in all, but that not everyone goes through all of the levels. Someone might skip a thousand mysteries, if that is what is fated.

These initiations seem strange to me, but then I have not even been through the first. I wonder if I will Walk on Water or turn Blood into Light. Ano says, "All Things in Their Own Time." She says I must now understand how the camel and the priestess are related, and, only then, will I be able to safely cross the Threshold of the Mystery of Red Love.

I wonder what could be unsafe about loving? Oh, Allat, my spirit dances in anticipation.

On the eighteenth day of the journey, I am weary. The desert sun beats down upon our caravan. We are weary, but thankful that there have been no demands or attacks from the middle tribes and that we have traveled thus far in safety along the well-worn east-shore trail.

But Baba is worried and the camels are stepping strangely. Some are stopping and we must beat them to move on.

The wind is picking up—the bells are tinkling all through the caravan—and sand drifts in the place where the route has turned inland. I think Baba feels the trail may be lost.

I do not know what he fears, but I can feel his trepidation, even from my place upon the ninth camel back.

I pull a veil over my nose and mouth, and slit my eyes, so the sand will not blow in, and I trust the camel to be my ship across the desert.

My camel stops suddenly, and with my eyes clamped shut, I automatically begin to beat it blindly with the stick I keep attached to the blanket. Blindly, I beat my camel, but the camel does not move. Abu, the boy, rides alongside me and hits my camel with his stick but my camel will not move. His camel, too, stops then, and beyond our control, both camels turn to face the wind.

However we beat them, they will not move.

Squinting my eyes, I see all the camels are stopping. All the camels of the caravan kneel down one by one, sealing their eyes and mouths and noses and stretching their bony heads into the wind.

The winds are rising.

The sands are blowing and Abu yells something to me. I cannot hear him. Then I hear, "Get down against the camel and cover yourself!"—and it is Baba yelling to everyone in the caravan.

All the camels are on the ground.

I have heard about this thing happening. I can see people around me securing things and I feel to see if my pouch is still at my side. It is there. And I tighten the knot. Even tightening the knot is difficult.

The sand is piling against the camel's side. I pull my robes in around me and lean forward on the camel. I lean into the wind. My heart pounds with fear. I want to be with my mother. I want her to wrap me in blankets as she did when I was a child.

But she is not here for me now.

I am with the caravan now, but, I cannot see them. I have the sinking thought that each one of us is alone.

I pull in my robes, gathering them all about me, tucking them under, making them like a tent to block the screaming sands and loose debris of the desert.

I am so scared that my legs begin to shake. And suddenly, I feel myself falling asleep and I am glad, for I would rather die sleeping.

I dream the sun is glinting off the ocean. The sky opens up and a man's voice booms out: "You shall not allow a priestess to live!"

I wake up as suddenly as I drifted away. I am so frightened. My stomach is in a knot.

The sand is screaming all around me. Bells ring violently. The sand screams, but I can still breathe. I say to myself, *I will not panic*. The only thing I can do is be calm. I am wishing for my prayer beads. Now, it comes to me that I left them carelessly at my mother's tent, glad that I would no longer be forced into chants at my mother's discretion. I feel for the white pearls at my neck. I take one between my thumb and finger and I begin the chant.

Hail, Allat, Mother of Form
Blessed art Thou amongst women
Blessed is Thy mystery of turning blood to light
Blessed is Thy creation and graced is the fruit of Thy womb, Life.

I hold the next pearl:

Hail, Allat, Mother of Form
Blessed art Thou amongst women
Blessed is Thy mystery of turning blood to light
Blessed is Thy creation and graced is the fruit of Thy womb, Life.

I repeat this mantra perhaps nine times, hoping it will bring me a sense of serenity, the calmness that comes when one taps into things of tradition. But I find I do not grow peaceful.

Rather, beneath the chanting, a memory begins to surface. This memory enlarges itself until it becomes the only thing in my spirit. It enlarges itself as the sand piles higher up my legs. It grows and grows until I feel there is no hope in living.

I remember a story I heard as a child, a story that was not meant for my ears, but was told to my mother by visitors in her tent while it was supposed I was sleeping. I did not sleep much when visitors were about.

I remember the guests were anxious even though my mother had given them dates and her finest coffee. They spoke of David, the northern Commander, the one who had killed the lover of the Daughter of our tribe, Zuleika, the one they called Bath-Sheba. He killed her lover, his own man, so he might possess her himself.

They told how David obsessed with Bath-Sheba, so taken was he by her beauty and teachings, and how he willfully took her into his possession, as if he could control the Mystery of Red Love.

They told how the people loved her, for she was a priestess who knew the mysteries of truths untold in Jerusalem.

She taught the priesthood about the Initiations of Love, Transformation, Water, and Fire. And the Commander was jealous.

They told how he called upon the people to enact the Law of Moses. That Law, according to the King, said, "Smash the sacred pillars." These ancient pillars celebrate the First Mystery, the Red Love Mystery, the Eternal Connection that generates Life.

So angry was he, they said, that he could not possess Love, that he chose to try to kill it, just as he had killed to acquire Love in the first place.

They told, also, how he had taken the sacred teachings of our tribe —what he learned from Zuleika—and put them into song. These songs he had claimed as his own, as if one could own a song of Allat!

They said he took Zuleika's prayer beads and burned them on her altar, that he smashed her images of Allat, along with the images of all the northern goddesses, the Mothers of Asher, Astor, Mari, and the settlements to the east of the northern sea, that he burned Zuleika's shrine and that, mad with lust for blood, he cruelly killed a multitude by the blades of his army, all in the name of the god he carved out of the mind-stuff of self-consciousness.

I remember this tale as I huddle close to the body of the beast. I am glad that I do not carry prayer beads or images.

This memory does not comfort me. I clutch my pearls and feel disguised. These pearls, they will be my prayer beads. I begin to repeat:

Hail, Allat, Mother of Form
Blessed art Thou amongst women
Blessed is Thy mystery of turning blood to light
Blessed is Thy creation and graced is the fruit of Thy womb, Life.

I know not how much time passed as I chanted this mantra of my people. I seemed to fall in and out of consciousness, alternating between peace and fear and peace.

During one moment, I awoke with the words *Mother of Form* hanging upon my lips, and the same voice I heard at the ocean pool began to speak to me again.

"Do you see now, Little Sister, why Trial by Fire is the highest initiation? Do you feel the heat of the desert? Do you feel yourself being buried alive? Do you feel the cold death held in the heat? How Life contains Death? How Death contains Life?

"Do you feel your hope fading? The uselessness of your happy ways? The profundity of your ignorance?

"Do you know, Little Sister, that I am with you? Do you know why the pearl I give you is black? This is your lesson, Little One. Hear me: You can love so much that it turns to hate. You can hate so much that it turns to love. You can go so far into Life that it becomes Death, so far into Light that it becomes Dark. In Death, you find Life. In darkness, flame.

"Feel the lightness of the desert close in around you. Feel how the burning sand encases you in darkness. Feel how David loved Zuleika so much that he killed for her. And then, when he could not possess her love—for a priestess is free—how his love became jealous and hateful, so hateful that he tried to kill her heart by smashing the image of her heart. And what was the image of her heart, but an image of me? And what am I but the soul of her own divinity?

"Feel how he hated her lover—Uriah—so much that he deceived him and had him killed in battle even as Uriah was defending David's own life. Feel how David had so much remorse that his hate for Uriah became penitential love and his love for Zuleika became a villianous mass of hatred, until, after years and years of confusion, David went mad with the contradictions he created.

"This is your lesson Alilat. Hear it and weep. Weep and gain wisdom. For freed is she who moves through Death to Life, through Life to Death. Strong is she who knows that the name of Life and Life Itself are not the same thing. Courageous is she who knows that Death and what they tell of Death are two different beasts. Know the source of the Fire Mystery, Little One, the Mystery of Saving the Hopeless, and you will gain the powers of Zuleika, a great woman of wisdom."

I know not how long I lay in deathly sleep in the desert, but when I awoke, the needling screaming whine of the sandstorm had ceased and the whole caravan was coming to as camels shook themselves out of small mountains.

The road was easily recovered as the stable markers were clear and known to Baba who left small tied offerings like little gift packages at each outcropping of limestone to honor the spirits of the lands through which we passed.

After six and thirty days of travel we reached the right fork at the crossroads of the caravan routes where traders from Amarna had been camped and waiting for three days, their boats moored at the inlet waiting to gain the stores our caravan brought from the edge of the world.

The transaction went well, better than planned, said Baba, and nine unhappy camels, whining and spitting, were draped with a thousand pounds each of the gold bars we would carry on the ten night ride to Jerusalem.

After one night's ride, our caravan stopped again and made camp. We set up tents and laid the carpets. We got out the sticks, tambourines, and drums, and laid a huge feast of local delicacies.

We drank Egyptian beer and we danced and drank and screamed and howled all through a day and a night, so great had our good fortune been.

Oh, was I in my element!

The trip had been hard, but now only nine more days until we reach the north.

I twirled and danced, clanging my finger cymbals. I danced the dance of the ten generations, from the time the first family of camels had been apprehended wandering in the desert. I danced the story of the garden and the first woman and man formed from clots of the woman's blood of Allat. I danced of the serpent that crawled into the man's foot and raised up his penis and then connected him to the woman in ecstatic rapture as they experienced the Mystery of Red Love. I danced the birth of First Child, the divine one, the sacred being whose halo flowed out like silver and gold flames. I danced how my tribe came into being and gained its riches. I sang the song of the tribal mothers while the drummers clapped the beat:

> *Honor to the Mother*
> *who births the Holy Child*
> *Honor to the child*

who rides upon the wind
Honor to the wind
who dances in the desert
Honor to the desert
who tumbles to the sea
Honor to the sea
who is eternity
Honor to the sea
who is eternity.

It became dark, the moon, coming into its fullness, rose up in the eastern sky. This was an auspicious time for us to celebrate.

There was one moment late in the evening, when the music and the song and the feasting died down and my people sat by the fire watching the flames. I watched the flames. I watched them lick and caress the wood, and came into my mind, the Trial by Fire, the Mystery of Azilut, and I made a connection between Saving the Hopeless and the dark day of sandstorm on the inland passage.

Amid the quietude and the crackle of the fire, I stood up and began to play my finger cymbals slowly. One-Two-*Three*. One-Two-*Three*. . .

My cymbals clanked eerily in the dark.

I beat out a slow, pulsing rhythm with my hands, slow and enchanting, enchanting and enticing, and the people of the caravan were hypnotically held, as if entranced, as I danced a new story.

I danced of tying down the cargo, clinging to the camel's coat in the whining storm, tucking in robes like a tent, trusting the camel to provide life and safety.

And, as I danced, my love for the wretched beasts grew, and I drew the people into their love for the beasts they so blindly tried to beat into submission, blindly and without thought. And I realized as I danced that no matter how much you beat a camel, it will not submit. It will not submit in its soul. It will not love you—and it occurred to me that priestesses and camels are alike in this vein.

The priestess is one who serves not out of duty or coercion. The priestess serves for the joy and honor of serving. The priestess serves no one, only her own sense of what is just and right and true.

I danced the connections between priestess and camel, the knowledge of Natural Law, of when to lie down and when to rise, the memory of even the remotest bush of thorns, the freedom of possessing one's own soul, the ability to close off the senses and dig oneself out of a sand mountain. The priestess knows these things and this is why she is a healer for the people. She heals their souls.

I danced slowly caressing the hardened earth with my unclad feet. I danced in circles to celebrate endless life.

And, at the end, I sang into the silent darkness:

> *Honor to the desert*
> *who is eternity*
> *Honor to the desert*
> *who is eternity.*

When I finished, the people did not move or speak, but seemed awestruck. Ano looked at me. She did not smile, but nodded her head, *Yes.*

I saw her unfasten her necklace of amulets. She took off a small carved wood camel, encased in gold, and tied it on a string around my neck.

She marked me as priestess. As priestess, knowing the power of the camel, I would ride into the Mystery of Red Love.

The valley is fertile and green with new grasses. It is like a long strip in the midst of high places, a strip which is the bed for a river or the basin for a sea.

We travel now by night and by day.

The people are tired, but excited, as we draw closer and closer to Solomon's city where, it is said, the streets are paved with gold and even the walls are hammered with precious metals.

In my mind, I imagine the city glimmering amid the high places.

It is said that King Solomon receives six hundred and sixty-six talents of gold each year and that his men and women enjoy a prosperity rarely known even in the far lands of India.

We travel by day and night and, after a time, a river does appear, and we travel on the eastern bank, even though it is told that Jerusalem lies to the west. This is because, Baba says, the way of the left bank is rocky and difficult and not fit for the movement of a caravan. Baba says that the river becomes the sea and there is a time before the sea when the caravan will cross back over shallow waters and we will make our way up the west bank of the big waters.

Loping along the west bank of the Big Sea, I feel something has changed in me. I was dark, now I am black. My hair is scented with the soft fragrance of the desert. I have packed my bells and jewels and ride free and simply. A camel-colored linen tunic I have wrap- ped about me. It is pinned at the shoulder. One by one, the red ribbons have fallen from my hair. My body is strong from the riding. I move supidely from a position of strength. I can feel my muscles rippling and this feels good and powerful. The simple camel amulet hangs about my neck and I feel the conection between myself and the camel. We have become one movement.

We flow across the desert easily, riding in the place between loose sands and the strip of hardened clay plains.

Further west, from time to time, high places rise dramatically out of the flatness. Ano tells me that there are people in those high places, living in small villages, lighting incense in caverns that look out over the sea.

The color is like I have never seen. In the mornings, the bright blue of the sea is illuminated against golden cliffs that rise and fall mysteriously across the land. The air is so dry in this place that it cracks my lips and burns my lungs. Ano gives me red ointment for my lips made of ox fat and blood, and this makes me feel sensual. I am not the same.

I cannot say what is different.

It is as if the child in me has danced away, and a goddess-woman has danced in. Lithe and supple. Sleek and simple. Oh, for the beauty of life!

We swim in the sea and purify ourselves. We shake out our hair and we comb it out. It flows around us, softly, beautifully, and it is as if we are all softer, more beautiful, for the hardship of our ride.

At the far end of the sea, we turn inland to follow the route that leads through the hills and cliffs. There is a settlement here—strange— but then I have seen strange things upon this journey.

Where the path turns in, there is a spiritual community and this community houses us for two days and nights, as we prepare with the guides who have come for us, for the final leg of our journey.

The community is nearly all men. A few women. Only a very few children. These men wear strips of ox skin around their arms and heads to tie on tiny little books which they say contain, in miniature, the words of their god. They wear these little folders containing the scrolls on their foreheads, so that they will remember to think about the words of their god. They wear them on their arms, so they will remember to do the work of their god. Ano says they tie them, too, around their middle, in places we cannot see, beneath their robes. They hang them there to remind them not to activate their penises for the world, they say, is filled with bloodshed, and the worst kind of punishment is to be born into the world. Their duty to their god, Ano says, is to father no child.

The women, too, believe this way.

There is no explanation for the existence of the children. Ano says they imagine the children to be their shame embodied.

Still, the children seem happy, running over the mounds of cut stone like little goats and leaping in the air like gazelles.

The women wear veils over their faces so as not to tempt the men with their beauty. These women have come to this community by choice and all feel this is well. They are uneasy with the people of our caravan, with our stores of gold bars, frankincense, and qat.

Their pots and jars are simple. They have no decoration save for the little leather books hung about their bodies as reminders to focus their attention on the word of their god. Their god lives in the Land of Death above the caves in the highest peaks of the highest places.

Ano says their caves are blackened with the smoke of incense because they believe their god can be seen in fleeting moments, his form illuminated in clouds of smoke.

They breathe the smoke of the incense because, they say, it may bring the essence of their god into their bodies and they may experience his presence inside their hearts.

The old men cough, and their voices are low and cracked from the dark clouds they have breathed. They look strangely at my lips, shining with the ointment of fat and blood and I feel these old men want me even though their sacred vow is to the Death God, the one who will grant them the gift of Death without Return.

They are uneasy, too, with Solomon's emissaries, the ones who meet us to take us west to Jerusalem. The emissaries come on stallions, the most glorious steeds, black as night, white as the sands in the inlet of the Red Sea. The horses are a special breed, bred for climbing, running and enduring, bred, too, for loving. They are not like camels, but are the friends of their riders. They gallop across the valley when the rider whistles.

Oh, what magic! Oh, what a broad place is this world!

Like the rising sun, our caravan enters Jerusalem from the east. From a far distance, I can see that the wall is not gold or even metal. It is not even completed. Mounds of stone stand everywhere.

Neither is the road we travel paved with gold. It is dusty and dry with use, hardened by heavy carriage loads brought from the mountains and sea.

The east gate is nearly constructed, and it looks as if it will be magnificent when it is finished—but the city is not glittering as I thought. It is all stone masonry and painted clay—beautiful, but nowhere near golden.

We pass under the east gate. In the middle of the crossbeam is a carved disk with rays like a sun with two huge wings stretching out to either side as if the sun is a bird with wings. It is like the sun flying through the sky and I wonder, for a moment, if the sun does have wings. I have never thought about how it crosses the sky.

The brood camels are kept by the gate. The rest of our caravan is led through the streets past new looking houses and the quarter of the dead. Then we arrive at the quarter of the palace of King Solomon.

There, our camels and stores are tended. The women are led to special chambers which have been prepared for our arrival. I do not know where Baba and the men go.

Ano and I stand in a yard under the streaming Jerusalem sun before a row of connected chambers. Two lovely women, soft in movement, full of grace, emerge from the dark doorway of a whitewashed building. The doorway is decorated with a wooden frame and the sides of the frame are painted with a network of pomegranates. Above the door, an Egyptian goddess kneels, her wings spreading out so, as if to encompass all who enter; her two-cobra headdress gives me a sense of relief.

We do not speak the language of the women, but we share some words in common. They smile gently and often, laughing with each other as they try to serve us.

The first chambers are simply furnished, but there are colorful rugs upon all the floors. The rooms open onto other rooms where women are chatting and weaving, painting and inscribing tiny pieces of linen and leather with sacred language and symbols.

The women are not all the same, but have come from tribes as far away as Egypt and India. There are Hittites and Edomites, Canaanites, Shunamites, women of Asher and Bethel and Adora. The women have come from all the high and low places to live in the beauty of the King's holy city.

We are led through the chambers into an inner yard which is closed to the outside world, but open to the sky.

This yard is like nothing I have ever seen, and after my initial disappointment with the dusty streets, I am stunned by the green spirit of this place. I am astonished by the exotic plants of every kind: palms, acacias, flowering hibiscus, big leafed plants from beyond Egypt, flowering apple. There are lotus pools with frogs and turtles. The most magnificent peacocks strut about everywhere, opening their tails like fans. The women have peacock feathers braided into their hair. There are exotic chickens and a baby deer which the women feed from a bladder with a nipple fashioned by tying up a little lump in the side with a leather thong.

There are babies and children. The women nurse their infants. The girls play games where they throw rocks and jump into squares and circles with symbols they have drawn with red desert chalk upon the stone pavement.

In the very center is the most incredible sunken bath. It is veneered with hammered gold.

The women, giggling at the size of our eyes, lead Ano and I to the bath and motion us to remove our clothes. We place our robes on benches. Our guides remove their clothing and we all enter the bath.

The water is cool and warm at once—so refreshing, perfumed with the most exotic scent of jasmine.

They lovingly wash our bodies and hair, ladeling water over us with gold containers, gently scrubbing our skin with plants from the sea.

How I feel! I feel as if I have entered paradise! I feel as if I will never know such a moment again!

More women come and they fawn over us and play with us, laughing, teaching us words in the language of Solomon.

At the edge of the bath, we lie on our backs upon cushions. A woman named Moon-Shun covers my wet hair in cloths, my body in a sheet, then sits cross-legged behind my head and massages the muscles of my face with the juice of cucumbers. How gloriously magnificent! She gives me cucumber water to drink from a golden chalice and I cannot believe my fortune!

Moon-Shun massages my feet with oils and essences. She massages my hands. I lie in the sun with a cloth over my eyes and all the time women are emptying and refilling the golden bath. A woman oils my whole body with an essence so rarefied I cannot describe it. Then Moon-Shun cuts my toenails and fingernails, filing them into perfect moons; she rubs them with henna and red ochre.

Another woman lovingly dries my hair and combs it out down my back. She anoints the sun-lightened strands with an essence that complements the fragrance of my body and winds my hair up into the fashionable peak of a priestess. She pulls tendrils down about my forehead and neck and these she cuts with a sharp knife; they curl into ringlets framing my face like a halo of radiant darkness.

When at last I stand, I am given a luxurious gown of linen which is clasped with golden pins.

Inside, we are given a special ceremonial meal of grains and cakes, raisins, figs, and the meat of a sacrificed lamb, cooked in spiced juices. We drink wine from gold cups. We eat from pounded gold plates etched with vines and flowers.

In the women's quarters are riches untold.

We are each given a room in which to sleep until all the tired weariness has left us, and my body, greedy for rest, falls upon the floor. In an instant, I feel the liminal state between life and dreams come upon me.

I am aware that I am in a chamber on the second story, that my window opens out over the street, that it is a night of no moon, that it is dark as pitch, that I have seen brilliant stars, the souls of gods and goddesses, twinkling so close, I feel I can reach out and touch them.

I am aware that I am in a heightened magical state. The netherworld becomes the Land of Dreams and my soul travels endlessly through time and space.

I dream of storms on the desert. I am chased by a cloud of sand that becomes the Death God trying to smother me. I dream of men with skin boxes hung upon their foreheads. I dream of sacred scrolls contained in large earthen jars. I dream of my mother in our tent chanting "Allat. . . Allat. . .Allat. . .," I dream she is saying to me, "Allat is the breath, the spirit, moving in and moving out. Ah comes in cool. Lat goes out warm. We bring in spirit, transform spirit, warmly send spirit into the world. Allat is our first utterance and will be our last. Allat. Allat. Allat. . ."

I dream of Ano and the red silk ribbons of the child I was.

I dream I am riding on the camel, the sea is glinting.

I dream I am calling out "Zuleika! Zuleika!"

I dream men are killing each other, calling out the names of their gods as if it is a battle between deities. I dream the Commander is screaming, "We must exterminate all the warring gods in order to bring peace upon the land. Yahweh shall rule!"

I dream the women are screaming, torn away from their babies, killed if they are not virgins, made slaves if they are.

I dream I am on a mountain, at the highest place of the holy of holies. I am in a cavern looking out over the sea and I am calling "Allat, Allat, Allat, restore my blood, for I desire woman-ness to be upon me!"

When I woke—a long, long time later—the cloak wrapped around me was bloody, and my woman's blood had been restored to me. I remembered, then, the dream and the prophesy: *You will be a ripe flower, open and ready to conceive life in thirteen days.*

When the women came to my chamber and saw the blood, they smiled and showed no surprise. They hugged me and kissed my head and led me to the inner yard. The yard was like a place transformed! Everywhere women, like graceful gazelles, sat on camel cushions, draped with red cloths. Their woman's blood flowed out of their bodies. The golden bath was filled with floating flowers and only the youngest girls bathed among the blossoms. There were boys, but for the first time I noticed that all the boys were very small children.

There were older women, too, who smiled lovingly at the younger.

Everywhere in the yard, images of goddesses had appeared. Golden. Silver. Stone. Wood. Clay. Bronze. Faience. Images of every kind. A great circular altar rested at one end upon the backs of twelve golden-horned cows. The sacred cows stood in a circle with their tails together, their heads looking outward. Upon this altar burned candles and incense. There were images of the goddesses from all the camps and settlements. I saw how lovely the women were, like the wildness of a forest.

Some of the women danced, telling stories with their hands and feet, making palm trees, barren hills, and spice gardens with their arms. These women spoke many languages, but the language of dance was the one they all shared. A woman sang:

> *I am the rose of Sharon*
> *and the lily of the valley*
> *Like a lily among thorns*
> *so is my love among daughters*
> *An apple tree among the trees*
> *so is my beloved among sons*
> *I sat down under his shadow*
> *in sweet delight*
> *and his fruits were sweet to my taste*
> *He brought me to the banqueting house*
> *and his banner above me was love*
> *He brought me to the banqueting house*
> *and his banner above me was love.*

I did not understand all the words that were being sung and spoken, but I understood the laughter. I understood the sisterhood.

The women, lovely as spring, went into a deep trance together and sought visions that would guide the continued creation of the holy city.

Ano was in the yard, but we did not speak. We bore witness to the sparkling mystery of womanhood in silence.

On the third day, there was a commotion near one of the doors and I saw an exquisite woman enter the sanctum. There was rapid whispering, muffled laughter and pointing, and I heard the words "Bath-Sheba." How my heart raced.

Oh, Bath-Sheba, how dignified. How stately. How like a great bird you float into the sanctum. How all the sisters rustle upon their pillows. How all the attention shifts.

Zuleika!

At that moment, I feel complete. She finds me, loves me, prepares and anoints me, guides me, counsels me, opens me, instructs me and takes me to the threshold of the Red Love Mystery. I cross the threshold alone.

> *What a wound Thou hast made*
> *my husband, my brother!*

What a wound Thou hast made
in this soul of mine!
The taste of your mouth is like
warm honeyed wine
Your eyes shine like stars
guiding me to Jerusalem
Your arms are like sunrays
wrapping about me
touching my heart
like a greenfield at dawn

Hold me close
Hold me close, my true love, my brother
And I shall hold you as bracelet fits
in the throbbing heart of love
in the throbbing heart of love

Hold me close, my brother
Oh, son of Jerusalem
Hold me close, my husband
Oh, son of Allat

We are one spirit
one mind
one heart
one soul

Light the candle
drink the cup
Thou hast taken me to the sacred bond
of love's holy song.

Yes, I see. Now, I see. The child Solomon, Ishraq, the Prince of Peace, was delivered unto the people by his mother, Zuleika, chosen daughter of the Great Allat, Mother of Life, and by his father, King David, chosen son of the Great Yahweh, Father of Death. The blending of energies made a holy child. The son of rest. The King of Love. Light itself. The Sun.

Now, I see! How he loves women. How he rises against his father's edicts! How he fights for the preservation of the goddesses of the tribes!

He has honored his father's enemies, placed Hittite warriors in positions of power; given everyone gold and grain: the Edomites; the Canaanites.

And the women, light and dark, he has loved with all his heart, and all love him as the Son of Love, itself.

He is the poet of the people, the Lover of the World, the man with the gentle song, the sweet tongue. My eyes fell upon his visage and I loved him.

Oh, hold me close!

I have loved him as the children of Jerusalem love him.

His breath is love. His breath is sweet as apples. His gaze is divine. He moves like a stag leaping in high, holy places.

My love for him is a mountain goat leaping in the crags.

He has taken me into the inner sanctum, and there I have seen the golden room, with the winged angels and the golden altar, and the ark of the covenant, and I have fallen to my knees and raised up my arms crying, "Yes! All life is sacred! Do not kill! Do not steal!"

And I have seen his shrine to life and I have seen his shrines to the goddesses on every hillside and I have seen the image of lifeforce everywhere—carvings of men and women loving, women giving birth, children at the breast—and he has quickened in me such devotion, such sacred callings.

In the inner sanctum, in the holy of holies, in the room all of gold, before the ark of the covenant, my eyes adjusted, and I saw the Great Wings holding emptiness, the Unknown, the Sacred Power, that which cannot be imaged. The Sun King touched my shoulder lightly with his hand and Allat cried into my ear: *On the thirteenth day, you shall be ripe like the red honeysuckle!*

On the thirteenth day, I was ready. I took his hand—they drove us to the edge of the city, all the servants left us—and we climbed alone. We climbed the hills to the sacred crevice of Ashtoreth above Jerusalem and it was in that sacred place we entered the Red Love Mystery.

I crossed the threshold, prepared by the wisdom of Zuleika and my mothers and sisters who had gone before.

I asked him mysterious questions with my eyes and he answered with his eyes, his mouth, his hands, and his soul. Like children anointed, we made love in the holy cleft. We would make a child to unite the tribes.

What is the meaning of a tear? A single tear drop on the cheek. Am I joyous? Do I grieve?

I am filled with such intensity I feel my lower lip stretch taught and quiver. My body tenses. Blood rushes. Strange pulsations.

I want to dive in. I want to run away. I want to open up. I want to close down.

We make love and everything happens at once.

This tear wells up and rolls over my cheek, down my jaw. I feel it hang suspended for a moment in time and I ask myself: *What does this mean?*

Oh, the riotous nature of Life living Life!

I conceived that day.

I conceived the holy child, wrought of the sacred blended energies of the Father and Mother of Life Itself. I conceived the holy child blended of all the tribes and races, the enlightened being born of the celebration of the sacred interplay of life and love and mystery. The blended energies of all holy truths.

In that single sacred moment of conception, I felt the souls of all the world's people come together under one tent to join hands and sing praises to Love, the glorious author of all that is.

All the angels of Heaven and Earth gather, the angels of Egypt and Moab, Sharon and Nubia, the angels of the Sea of Reeds and the Dead Sea, even the angelic guardians of the poor celibate priests on the northern shore. The angels of all the tribes, great and small—the angels of animals and plants, fish and foul, of all the herds and herbs and heavenly orbs—come together like night filled with brilliant shining stars to proclaim to the universe endless radiant love for every single being in every quarter and throughout the endless worlds beyond.

Oh, joy! Oh, harmony! Oh, happiness! And all these—all these angelic forces—are united by the guidance of one Supreme Lifeforce, one Eternal Being, who reigns over all and the name of that being is Love. The name of that spirit is Love.

Sisters of Jerusalem, the trading is completed, the gold and herbs stored in the palace, returning camels laden with gifts from the Prince of Peace. But no gift is greater than the gift of Love I carry in the pocket under my heart.

May I carry this Light Being with the reverence of the priests who wear the tiny scrolls tied upon their heads.

May I carry the Light of my Soul, the Blend of the Races, safely home to the tents of my people who dwell at the edge of the world at the end of the sea.

May the holy child and I, like Queen Zuleika with her loving son, ever carry the hope of the Great Being behind all illusion, called by those with voices to pray, the Great and Enduring Spirit of Love.

I, Alilat, lover of the Divine within, in all that is, convey to you this wisdom, the wisdom of the camel, the one who moves with little sustenance over great distances in extraordinary strides: Every moment is a new beginning.

At this moment, become what you will. You are free.

Accept freedom. Emit love. Emit beauty.

Make amends, atone, forgive. Enter the warm circle of the vast and magnificent human tribe. Enter as a lover—full with compassion—and you will come to love. The loving world you seek has sought your love forever.

∝

Night was falling and the velvet curtain of consciousness seemed to close. I became very aware of my breath and my surroundings though I had not thought of either for hours.

I saw the candlelight shimmering, heat waves rising in the cool air blowing in off the ocean. It seemed as if my eyes had been closed all day.

Quiet and gentle, it seemed as if Riavek touched me on the shoulder.

"Yes, Yes, Riavek," I whispered, "I feel your question. I feel your touch. As Sister Alilat, I learned that there are many ways to perceive the sacred. I learned that all worshipful expressions are valid. Shall we kill each other in the name of gods? Oh, Riavek, my Brother, Let all peoples be like Solomon. Let us honor and celebrate diversity. Let us cherish peace. Let us celebrate the divine in all, the feminine, the masculine, the emitting, the receiving. Let us love one another and cast no-one's love asunder. . ."

CHAPTER 8

ELECTRA
ANCIENT GREECE

Delphi, 186 B.C.E.

Imagination: Images play and repeat, dip and surface, skim and dive, scalloping through the conscious mind like pelicans grazing in a rich summer sea.

The elusive mystery of imagination is a deep rich velvety vault, as powerful as the human dream of birth, death, and resurrection. We hold the world in our reflection. Be still.

On the fourth day of meditation in my place above the ocean, I sit in the doorway of consciousness with the sacred channels open to every nuance of past and future. I perch on the threshold to forever, the portal of dreams and visions, and I feel I am standing in a hall of mirrors. My image reflects endlessly out in every direction, an image of light repeating endlessly through the darkness of the space between breaths, between heartbeats, between sounds, between thoughts, between bodies, lives and worlds.

My garment billows slightly and the silken folds of every image sway. I raise up my arms; every being raises hers. Moving together as one silent sister, we petition higher forces with open hands, standing firm, calling for guidance: Ours has been the quest to know.

Is this arrogance? Is this humility? Do I stand in fear of awesome forces? Or do I stand fulfilled in a state of unraveling and unrelenting bliss?

Spirit steps in and out of body. Akenaton says the body is a temple. He calls himself Pharoah. Pharoah means temple. The temple houses spirit. It is a holy dwelling place for the spiritual entity, a container built at the vortex where converging energies meet, created to house the still, unmoving mover who lives in the eye of the storm.

He says spirit is light: The Sun's reflection.

I mirror world spirit, the power of life behind being. I reflect it back and contain it in soulful forms: A moving picture of the goat pen at a mountain shrine where olives grow, the thick wafting aroma of juicy beets boiling on an open fire, wine-softened laughter mingling with the sound of cooing doves roosting in the evening. All this playing on a vast and endless inner stage. I step in and out of awareness, imaginings, in and out of universes and material forms. I engage and disengage in cosmic forces beyond coherent rationalization. I create life, fill up temples with hair-raising cosmic power, rise and fall and rise again like pillars in a temple, like lilies in the field. I do all of this and yet *I* do nothing. This is the paradox.

I raise up my arms in the hall of mirrors, every image raises arms, and there is no telling who moves first or is real.

All images move at once, a perfect reflection from every possible angle. The holographic image fades and disappears in the distance and yet there is no distance. I can touch the reflection before me. I reach out and she, too, reaches for me—we try to clasp hands in human warmth and bondage, but we cannot, there is nothing there but illusion—and I search imploringly for code-breaking details, details that might release the power to touch, that might separate out the endless images, distinguish each from the other as independent entities through time.

The candle flame moves against its reflection in the hall of mirrors, like an illuminated path of pine torches on the dark hillside, and I am caught, for a split-moment, wondering if my soul is disintegrating or integrating, and in the same split-moment, Riavek speaks: "You must dis-member before you can re-member," and I know I am in an initiation from which I will never return. The road moves one way, up and down at once, curving in the direction of knowledge of the heart.

"Even the name you chose, Pam-ela," Riavek says, "means *All Light* in Ancient Greek: All Light. All things considered; all things illuminated. You have awakened, Pamela. In *light.* You have traversed the dark beyond the River of Forgetfulness. You have moved stones before the Portals of Forever to release the ancient memory, the ancient songs and laughter, the dances, and now what was dead and forgotten stands resurrected. Beauty stands revealed. Horror stands revealed, also. You have chosen to see this, to awaken even that which you once swore would be put to rest forever. You have chosen to view every image, all angles. Hold up freedom, then, and examine its edges. Hold up tragedy and explore it. Hold up death. Hold up *love.* See it. Feel it. Smell it. Hear it. Taste it. Touch it. Let joy and heartache crack open the walls of your heart like winged bodies shattering

Time's dark glass. Search for meaning. Then you will know why you chose this mission.

"Blink your eyes and enter the altered state. Travel the path that goes higher and deeper. I will count from five to one. Breathe deeply and wake on a mountain at the edge of the sea. Wake at Delphi, the womb of the ancient world. Delphi means *womb* in Greek: Womb of the Ancient Mother. Now. Five. Four. Three. Two. One. . ."

Five: I closed my eyes and visions spun. Twisted cypress. Marble. A rocky coastline. Four: The smell of sulphur. Lamb turning on a spit. Fragrant star jasmine. Red wine. High white columns. High-pitched singing in strange tongues. Three: Red flowers and opium. Torrid vapors of smoke settling. Opiated wine. A drugged stupor. Two: Nothing too much. Nothing too little. The middle way. Poppies. Olives. Onions. Sesame. Round bread cut with crosses. Fat beets in thick, bubbling juices. Red eggs. Eggshells burning in sulphur. A curious stench. One: Fresh blood dripping down the sanctified altar.

Riavek speaks, "What do you see?"

I look through a portal. Everything becomes more apparent. I see a wild mountain meadow. A little girl. Maybe 7 or 8 years old. A small flock of sheep.

"What is the girl doing?"

"Tending the sheep."

"What does she look like?"

"Big gold eyes. Tan olive skin. A straight nose. Dark brown hair curling in ringlets around her face and bare shoulders. White teeth. A big smile. She is singing to herself and dancing. A short brown dress caught with some kind of sash. A scuffed knee. . .She must have fallen. The meadow is rocky. Down the gorge, I can see fingers of water. The sea. There is a low rock wall. Blue sky. A veiling of high white thin air. A few clouds. The girl shakes a rhythm with a container filled with pebbles. What is she doing with that?"

"Go deeper. . ."

I go deeper.

"She uses it to control the sheep—I see—to make noise to get them home."

"Who crosses the meadow?"

"An old woman. She is old. Not ancient. Maybe 60-something. The girl sees the old woman. The old woman is coming close to her. She is speaking. She is asking, 'Where is your father?' The little girl says, 'I don't know. Maybe in Corinth. Mother told me but I forgot.' The old woman says, 'Your mother and your sister have gone away to talk business with the Romans. It seems the centurion is fond of your mother's wine.'

"The girl stiffens. She seems very confused. The old woman has tears in her eyes. She says, 'Come with me, my girl. We'll take the sheep to the city shed for safe-keeping.'"

Riavek says, "Move foreward. Switch scenes. What do you see?"

Immediately, I see a white stuccoed mud-brick house, simple, very elegant, clean architectural lines. It is very early morning, not yet dawn, damp, cool, gray, smells of pungent salt air. The sun is not yet up.

"The little girl rises from a soft sleeping pallet," I say, "still in her woolen dress, now very rumpled—her little brown feet bare—and she slips from the house and runs, hopping and half-skipping, goat-like, down the hillside on a zig-zag path through what appears to be a small city of marble. There are columns. Ruins. Animal pens. No one seems to be awake. She runs on a path through a forested area of bay and pine to a level place where a stone dwelling stands alone in the midst of thick, old grapevines and an ancient olive grove. Fat lemons have dropped from the tree. Cautiously, the girl approaches the house. Quiet now. Moving slowly. Stalking like a cat. She comes very close, up to where she can see the chickens and hear them clucking quietly. The aroma of crushed grapes hangs in the still air. A man sleeps by the door. She studies him. He snores. A rooster crows suddenly, and the chickens start to create a din. The man bellows in his sleep. Someone shouts a foreign language from within the house, and, just now, the girl sees fresh blood dried on square stepping stones. She knows something is very wrong. These stones have never been the killing place. Her eyes open wide, as if to better see. Her heart pounds in her chest. She is frightened. Like a wary animal, she turns away and runs. Quiet. Fast. There is shouting in the house. She runs, running now through the forest. She runs and runs. Her little chest heaves. Her breath is shallow. Her face streaks with tears. She brushes a tree, a small branch breaks, gashing her thin arm.

"She is whimpering. Something has happened. Something bad. She is saying, 'Where is Mother? Where is Cassiopeia?'

"She runs back into the village and zigs up the jagged path. Women are outside now, collecting water, watching her. They exhange long glances with each other as the girl runs by. She runs to the home of the old woman who stands by waiting and collapses in her arms. Her chest still heaves. She begins to sob. The old woman holds her close and weeps softly."

Riavek interrupts: "Who is the girl?"

"She is me."

"How do you know?"

"I feel dirt up to my knees. My arm is bleeding. I feel the heat of the old woman's bosom."

"Change the scene. Move forward. Move forward until you can see again."

I feel I am in a tunnel, moving through a tunnel. It is as if there are openings on the sides that look out onto different scenes.

"Follow the path," says Riavek, "and you will learn that the dark road itself is the question. It is also the answer. Follow until your heart commands you to stop."

I follow the road and it is as if I move in the midst of mirrors between rows of pine torches, torches that mark the mountain in all directions. Yet there is only one way I can go. I am moving up and down at once. In and out. I am floating. Then I feel it; flashing images stop.

I am looking through a portal at the girl. She is much older—18 or 19. She sits on a stone bench watching a woman cooking. It smells delicious. A fabulous open air cook-fire.

Riavek says, "Move inside the girl's body. Allow your consciousness to take up her form. You are safe. Freely move. Feel yourself inside her hands. Feel yourself inside her feet. Occupy her form. Feel her heart beating. Feel her lungs breathing. Feel the ebb and flow of life as it moves within her body. Feel it move within yourself."

I can feel it. I can feel her body. It is strong. I take this body on as my own. I can feel dance in my arms and legs. I feel tall. I grow straight. This body is alive, filled with keen awareness. Deep sensitivities.

I am watching Nina, the dark-eyed cookgirl who has been with the Pythias since her father, acting on the prophesy of the oracle, gave her into service. She brings to mind Cassiopeia. A pain for the loss of my sister ripples through my body like a wave passing through a pond. *Cassiopeia, my sister, I pray you are alive and well and living in Rome. Perhaps you married a Roman citizen. If you are but alive, I know you have not relinquished your spark, even if you dwell in slavery. Some things are too precious to sacrifice, dear sister, no matter what conditions befall us. Remember? As our father might have said, What would a Roman know of freedom? Even free, they work together like wood slats in a wine cask. They are more worried about appearances than anybody else in the world, ever reacting to what other people think, acting always from the outside in. Perfect organization men.*

You and I, my sister, know the meaning of true liberty, the importance of idea and dissent, and we know the price of freedom, too. Every Hellene knows that physical freedom may be gone in an instant—they will ever try to grab your holdings, however meager—therefore maintain, above all, freedom of spirit. Always be free in heart and mind. Even if they force you to bear a litter of baby soldiers for their state. Remember, you are of Delphi and Delphian you shall stay.

In the dappled light of this olive tree outside the house of the priestesses, Nina stands laying the wooden table with round loaves placed on silver trays.

I sit remembering.

Much of my experience of my early years eludes me. I can vaguely remember my mother and father, how my father owned the vineyard and orchard before the Romans came. I remember playing in the vineyard, hiding in the rows of grapes. I remember taking the sheep to graze.

They say the Romans occupied our house and that I, alone of my family, escaped because I was out with the sheep, and the old priestess found me and hid me in the Pythias' quarters.

I remember how my father disappeared. Delphi and Corinth were taken by Romans. I never knew what happened or why. Suddenly my world collapsed.

The old ones say Greece had appealed to Rome for assistance—we had sent ambassadors—and the Roman idea of granting aid was to conquer us in our weakness. Not all at once, but over time. The old ones say the year after the Romans overran Delphi, they granted us freedom. What does that mean? My mother and father and sister were gone. I was just a little girl torn out of the soil like a dead grapevine.

I wish I could remember my mother better. She was 29 when they came. I remember her feet, stained purple from working.

Watching Nina placing the bread almost brings a memory. The smell of beets and onions boiling for the feast almost brings a vision of my girlhood. Red eggs dyed with beet juice, placed in the center of the loaves, elicits in my soul a feeling of strange peacefulness, as if maintaining practices of happy ways could placate certain monsters that rear up their ugly faces from the past.

They take out the gnarled old grapevine, dig it up out of the earth. What once lived, no longer of use, is stripped of its protective sheath and forced to reveal its long submerged nature, the part of itself that groped in darkness, fingers curling about bits of dirt, reaching deep in receptive areas that accepted penetration, reaching only into places where intrusion was allowed.

Inverted now and suffocating, dying roots dangle emptily toward the skies pleading to the Mother for her warm embrace, pleading to the

Unseen Power to restore spirit. The petition is denied. Life is not rekindled. The only thing the dead wood shall grow is the Equinox Fire.

This is how it feels to be uprooted.

I remember the Romans lounging in front of my father's house. They believed I possessed the Power and the Sight, and, because I was so young, they accused me of the Evil Eye. It was because of the way I looked at them. I am sure my eyes shot daggers. They had torn me from the land and my quavering roots shook with anger.

Old Pythia, the high priestess and sister to my father's mother, did take me in and instruct me in the high arts of trance and divination. She taught me the sacred language: The Power of the Oracle.

I was not mute, they say, the day Old Pythia took me from the pasture, but when I realized what had happened, they say, I became silent.

I did, the old woman told me, sit in a corner and rock my body. I did sit and rock—my eyes staring blankly at the wall—for many weeks. I do not remember this rocking. I do possess the Sight, but the first eight years of my life now stand like the gaping hole to the womb of the earth—dark and unknown.

They said I was in mourning, and that is why I did not speak. I do remember waking.

The old woman did take me in from the field.

She is so much older now. A seer, prophetess, visionary. They call her the Old Pythia of the Abyss.

She took me to her home, the place where the priestesses live, and when I realized what had happened, I screamed and screamed, wailing for my mother, for my Cassiopeia. I screamed and wailed and moaned and cried, then they say I went silent, and for weeks, sat on the floor, blank-faced, unsighted, unfocused, rocking, my arms around my knees, rocking, and they tried to straighten my body out, but it was fixed in rocking until finally it began to unwind and straighten out of its own accord. Then it rolled emptily over the floor.

I was young and did not speak after that.

I did not know who had betrayed me, or even if I had been betrayed or if I had been abandoned. Old Pythia said they would have had me, too, had I not been in the meadow, and my mother claimed no more children, only Cassiopeia—who had been with her working in the winery—in an attempt to have me spared.

Later, Old Pythia said I could never return to my home or they would know me as a daughter of the house and claim me, so she changed my name and claimed me herself whenever the Romans came for tellings.

I have vague memories of priestesses trying to talk to me, trying to hold me, of them feeding me tea—I vaguely remember Sister Selena's face and Philanna's—while I rocked in that oblique state, but I did not come to until I realized Old Pythia was offering me the magic powers of the sacred beans. I was a child after all. "Do you want the beans?" she asked. I woke up and nodded yes.

Those two little beans altered my course. One bean was black and one was white. There were identical in size, shape, texture, weight, and temperature, so if you held them with eyes closed, you could not discriminate between the two. White was yes. Black was no. White was venture down the path toward cosmic light. Black was the dark road and do not go. But this was simplistic—of course I was only a little girl—but later I learned how essential it is to explore the black abyss.

I did not speak, so the priestesses spoke to me with yes-no questions. I did not look at their eyes. My stomach hurt.

I put the beans on the floor. I touched the white bean for yes. The black bean for no. Did I want water? No. Did I want to bathe in the spring? No. Did I want bread and onions? Yes. Old Pythia told me she could teach me how to know the future by the beans, to know about Mother and Casseopia.

She said, "Do you wish to know this?" I remember scooting away from her. She was sitting on a wood box by my mat. I must have seen her out of the corner of my eye because I remember her eyes looked sad. Her eyes were seeing into me as if I were a cleft in the mountain. I doubled up my fist and reached out and hit her with all my strength. She did not move. She did not flinch at all. So, not knowing what to do, I touched the white bean.

The Old Pythia told me that knowing about people who are far away is the gift of the priestesses of the Oracle at Delphi. She asked me if I understood. I touched the white bean. She asked me if I wished to join the sisters of the priesthood. I got very cold then, even though the sun was bright and all the priestesses were inside fanning themselves. The hair on my head stood up and the flesh of my little arms and legs crawled up into bumps, and my whole body shook and shivered. I began to gasp. I could not breathe. I fell over. My legs and arms began to jerk, and my head went back on my neck. My eyes opened wide. I felt this happening and it was like cold lightning struck me. Old Pythia and the priestesses rushed forward. Selena lifted up my head and talked gentle words into my face. "Hold the spirit," she said, "Hold the spirit in you." She repeated and repeated, whispering, "Spirit, do not leave this child." The priestesses placed their hands on my arms, legs, and belly. They held my hands. Philanna held my feet. Old Pythia said, "Still the cosmic fire. Still." They all sang the same note over and over, deep and low, until my whole body relaxed and went limp. My eyes came back to the front of my face. I remember my eyes had turned in when the lightning came and they looked on the inside of my head. It was dark there, but I saw there a tiny, blue star sapphire glowing like a queen's jewel. I watched the sapphire's glow for what seemed like a long time. When my eyes came back, I sat up. The priestesses helped me. Then, with a trembling hand, I picked up the white bean and held it up in front of my cheek. At that moment, Old Pythia spoke. She said, "Our littlest sister: Pythia Electra." And so I became the child of the Oracle.

In my mind, I consented to live that life, the life of a priestess, but in my heart, I vowed to live that life in silence.

How can I describe the thick and luscious aroma of the boiling beet? It sings to my soul. Sensual. The beet is wine in solid earthy form. Round and rich to bring on fertility. The smell of beets boiling permeates my senses, unleashing juices all the way to the core. At the break of spring, when sun and moon stand even, we cook beets to celebrate Earth Mother's resurrection as she brings forth life again.

We add a huge abundance of chicken eggs to the mix, and the shells turn red, dyed as they are by the thickening fluid. The dye is fixed by herb vinegar. All is well. All is *Paradise*.

Sometimes it seems we live in Paradise right here in Delphi. When the poppies begin to bloom, when the orange blossoms issue fragrance, when the jasmine erupts, when the grasses green, when the sun hits the mountain in just the right way. I learned of Paradise when my moon-blood came and I was allowed to attend the Winter Solstice ceremonies. This was my first real initiation into the priesthood.

Paradise, they told at this ceremony, is a walled garden, the most beautiful place you could ever imagine, a place of endless Light. Paradise, they say, is entered by Good Thoughts, Good Words and Good Deeds. It is safe. No enemy may enter. It is as safe as any passage on the Isles at the time of the Sacred Games. And everything you need is provided for you. There is an abundance of food and music, flutes, pipes and lyres, and everyone is happy. Everyone is beautiful. Everything is excellent.

This is the place, as priests, they say, we shall enter upon crossing the River Styx. We shall enter this place, they say, because we have honored it and worshipped it and because we have been Good. It was Zarathustra of Persia who taught of Paradise four hundred years ago, and these teachings have been passed from mouth to ear through the Delphic Mystery School in which I have studied as a priestess. I have listened, I have attended the rites, and I have read also of Paradise. I have read Zarathustra's teachings in the *Avesta-va-Zend*, the story of Ahura Mazda, the god of goodness and light, the god of the sun. Ahura Mazda is a sun god like Apollo, our patron god of Delphi. Ahura Mazda lives in the Goodness of Aisha, the Light of All Life.

Aisha,
the Cosmic Order
Pervading all things pure
Whose are the Stars
in Whose Light
the glorious Beings and
Objects are clothed.

O Holy Aisha
Art in the Tree of Life
that standeth in the middle
of the eternal Sea
That is called
The Tree of Healing
upon which rests
the seeds of all we invoke.

We invoke Thee, O Aisha
the sovereign endless Light.

Ahura Mazda fights Angra Mainyu, the demon of evil and darkness. Apollo, living in Goodness like Ahura Mazda, fights the deadly Python who dwells in dark Earth. Who do you think triumphs in these battles? Who do you think wins?

Ahura Mazda creates, Mithra preserves. They battle the forces of evil together. Mithra dies and is resurrected as they say we shall die and be reborn. Ahura Mazda and Mithra remind me of Arjuna from the far east. Arjuna is taught by Krishna, the Sin-Bearer and Redeemer of Souls. Arjuna must also fight. . .*Is life, itself, a battle?*

They say if we understand the Mystery Teachings, the meaning of resurrection and immortality, when we die we will be reborn into Paradise. That is, our *soul* will rise out of our dead body and journey to this place called Paradise. A person has a soul, they say—a thinking and feeling *spirit* which leaves the body when that person dies. This soul, they say, is immortal. For those who understand the Mystery, for those who have Good intentions, the soul will dwell in a happy light forever. For those who understand the Mystery, the soul cannot be killed, and, to understand this better and to remind us who we really are beyond our physical form, to remember that we are moving toward light, each year, four days after the longest night as the days begin to lengthen, on Mithra's day of birth, we of the priesthood worship Paradise. We celebrate the birth and resurrection of Mithra, the Preserver of Life, by recreating the abundance that they say exists in Paradise.

The ceremony is fantastic. We gather in the heart of the temple. There we honor Dionysus, god of ecstasy, Apollo, god of light and music, Ahura Mazda, Mithra and Isis, Osiris, and Horus, the holy family whose teachings came to Delphi from Egypt.

Mithra opens the ceremony, calling the priesthood to remember the beauties of Paradise, calling the priesthood to remember the gods and the protection and happiness they offer. There are abundant sacrifices, abundant gifts and food and wine. There is a play in which a priest is killed; his soul rises from his body and enters the excellent walled garden where he is shown to live forever in safety and prosperity, harmony and happiness, with fine music, olive oil, garlic, bread and wine, guarded by the eye and sword of the all-powerful Unseen Power.

Only things of spirit, they say, *survive.*

At the very end of the beet cooking, we throw in the beet leaves. Dark green, red-veined, mysterious. Like pulsing life itself.

Underground grows the beet root. Above, the greens. In between, strong stalks. Red and white and green, veined, alive, pulsing, the consecrated meal, mixing together to honor the Earth Mother Ge's annual birthing.

Nina stirs the brew with a big wood spoon. Beets and eggs shall serve the priestesses—and even Apollo, himself—before we begin the fast that precedes the sitting to seek visions for the future.

Will the Romans retract the freedom they gave us the year after the occupation?

To be Hellene is not easy. Our task is to teach ourselves as well as to educate barbarians by example, is it not? And yet, year after year, century after century, barbarians invade us from every side. But let us not think of that now. The beets are almost tender.

The sisters have bathed this day in Castalian Spring. They have drunk only of the pure and sacred water. They have donned their consecrated clothing, white chitons, red hoods. In silence, they assemble at the main East Gate and, in silence, anoint themselves with holy water from the basins. Singing the seven holy intervals of Pythagorus, they walk up the Sacred Way toward the Great Altar outside the Temple. Today no sheep nor goat will be sacrificed there. This day, Brother Apollo receives succulent red beets and eggs, onions, and crossed round loaves presented upon our finest silver from Athens.

Nina decorates the silver trays—beds of raw, red-veined, thick and succulent leaves, round loaves cut with the cross of equal arms, and, at the vortex, a red egg.

The egg is meant to be moving inside the cross. This means life begins again. Eternal life has triumphed.

I shall tell of the bread. It is the Bread of Life. Cut in quadrants, it symbolizes the four elements of which everything in the world is made: fire, water, air and earth. Each quadrant represents an element. Earth Mother creates by combining elemental properties. Fire is the lightest solid, and looking deeply into its structure through meditating in trance, you would see it is shaped as a tetrahedron. Water, heavier, is icosahedral. Air is octahedral. Earth is the heaviest. It is everything that is palpable, everything that can be tasted, touched, smelled, heard, seen. Earth particles are cubicle; they have the most stability. Spiritually and philosophically, fire represents spirit, water symbolizes love, air, the mind, and earth, the body. There is a fifth element, and that is the endless, the eternal, the thing that bonds the four solids and makes them work together as one cohesive structure. It is the aether, the akasha, the illumination behind all things. The fifth element is the Unseen Power, Aisha, and it is circular or spherical and that is why the bread is round. The round loaf contains all five elements. It is labored over with prayers and imbued with mantras for the continuation of the cycles, for the return of the Great Mother's fertility, Aisha's sacred seed.

Nina bakes the bread with the greatest care. She labors over the beets and onions. She labors over the eggs, treats them gently, like baby birds. She places the egg in the center of the bread, at the vortex where all the elements swirl and combine, and the beginnings of life stir.

The whole presentation is bountiful and elegant—fat beets and thick, juicy onions placed all around the loaf—a feast most fit for any god, goddess, power, or intermediary.

This is my job: I shall, myself, place upon the Great Altar, the five silver trays, in that the aromatic scent of this great meal—may float to Brother Apollo. We will attract his attention and petition him to petition to the Earth Mother and the Unseen Power on our behalf.

I record this picture for you and you will ask me how I know so many things since girls are taught to see as little as possible, hear as little as possible, so we will ask as few questions as possible. Here is the answer: I have not been raised as other girls. I have been raised as a priestess.

Old Pythia took me as her own. She brought me up as a Pythia of Delphi, so for the last eleven years, I have received the benefits of the priesthood, even though it is not fitting for women to practice until they are 50 years old. At 50, they say, the highest wisdom becomes accessible. They say there is some fear, also, that younger women might be attacked. They say this happened once, that a young Pythia was once raped. I do not know if that is correct.

I am not terribly fond of this restriction, but it is a restriction nonetheless. And, as a result, I am deemed too young to walk in this processional. So, I have the honor of serving the god at the Great Altar. For public ceremonies, they refer to me as Altar Girl.

I am a girl no longer. I am 19, way beyond marriageable age, but I shall not marry. I am in service to Apollo, and Apollo shall ever my bridegroom be. With that I am mostly content. Were I in Rome, they would have me make babies for the state.

I detest the Roman mind. They took my sister. What became of her? I fear the worst.

There is a young Roman soldier, *Tonio*. . .

He was conscripted into the Roman army and did not willfully go, but there he is, even now at my father's house. And I must *never* claim clanship to that house; I am Pythia Electra, and the girl Cynthia who might have once lived there, is 11 years dead and might as well lie decaying in a funeral pot under the mountain.

Tonio: I abhor him and what he represents. I know they teach me it is not the way of the priestess to hate, but to find compassion. So, I would not *say* that I hate him but he is of *Rome*. And also he distracts me.

He distracts me day and night, night and day. His eyes are set close together, right next to his nose.

One day, we met in that same meadow, both of us alone walking, each of us on errands. He stopped me. He asked me to sit. This was unusual. Men talk to men, women to women, But, I sat with him on the low rock wall and he spoke about death. I did not expose my feelings, but I listened.

He is alone, Tonio. His mother died when he was born, and he asked me if I believe his mother had a spirit, if her soul would go to *heaven*. He knows I am a Pythia and he thought I would know. He does not believe what the Romans or the Jews have said about death. He did not know I do not speak.

Since I do not speak, I did not speak to Tonio. I listened, and as I listened I looked into his soul to see what I could see. I saw *sadness*.

By Delphic standards, I am very well educated, and yet I am not sure what I know. I have studied all forms of knowledge in the world:

letters, history, numbers, geometry, philosophy, music, dance, and the Mysteries of birth, death, and resurrection. Frequently, the best orators lecture at Delphi. In the last year alone, we have been instructed by Marcus of Rome, Lysander of Corinth, Phyllis, also of Corinth and Roxane, who traveled from the North to speak of mysteries and events that we had not before known of. It is absolutely essential that the priesthood have a firm grasp of world knowledge. Our proclamations arise from the soul of Mother Earth and affect the course of world history. To remain in ignorance would be an insult to the gods and a crime to all humanity.

Old Pythia goes with the others to symposia in Alexandria every few years to exhange information with other members of the Collegium of the Adepts, scholars of the Mysteries, who travel from all over the world to the Temple and Library of Jupiter Serapis. I will accompany Old Pythia on her next trip to Alexandria. I am ever so excited about this as I have never yet left Mount Parnassus. We will go by boat, crossing the sea in early summer. We will stay in the quarters of the Temple reserved for visiting adepts. Since I am legally too young to make the trip, the sisters will take me as their daughter-server. With this I am content. To see Alexandria! To experience the adventure of converging with people from the whole world!

The plates are nearly ready. Nina signals me. Five platters will I place upon the Great Altar that their scent may waft toward Apollo and stimulate his appetite.

I rise from my sitting place and, with great solemnity, I carry the first platter.

Apollo, I call inwardly, *Wake and feast!*

I hear the processional of priestesses moving along the Sacred Way. They have purified the body by fasting. They have purified the mind by chanting. They have purified the heart by bathing in Castalian Spring. They will purify the spirit as they enter the fiery chasm in the heart of the Temple after partaking of the sacred feast.

I hear them coming, toning the seven intervals of Pythagoras in fabulous harmonious strains. They call Apollo with their music. My heart thrills. I place the third plate.

Pythia Athene plays the kithara, sacred to Apollo, as Pythia Selena's voice rises in a wordless melody, sweetly appealing to the Brother to awaken.

Old Pythia is carried on a dais. Her ankle is swollen and she has trouble today with the walk.

My only regret about choosing silence is that I may not sing. I tried to sing once, in the meadow alone, and a noise came from my throat like the screeching howl of a night bird or a wolf at early hunt. I have chosen silence and silence has chosen me.

I can almost hear their feet stepping now. I place the fourth plate. *Wake, O God of Music, Laughter, Love! Wake, O Young Man, Sun God, Wolf God, guardian of the Python's seething cavern.* The sun soars up over the hill. Warmth permeates the holy close. I place the last plate.

Apollo, most precious guide through the veils, of your many forms, to me you come as a wolf. You come to me with the admonition, *Speak with the tongue of the Wolf.* Speaking with the tongue of the Wolf is speaking *truth*, even though we well know, truth changes over time. The river of life continually moves—we have studied the teachings of Heraclitus—and we continually move and change within this river. Still, there is truth and there is falsehood. Falsehood is acting according to external pressures, according to the conditions and judgments of others. Truth is deep assessment that rises from internal spirit. Truth is given by the Unseen Power. Truth arises from the deep abyss within the self. People fear truth as it has the power to disrupt the social order. Look at Greece! Chaos! Romans, especially, fear the truth. Organization men. They cleverly dictate what they cleverly calculate to be *real*. They manipulate the people with stories about the treacheries of the gods. Hellenes do not seek control and power in this way. Greeks do not live in fear of the gods. We are free.

As free beings, we think for ourselves and honor individual assessment. As Greeks, we exalt the *question*. We travel within for answers. *Quest:* the search; *Ion:* to enter into. Education, for us, is about *asking*, about *drawing out* deeper and deeper truths. Education for the Romans, is about providing answers, a well-conceived explanation about what is. This is all designed carefully, of course, to re-create and maintain the power of the state and to command allegiance to that power. To sustain this kind of power, all minds must be trained alike—people must be trained to be intolerant of differences—a practice which we of the Delphic priesthood find detestable. In certain ways, though, the Romans must be admired. Together they constitute a machine, a well-oiled framework with fixed and moving parts, forever building their networks to tie up the whole world as with streamers radiating out from a Tree of Life, ribboning like spokes on a May Pole, with Rome as the hub. Inwardly, I admit that is *impressive*. Do we, as free and independent Greeks, not continually beg them for aid? Aid to stave off the North. Aid to fight the East. I suppose people with Roman ideas are required in the world. I don't know.

Oh, I know so many things, and, at the center of my education, I am not at all certain that I know anything at all.

Suddenly, I am charged with energy. My hair is on end. That is truth to me, when my body speaks its own language. My body speaks now. The sisters arrive at the Great Altar singing. The strange intervals create chills. The smell of beets drifts outward. My hair lifts itself up. Apollo wakens. I *feel* him wake. I stand with the sisters. All raise arms. Firm and steady we stand, not in fear, not cowering before the god, but strong and steady, for he is our bridegroom, he is our beloved, and behold sisters, he wakes! I am ready.

Old Pythia leans on me, holding my arm for support. She shifts her weight betwen Philanna and me. She is nearly 80. Her ankles are tired.

I see the Wolf with my inner eye. He stands by the Altar. He rips into motion. He tears apart beets. Gnashing his teeth, he devours eggs and onions. His teeth redden with the fresh blood of this succulent sacrifice. He gorges himself on the sweet Bread of Life. He leaps, feral beast, into my heart to guide my dark journey into the body of life, the Earth Mother. We shall implant our shells in her womb year after year, that we may be filled with life forever.

Pythia Selena drops her note and swoons. The sisters reach out for her, catch her and lower her gently to the ground where they cradle her as she writhes and speaks in the language known only to the Pythian priesthood. She writhes and screams out: "Apollo is risen. He feasts at the Great Altar! He eats the beets! Is energized! Is purified! The black gate opens. Earth Mother stands ready. Dark forms fly from her chasm. Creation begins. Dark days await. Light nights await. Life springs anew!"

She falls back and after a minute begins again: "Earth Mother will receive us. The bridegroom opens the guarded way. Now we shall eat. Then we shall prophesy. Bring forth the torches. Light the dark. Heat the dank. Fire the belly. Fire. Water. Fire. Water. Father. Mother. Death. Life. Earth. Death. Return. Renew. *Rejoice.*"

Selena closes her eyes and collapses. Six priests rush in, come running from the small temple to hear her sacred words, but now Pythia Selena speaks no more. Priests and priestesses, then, stand together at the Great Altar, chanting, toning, raising up the universal energies. Old Pythia is held by Nina and Philanna as I pass the trays. The priesthood feasts. Some of the priestesses rub the ruddy beets on their cheeks and fingernails. The juices stain their skin. Spring returns.

We eat greens and onions and eggs at the Great Altar, carefully replacing the empty egg shells on the central platter where they will be crushed to be carried under cover of nightfall into the deep, black cavern of the sleeping Python. Oh, God of Light, Healing and Music, Wolfen Brother Apollo, it shall be a long night.

Riavek interrupts my reverie. "Stop. Change scenes. Move forward in time. Move forward until your conscience opens a new door."

Suddenly, I am in the hall of mirrors again. I am moving through a tunnel, down a dark road. Vague ideas spin: *Greece: Art. Thought. Freedom. Material insecurity. Independence. Question. The journey inward. Spirit is the only lasting power. Know thyself. Chaos. Rome: Authority. Obedience. Discipline. Material acquisition. Answers. Organization. Power is a matter of will. Force.*

Spinning. Going deeper. Getting darker. Darker. Darker. Then I am at the chasm, deep inside the Temple. I am at the chasm and I stand alone by the cleft that reaches deep into the body of the Mother. It reaches so deep: The steaming crack from which all life emits. The steaming crack to which all life returns. We emerge from her womb, our umbilicus tied to her placenta, sucking in nutrition, drawing in life.

This is the womb: Delphi. The omphalo of the world. The center. The navel. The hole in the axis. The hole in the soul.

I chew the treated bay. Its flavor is acrid. I hold it under my tongue. It releases its narcotic powers. I feel dazed. It releases its powers to energize. I am tranquil and terribly excited. It is dark. I stand alone.

I see the tripod, the sacred chair, golden snakes intertwined about its legs, positioned above the smoking chasm, the simple throne taken by the Pythia as she moves into ecstatic meditation and begins to sing her revelation. In prophesy, she speaks the sacred tongue, the secret language. Her divine pronouncements come in prayers. Scribe priests stand by listening, holding their paper, holding their pens. They translate her words into Koine, the common language, write it into poetry, the most sacred form of the written word, and this they pass to those who wish to know, to those who have *paid* to know.

I do not mount the tripod. I have come not to prophesy but to honor the Unseen Power and the Great Mother as she writhes in ecstatic pleasure giving birth to the world again.

I have brought fragments of crushed red eggshells. I ate of these eggs. I crushed these shells. I folded them in purple silk and now I carefully unwrap them to scatter them in the chasm. *Great Mother, heed these shells. May spirit be reborn! May spirit burst through as a baby bird or die! As serpent cracks the shell, life lives! Resurrection!*

I feel her breath upon me. Her form. Her shape. I smell her body. Heat. Sulphur. Sweat. Steam. She pushes out life. Spring comes. All is renewed. *Rejoice.*

They say Apollo slew the Great Python that lived in this hole. They say the Python destroyed the sacrificial beasts—cows, goats, sheep, chickens—stealing them from pens and fields and eating them whole. They say the Python threatened to steal babies, children, so insatiable was its appetite. They say the god Apollo, patron of light and heat and music, mediator for the Unseen Power, translator for the Great Mother, slew the serpent and threw the dead carcass in the Great Mother's hole, this place where I now stand scattering the shells of old life and praying for rebirth.

They say Apollo saved the people of Delphi from a treachersome fate, but, as I stand here, the warm wine of Dionysus turning my thoughts inside out, masticated bay burning a hole in my mouth, I must ask the question: *Did Apollo slay a dragon that threatened Delphi, or did he rather, slash the umbilical cord that connected the Great Earth Mother Ge to her people?*

Suddenly, I have a vision of my mother and Cassiopeia. They are enslaved. They are not together, not even in the same part of the land. I know this to be true, and yet I fight the knowing. I push the vision down, repress it, struggle to see something else, a happier story.

Only things of spirit survive. Only spirit has power. All other concerns fade. All other freedoms disappear. Matter is fleeting. Spiritual wealth endures. *Oh Mother, Oh Sister, be rich in spiritual holdings. Be light in the midst of darkness. Chained by poverty, prosper in spiritual wealth. Chained by slavery, rejoice in spiritual strength.*

As I stand at the edge of the abyss, Brother Apollo approaches me, moving tautly as a wolf. He takes his agile wolfen form—and becomes my seeing guide in darkness. My shells scattered over the ledge, my shells burning in her inner flame, I stagger, entranced, and fall to my knees. I close my eyes. *Apollo, Wolf Brother, guide me into the cavern that I may be gifted with the Power of Sight.*

Apollo takes me down, down, down, deeper, deeper, into the birth tunnel, wet and steaming, smoothed by the passage of the thousands and thousands who have gone before. I move down, down, down, falling in a deep trance, deep hypnosia, down, down, down to the world of dreams, the elusive liminal world between wakefulness and sleep.

Apollo's eyes glint as he gallops beside me; he glances over and gold lights flash from his eyes as we travel between worlds. I hear the sacred language: *Speak with the tongue of the Wolf.* We fairly fly to a roomlike cavern deep inside the darkest interior. Her red-black walls heave, sweat and contract with the heavy labor of creation.

We reach a deep, dark inner cavern, smelling of sulphur, strangely illuminated as with green phosphorescent stone, and I see that the Old Pythia, great Pythoness, Prophetess, Seer and Teacher, stands waiting, stirring up a mix in a great black cauldron. A cloud of burning opium fills the room. Apollo waits by the door. I enter alone.

Old Pythia speaks in the sacred tongue. Her voice is shaking: "I have summoned you, Pythia Electra. I have summoned you, my spiritual daughter, to consume the potion that will open your powers of wisdom. Long have you been my pupil, my charge, my beloved daughter. Long have I loved you. You have been my beloved since the day I found you in the meadow herding the sheep and clinging to the little rock rattle. Long have you lived with the Pythian sisters, drinking the sacred knowledge, making the spiritual journey, learning the techniques and results of liminal consciousness through deeper and deeper states of hypnosis. Well can you trance travel. Well can you see in the dark, hear through the veils, feel the meaning of portents and omens with your heart and hands and head. Yes, my daughter, faithfully have you drawn out the magical beans—the black and the white—and tested them over these last eleven years to prophesy the course of human events."

The beans she gave me at the moment I awakened—even now I carry them. Of equal shape, equal weight, I draw one from the pouch without looking. It tells me yes or no. I weigh the indication against my conscience. This is as I was taught by the Pythias.

"You have learned to know, to read the secret tales, to speak the sacred tongue. You have prophesied well. So be it."

I moved close to Old Pythia. I could see her hands shaking, hear her voice trembling, see her stirring and stirring.

She motioned me closer. Her cauldron flared.

"Pythia Electra, drink the cup of fire," she said, "Drink from the fiery cup and words of fire shall flare from your blazing heart. Drink the cup of truth, Electra. Drink the cup of freedom."

Her trembling hand held forth the flaming chalice.

"Pythia Electra, daughter of my own life, consume the fire in the caul, spark of my being, ignition of Unseen Power that makes my heart to beat, my breath to breathe, my brain to think, my soul to soar. Drink, that I may pass to you the spark of Aisha that served to animate this humble soul."

I did not understand.

"Pythia Electra, I move deeper into the Mother's womb. I fade into these black walls. By the way I came, shall I take my leave. I move into shadow. Drink the cup, so this form may rest in her fold. This body is tired, Cynthia. This spirit will rise."

Cynthia! She speaks like my own mother!

"Priestess, *drink.*"

She dropped the cup, so feeble was she, and I caught it mid-air and quickly drained it. Every drop.

Old Pythia fell to the floor. My tongue blazed! My throat burned! My belly erupted! Flames! Fire! *Lightning!*

I screamed and screamed and screamed and screamed.

Pythia Selena shook my shoulders. "Electra! Electra, stop! Electra. Be still. Electra. *Electra. . .*" She called and called for me. Her voice traveled slowly into my consciousness like fish song through water. "Electra, be still. . ."

Eventually, I stilled. I calmed. I snapped awake and looked into her deep eyes, swimming with a flood of tears. Seconds passed as we knelt at the edge facing each other, studying each others' eyes, looking past each others' eyes, through the windows of the physical temple to the deep, inner oracle inside each of us, the inner shrine, the place of light, the holy of holies where we two could meet unmasked, and commune, soul to soul.

Wolfen Apollo stood guard watching by the shrine wall.

"Electra," she whispered, "Old Pythia is dead."

"I know," I said.

Both of us were stunned by my words. Like the egg tooth of a baby python, they cracked the shell of eleven years of silence.

The priestesses walked slowly through the passageways between the dwellings, humming and pounding out a low eerie rhythm on drums and sticks, while the priests followed behind and spoke to the people of the Old Pythia's death. They moved from house to house, calling the people to the funeral games. There would be wrestling, running, boxing, stone-throwing, with dancing by a Pythia in training and singing and flute competitions. The games would be solemn, the feast unequaled.

I stayed behind to attend the Old Pythia, lest her spirit should call out for condolence. Laid out on a bier, covered to the neck with the rich purple pall, oil burning at her head, oriental poppies and delicate orange blossoms strewn all about, Old Pythia looked serene. At last, she rests.

She does not look, though, as the guardian I have known in life. Her mouth is set in an unfamiliar line.

I am a bit frightened though I would not *say* it. My stomach quivers. The boatsman Charon is near, the veil between the worlds is open, and I would not have the funeral ferry take me, too, over the River Styx.

Men build the funeral pyre by the place of pottery making outside the village. Construction of the pyre and the litter upon which Old Pythia will be borne is completed on the second day.

In the evening, the funeral begins.

Old Pythia, do you really need that coin the priests have placed in your mouth to pay Charon? Who, on the other shore, will eat the honey-cakes you carry to the flames?
Mourners surround you screaming and crying, old women in black dresses crouching at your feet wail and moan, their wrinkled tear-streaked faces speaking the horror of death. You are silent now, as I was then.

A beautiful long-haired goat with sensitive and expressive eyes, her white fur washed and combed, is brought up to the Great Altar. She looks around gracefully and tentatively. Her horns have been guilded, coated with shining gold foil. About her neck is a garland of the most beautiful spring flowers: poppies and daisies, narcissus and daffodils, intertwined in a delicate wreath. She gazes directly into my eyes. Her eyes are sweet, tender, innocent, loving.
The Great Altar is already streaked and stained with fresh, hot blood. The priests sprinkle the goat with holy water. She bows and shakes her head, shaking off the water, and all agree this is a good omen: Old Pythia's passage will be clear and open. The Old Pythia is favored by the gods, favored by Earth Mother Ge, favored by Apollo, by Dionysus, Ahura Mazda, Mithra and Mother Isis.
The goat is stunned with a blow to the head and the high priest quickly slits her throat. Blood spills out, caught by a priest in a holy grail. The bowl of blood is poured out onto the altar, an offering to Apollo. Ghosts, too, crave blood. The village flows with otherworldly energies. The spirits of the dead have awakened and move among us.
Two more goats are sacrificed, two lambs and a wild boar who comes screaming and crying out just like a human child.
The animal flesh is opened. The entrails are analyzed for prophesies. Fat is cut away and collected in huge earthenware jars to feed the funeral fire. The rest is skewered and placed upon spits where it will be turned over open flames first for the olfactory pleasure of the gods and second to satiate the athletes and mourners who will be weak from praying, gaming and fasting.
Bread bakes in the ovens. Wine casks are full and waiting. Jars of honey drip.
The feasting begins at dawn.

I hear Tonio will enter the running race. My heart skips a beat. He stands to win. He will win. Upon his head, the high priest will place the crown of olive and bay laurel. *With whom will you celebrate, Tonio? With whom will you share your joy? I don't know what happens to spirit,*

*Tonio. They say Charon rows it over the Styx to the Realm of the Dead.
Over the edge of the abyss, down, down, down in the steaming chasm, far
below in the Earth's most secret places, they say, is the gate. They say you
must feed the dog who guards the gate a honeycake so he will let you pass
into the beautiful land. Will you see your mother there, Tonio? Will I see
mine? Will we dwell forever in Paradise? We are young, but soon, laurel-
led boy, we too, will be ashes piled under the ground.*

What am I thinking? Unknown feelings stir within me.

The fire burns all night.

They have carried Old Pythia upon the litter, all wrapped in purple, her face covered now, all strewn with herbs and flowers, and they
have placed her upon the funeral pyre with honeycakes and coins.

Her spirit is already gone, called away by the wails of mourners
and hired flute players; she feels no pain now. The Old Pythia feels no
pain as the flames of the pyre rise higher and higher.

They have placed the fat of the sacrificial beasts all about her and
anointed her liberally with consecrated oil. All around dried wood is
heaped and the flames rise up like greedy tongues to engulf her abandoned body.

Through the night heat waves shimmer, the smoke-filled world
appears to dance and move all about. Death songs are sung.

Late, late, when it is very dark, far beyond the middle of the night,
the burning of the bones is ending. The fire burns low and the glowing
embers are doused with watered wine. The pyre cools in damp darkness. The high priest sprinkles wine here and there as Pythia Selena
sings eerily in the sacred tongue. I huddle with Nina in a nearby grove.
She and I embrace against death's dark horrors. *We are so young, Nina.
Let us not soon feel the glimmer of Death's Evil Eye.*

Priests and priestesses gather about the pyre, cooling the hot bones
with wine, placing them aside, letting them cool, placing them in purple cloth, wrapping them tightly. They will place the whole bony pack-
age in a large gold urn from Thasos to be buried beneath stones of the
side of the mountain. The priesthood moves methodically like white-
cloaked ghosts under the black pall of mid-night.

All at once, I am compelled to take ashes. I *must* have ashes. Impul-
sively—forgetting to use my words—I break away from Nina, move
quickly and silently toward the pyre, sweep cooling ashes into the skirt
of my bleached linen chiton—no one even attempts to stop me—and I
run, carefully, clutching my dress like a sack of flour, into the meadow
where once, a long time ago, the Old Pythia found me herding sheep.

Holding the skirt with one hand, I scoop out Old Pythia's ashes with the other. I throw them to the air. They fall like rain on my hair and body and skim across the meadow like heavy pollen from pine trees.

To the east, I throw ashes. Heavy gray-white meal, bits of bone. I throw this to the east, the place where life begins, the place of birth, new days dawning, years beginning. I throw ashes to the south, the mid-summer, the heat of mid-day, the bright light of noon. I throw ashes to the west, the place of endings, the dark of night, River Styx, the Great Ocean. I throw ashes north, to the mountain, the chasm, our home.

I throw Old Pythia's ashes up to gods and goddesses of light, down to gods and goddesses of dark. In a frenzy now, I whirl around, throwing ashes to the Mother, to the Unseen Power. I drop ashes in a circle; I surround my own body. And still there are more ashes.

I sit in the middle of the circle surrounded by the burnt crushed shells of Old Pythia's ruined temple. Tears come and I weep. I shake. I shrink from the horrors of Death even as I am drawn to know it.

Old Pythia, what is the Truth of the Other Side?

Revelation: I *eat* the ashes. Suddenly, I just shove them in my mouth. As Death tastes Old Pythia, I taste Death. I take Death in me. Dry. Warm. Like dirt. Dirt with pebbles. I chew a bone. I must. I *must.* Dry. Deathly. I am not afraid. I am *not. I will eat you, Old Pythia and I will know Death. I will know Death, for am I not Death? Am I not Death myself? A bag of ashes? A bag of bones?*

In a frenzy, I rub ashes into my skin, my arms, my legs, my face. I draw lines on my face. Barbaric.

I am Greek, Roman, Jew, Barbarian, Past, Present, and Future.

I am the Dance of Death.

I rise up and dance in the circle. I step outside and dance around its perimeter. I am Death's Dance, whirling and twirling, embracing all.

I begin to sing. I am Death's Song and my tones are clear. I sing from the belly and feel the vibration.

I twirl and whirl; my hair swings wildly. My hair swings heavily, coated with bonemeal.

The sky grays and lightens. Tall trees stand around the meadow like black centurions. My eyes see sharply—wolf eyes in the chasm.

Tonio stands alone, watching beneath a tall pine. The wreath of laurel is shadowed on his head: Tonio, the Victor.

I am alerted—he has watched me dance.

In the sacred language of Pythias, understood only by priests, I begin to chant:

Come Tonio
join the Dance
Risk Death
to Live.

I dance like Apollo. I dance up the rising sun. I dance down the dark chasm. I dance before the living and before every ghost and shade. *Charon, you cannot hurt me. I am free. With Wolfen eyes, this soul has seen. With Wolfen heart, this captive tongue has finally learned to sing.*

∽

What is freedom? To be free is to not be under the control of some outside person or some arbitrary power. To be free is to be able to act and think without compulsion or arbitrary restriction. To be free is to be independent, unrestricted, to enjoy the power of one's own potential, to experience one's nature, to test one's limits. To be free is to journey deep within to seek one's own conclusions.

As the candle burns low, I contemplate freedom. *Free:* Without obstruction. *Dom:* Domain, dominion, a state of being.

Freedom to think. To laugh. To dance. To eat the ashes of the dead.

How can I take as true that which my body will not believe? How I feel inside my body generates my spiritual beliefs. I react *physically* and my physical body decides what *is* and what is *right.* Believing is an emotional experience. *Be* is the state of; *lief* is love, libido. Libido is sexual energy. If I am to *believe* something, it must generate electricity within me. My hair must stand on end. My body separates truth from falsehood. I *feel* my way to truth.

Belief systems are set before me. How shall I choose?

Riavek calls softly. "Rest now. Eat. Boil beets and cook onions. Dip your bread in olive oil remembering the ancient ways. Fondly reflect as you prepare for ordination."

He asks: "What has Sister Electra taught you?" I say, "To trust my own—my *heartfelt*—experience."

A soft breeze flows in and the candle fizzles into obscurity. I pour myself a glass of wine and retire for the evening.

CHAPTER 9

HYPATIA
LATE ANTIQUITY

Alexandria, 415 c.e.

$\mathbf{R}$iavek says *you must dis-member before you can re-member.* I consider this statement. On the fifth day, it is still too early to assemble the fragments of this visionary encounter and yet, even without all the pieces, a certain structure begins to emerge. Lessons come, one by one, emerging from subterranean depths like the bones of an ancient skeleton scattered through space and time. It is my task, I am sure, to recreate the correct design.

I work with bones and bits, glances, glimpses, phrases, assembling pieces like an artist who scavenges the ages searching for truth.

I begin to understand disintegration and reformation. I begin to understand what it means to dis-member: It is as if the visions take me apart, shatter my ego, break down the whole into constituent parts so that I might understand what makes me and grow strong. It is as if I struggle to remember my core purpose or the path of my soul or perhaps the path of woman's experience through time so that I might find a sense of meaning and wholeness in an otherwise piecemeal world.

Moment by moment, I doubt my *self.* I question who *I* am, *who is the journeyer?* Is identity born or formed? Does new identity create itself through spiritual birth? In the process of initiation, does the old self die as a new self is revealed? The spiritual initiate, they say, must voluntarily relinquish the personality to separate the callings of the ministry from the callings of the ego. Only then, cleansed and freed from destructive attachments, will she be able to properly heal. Only then can the minister properly serve.

The traditional initiation into the sacred realm, it is said, inherently contains the experience of dis-memberment or suffering, death and rebirth. This sequence of events is a means by which the initiate is broken down and reconstituted as a technician of the sacred—sometimes by way of devastating or traumatic events. Body, mind and spirit dissolve, ego disintegrates. Through this process, one offers oneself over to a greater power to be reborn in a light which reflects the right use of universal energy or will, *always* the will to goodness, *always* the will to healing. The right use of will demands the egoless translation and transmission of sacred energies through one's own body. One's being becomes a tool, not as one who is enslaved as a draftee in "boot camp," but rather as one, who filled with light and meaning and the power of wholeness, *desires* to serve. To remember this truth is the task of the priestess.

It is early morning and I am rested and ready. I sit very still, light my candle and call upon Riavek to join me at my altar. As if he has been waiting, he is there immediately. He appears in golden light. He sits facing me, cross-legged, his hands resting gently on his knees: We are each others' mirror. My heart is full with utter gratitude. I bow.

"This will not be an easy day," he says. His tone is reserved and concerned. "But you have eaten the ashes of the dead and so prepared yourself. It is necessary for you, Pamela, on the fifth day of your final preparation, to learn the deep meaning of dis-memberment. You will be informed as to what has gone before and what is yet to be. And then, even in the small town where you live, you will be able to verify many aspects of the incarnation you will shortly witness. It is documented and contained in the canon of the planet. You will remember why you were born to your mother on the twelfth day of the third month. You will remember why a deep, deep fear has imbedded itself within you and you will begin to overcome it. Breathe now, breathe deep, and move fifteen hundred years back in time into the body of Hypatia, esteemed professor of philosophy and mathematics in the year 415 of the current era. . ." So quickly then could I see. Before Riavek had finished speaking, I was already on the boat.

The harbor teems with electric activity as I sit on the deck of R's ship debating about whether I should compose some kind of letter of explanation for my students. What can I say to them that I have not already said? And yet what will they think when I do not show at the lecture hall tomorrow and they find I have disappeared without so much as a trace? I fear they may think Cyril got me.

I await this voyage with more than a little trepidation.

When R and I were children, he sent me love letters on the finest, whitest, softest parchment written with ass's milk. It was our little game: invisible writing. When I received R's blank page delivered by way of his accomplice, my nurse-maid, I would wait until she was gone, then rush to the brazier, take ashes and scatter them on the page. They would stick to the dried milk and the message would be revealed. "8, beauty everlasting, brilliant as the sun, I shall 9 thee forever and ever. 9-18" Eight is the number of my name, Hypatia. Nine-eighteen is R's name number. Nine is love. "Hypatia. . .I shall love thee forever and ever. R"

I had completely forgotten this game until, under the black cloak of midnight long before the first hour, I received a blank scroll of rough papyrus delivered by a beggar into the hand of my father's door eunuch who gave it to my maid-servant who, in turn, awoke me from a deep dream. Between my late-night confusion and the dim light of the oil lamp, I forgot at the moment I broke the unrecognizable wax seal, to attend to whether or not the seal had been melted and resealed. All I could think when I opened the blank page was that this was some kind of prank on the part of one of my younger students. I had been dreaming of a beautiful garden, jungle-like, with a stone bench. There was a white bengal tiger who seemed to be conversing with me, lotus pools with flower heads following the sun, waving papyrus in bloom, fresh water streams and a soft mist, and I hated to be jarred from this paradise into the sudden blast of waking. After opening the strange scroll and seeing nothing there, I sent the maid-servant away and began to fall back into sleep. *Oh, to be in the company of that tiger again. . .*I drifted softly and slowly into the languid, dark and cradling waves of night—and then, suddenly, shockingly, with a huge surge of energy that shot my body bolt upright in bed, I remembered R and our childhood game of invisible writing. With haste, I clambored up, pulled the bedsheet around me and rushed to the brazier. I brushed ashes over the page and, yes, the ashes stuck to rows and rows of strange numbers. The black night electrified. Fear surged through me and my very hair stood on end. It could only be that the worst had come to pass. The note read:

$$8$$
$$A\ 8, 15, 21, 9.\ \ 7, 15.$$
$$3, 25, 9, 9, 12 = \dagger$$
$$1, 23, 1, 9, 20$$
$$999999999$$
$$9\text{-}18$$

I immediately recognized the signature. It was from R, but the letters and numbers were as foreign as Sanskrit. *It is so hard to think in the middle of the night.* As in childhood—and yet this moment was no childhood game—I pulled reed, ink and paper from the box, sat down and made a chart correlating letters and numbers, A=1, B=2, C=3. . . The letter began to reveal itself:

"Hypatia
1 HOUP GO
CYIIL =†
AWAIT
Love
R"

The word "love" I understood easily. It was nine times nine for the full power of love which equals 81. 8+1=9. Multiples of nine return to nine as love returns to love. *Yes, R, I remember.*

I looked at the words on the page, but still could no more decipher them than if I were looking at ancient Akkadian. *1 houp go. . .1 houp go.*

Suddenly I remembered that as children we had used a trick in case we were found out. Any letter, word or number adding to a multiple of nine, such as 18, 27, 36 and so on, we would code as nine. We called that the "love blind," since these numbers always returned to nine as love returns to love, and it made our letters all the more secret. I re-added the scratchings and the message became clear: "Hypatia. 1st hour. Go. Cyril equals death. Await. I love you. R."

Immediately, I intuited what was happening. The bishop Cyril had finally issued a warrant for my death. As he had long threatened, he had at last sicked his fanatical parabolans and monks on me, just as monks might sic a pack of dogs on a sacred ibis. With all our speculation, we hoped this would never happen. But, as that which can be imagined can also quickly manifest, the worst thoughts I have ever had instantly became physical reality. How rapidly life's circumstances can change! And now, I sit here facing the choice between truth and life, a choice I never believed I would have to make. And yet, as I sit on this deck, it seems I have already chosen. The ship prepares to sail for the Greek isle of Delos. Even now, men lower cargo into the hold.

R knows something about my fate that I need to find out. I have yet to see him since I came on board, and I hope he returns soon. At this time, I am certain of one thing only—my life is in danger. As a man of great wealth, R is privy to a great many things. I trust him. If he says, "Wait," then wait I shall. If he says, "Be ready to leave at the day's first hour," be ready I must, for this is something R would say only in the midst of the most extreme circumstances. I am not at his command, far from it—I answer to no man—but perhaps, I don't know, perhaps I have always loved him. Or, in any event, perhaps he is the only man who has truly cared for me. We discussed this once, what to do if Cyril ever actually acted against me. And now it seems that this has come to pass. I received R's communication in the darkest hour literally and figuratively, the dark hour before dawn, and with only one hour to ready myself I realized how truly unready I was. I fumbled with my clothing—my hands shook and I had an anxious feeling in my heart—trying to think, trying to wake up, trying to remember what to take. What is important? I clutched the golden ankh around my neck. That seemed important.

While my books on *Arithmetic, Astronomy,* and the *Conics of Apollonius* only elicited contempt and ridicule from the Catholic bishopric, and especially Bishop Cyril, I know it is the publication of my new work, *Indigenous Origins of the Christian Allegory* that set Cyril off. Not that this book is any different from what I have said from the lectern for years and years, but it is the volume of sales. Even I was astounded. The first five hundred copies were sold before they were finished, and the second five hundred sold within the first week of the book's release. Thereafter, my students could not copy fast enough to match the demand. Naturally, this is unheard of in Alexandria—a good book usually only sells about five hundred—and so the political polarization grows hotter and hotter.

Cyril, by the way, was not always a bishop—but does a power-hungry man not always move in the direction of power, no matter what truth must be sacrificed? I watched him gain leverage over the years, but I never thought he would get in a position where he would actually have the power to command death. Even I, who have held the distinguished chair of philosophy for so many years, who have studied all manner of social organization, am awed by the amount of power Cyril has been able to amass. He zealously calls the people to have faith, to believe, to witness his transparently ridiculous miracles. And they do believe. They are "stunned" by his trickery, they fear him and follow him blindly. He offers an easy solution for their problems and so they believe. They believe because they want to believe. Any educated person can see through his hypocrisy. The problem is that the ignorant ones are angry because they have been excluded from schooling, and they are tired of paying taxes to fund foreign wars. I understand this. The Christian organization—seeking that tax money, of course—tells them they can build a new world wherein a Greek education is not required. Plato, they say, selectively serves the wealthy, "expensive foods with fancy dressings," but the Christian Apostles feed the masses from a wholesome soup kitchen. How much the better! You don't need to go out and *learn* anything, they say, you just have to *feel* the mystery, take it into your heart. With so many massing toward Christianity, what can leaders do? Is it not better to adjust one's own views and stay in leadership? Leadership is power. And so the leaders, one by one, are "baptized."

Look at my student Synesius, the bishop of Ptolemais. He only consented to "speak in myths" in the church if he could be free to "think as a philosopher" in private. What can this mean? I do not doubt Synesius' character, but I deeply fear for the course of civilization.

I feel now that I stand alone, all but for my father Theon, grown so ghostlike now, and R who I have always trusted. I have many devoted students, but who among these would seek to walk in my sandals now?

I have always been a scholar and a teller of truth insofar as whatever truth is, is discernable to me. My beloved mentor Plutarch always said that truth is elusive. What we so strongly believe to be true at this moment, we may totally reject five years hence. That is the nature of life. We must be open to grow and change. Ego, self-centeredness and pride are the deadly enemies of pure understanding. This, Plutarch taught as he taught, through allegorical accounts, the secret of the ancient mysteries of birth, death and resurrection. This mystical knowledge and its preservation through the sacred mathematical formulae we owe, Plutarch said, to the founder of all learning, that wise old ancient, Thoth Hermes Trismegistus.

As I fumbled with my robes and my cloak in the dark morning so early this day, I remembered Plutarch and then Socrates, Plato, and Aristotle. What would they think? Socrates. . .the *hemlock*. . .condemned to die for his ideas. I would never dare to compare myself as a teacher with that master of masters Socrates, but just now I feel the deep fraternity of indignation that comes from knowing one is wrongly persecuted. What is important? Earlier today, I slipped on my poison ring, a secret container carved of the finest lapis lazuli. I call this carved lapis my "Philosopher's Stone"—ironic—the lethal poison is still there. I had this ring prepared for just such a moment as this. Lapis, a beautiful cobalt blue glowing with specks of golden stars like a magical skyscape in the late of evening. How inspirational! But the Christians disdain such beautiful stones. They do not know—because they have not been taught—that the jewels of the priests and priestesses represent all manner of spiritual energies that radiate from the human body. Streamers of electric force pour forth and we are luminous. We learn to control these energies, to harness and transmit them, to use them for healing sicknesses of the soul.

Are the same individuals who now reject and condemn us not the very ones who earlier sought our healing services? The Christians imagine that our jewels represent wealth. They do not realize they symbolize, and even invoke, levels of initiation in the sacred mysteries. Remember the statue of our god Serapis that stood in the labyrinth? It was made from a single emerald to activate the healing rays. And the statue of Serapis at the Serapeum? It was made of filings of gold and sapphires, hematite, emeralds, and topaz. When the Christian monk struck it with his ax, sparks flew and the ax shattered into pieces. Such is the power stream that flows from Serapis.

As a priestess of Serapis with the highest degree of initiation—as conferred upon me in Theon's school—I ask myself: Now what I will do? What fate, for me—a priestess now hunted in the very city she loves—shall come to pass? Will I die by my own poison? Will I escape to Delos and write from exile? Will the arch-demon Cyril at last overtake me and do with me what he will? *Gods and goddesses forbid. . .*

Men came this day as soon as I had donned my cloak, R's men, walking briskly. They draped a man's cloak over my head, put men's boots on my feet and took me quickly to the coach even before the first hour had come; we traveled in still darkness a roundabout way to the harbor, so I had no time to gather anything about me. They said, "Your life, dear lady, is all that matters now." Only my writing kit, only reeds, ink jar, and paper did I slip into my robe, for I felt I could not leave these precious tools behind.

I turned over the pot on the table as I walked out the door. As my father, Theon, and I had agreed, this would be the signal should I ever have to leave and he would know to cover for me. I knew my father's man would care for him were I to not return, and yet I believed my absense might possibly kill my father. Still what choice do I have? Theon is so weak now. And, of course, that is why I never married. Upon my mother's death, it seemed like his soul died also. All these years, twenty-four years, I have carried him. What the outside world never sees!

If only the Christians could see! What difference is there between their new Jesus and their ancient Alexandrian Serapis, both forms of the god of birth, death, and resurrection? Are these not one and the same, with Jesus being merely an updated version? Do both Jesus and Serapis not represent the holy spirit incarnated in physical form and transcending into eternal life?

When we understand how to activate the fiery healing energies of spirit as it is incarnate in our bodies, all of us, *every one*, becomes as radiant and immortal as the guiding gods: Jesus the Christos, Serapis, Horus, Apollo, Mithra, Krishna, and the Buddha, all of whom are symbolically born to the world through the Great Mother at Winter Solstice, the birth day of the Sun. On this day, as all variations of the supreme story tell, Light as Life is reborn in the world. The Solstice symbolizes resurrection, renewal, hope, a symbol of the incarnation of the holy spirit. The Sun Gods, the Sun Kings, emerge from the labyrinth as newborn babes. Is it not curious that the Christian organization has set the birth date for Jesus on the same day as all the rest were born? Mithra, Horus, Apollo, Krishna and the Buddha? The same day as the birth of the Sun?

Awaken, Christians, all of these gods are Sun Gods, healers—the power of Light runs through their veins. The ancient stories are meant to guide us. How can you believe that Jesus is "the only way?" Did not Mithra come from heaven to redeem us from our sins? Was the master healer Horus not born in a lowly stable to his virgin-mother Queen Isis, the Great Goddess of all that is? When Apollo's mother Leto was in labor, did not all countries and islands refuse to give her a place to birth, just as the inns of Bethlehem would not accept Mary, the mother of Jesus? Did not Leto end up birthing Apollo on Delos, the most desolate of all isles? (And is that desolate isle not the very place for which this creaking ship is now headed?) And, as for Krishna, it is told that his foster father Nanda was in the city to pay a tax to the king when he was born. Were Joseph and Mary not in Bethlehem to pay taxes? Krishna's birth, heralded by a star, took place in a cave which became mysteriously illuminated as he emerged from his mother's body. Just after birth he spoke to her, the virgin goddess Devaki, just as they say the baby Jesus spoke to his mother, the virgin Mary. Krishna was adored by cowherds who followed the Star, just as Jesus was adored by shepherds. The Buddha, like the Christos, was born to the Virgin Goddess Maya, who is *also* called Mari. In Buddhism, Hinduism, Mithraism, as in Christianity, the dead are delivered from pain and misery through so many similar rituals. O, thinking citizens of Alexandria, is it not then an outrage that the bishop Cyril should posit that anyone believing any story other than the one he puts forward will burn in hell eternally?

What I fear is this—the ancient knowledge we have painstakingly collected and the rational mind we have carefully evolved may be facing total annihilation. The Christian movement is about thought control. Can you see? Any idea, image, or person that challenges their "truth" is systematically eradicated, burned, pillaged, smashed. Witness the actions of Emperor Theodosius. He made Christianity the religion of the state—remember? That was only in 381—and he prohibited the practice of pagan rites. And then what happened? The ignorant Christian monks and mobs—with full governmental approval—systematically leveled every ancient and sacred holy site, temple, mystery school, and bastian of knowledge—the Oracle of Apollo at Delphi, the Temple of Artemis at Ephesus. Such tragedy. Then he granted Jews immunity from persecution, but forbade them to spread their religion, build new temples, marry Christians and enter government service. Twenty-four years ago—I was 16—he issued the edict to destroy Alexandria's own Serapeum, our Library and Temple, the Temple of Serapis, the God of the Sun. Monks ruined our glorious statue; *six hundred thousand books were burned*. That was only twenty-four years ago, but how fast people forget. I, however, whose mother died of grief, shall not forget, could never forget, but all this I have told in my book, *Indigenous Origins of the Christian Allegory*.

I sit on this shifting ship deck, my pen and paper waiting, and wonder how to address my students.

I am transparently invisibly hidden from those who might seek me out for love or counsel, death or torture, and I am caught up in thought, but even so I cannot help but notice, at least to some extent, the liveliness all around me. What ships! Wheat ships. Corn ships. Ships with fishes and spices, colored glass and gems. Their massive masts rock like the Forests of Lebanon must rock. Hulls groan imploringly. Hemp ropes roll on squealing pulleys as a hundred languages bellowed from bow to stern, port to starboard, boat to boat, call out greetings and directions, reprimands and jovial invitations. There is so much noise—it is interesting how one can block it out when one's inner thoughts are active and weighty. A whip cracks, a slave falls, all pointing to the abundance and prosperity of these proud and ancient quays.

The sun now rises.

O, citizens who can think, it is you with whom I would have liked to have spoken! And still, I would seek to petition you further in writing, as if the written word could somehow be more permanent, more provocative, or more powerful in swaying you toward reason than words I have already spoken. It is the prosperity I see all around me that troubles me, for what soul, if given a taste of riches, might, or the freedom that wealth seemingly purchases, would not seek after more of the same until the grievous longing is satiated and greed sickens and dies at last? And when the powerful weary at length of the price of administration, will there not be legions of others rattling chains and chomping at the bit for their chance at ascension? Will this race for accrual not continue anew, class after class, mass after mass, until humanity lives and breathes no more?

Sea foam thickens and weakens moment by moment, day by day, month by month, depending on the mix, the tides, the currents. Citizens, do you honestly believe it matters whether the mix in the human sea is Hellenic, barbaric, Christian, horse, ass, or mule? Take the monk who is sworn to poverty, chastity and obedience, give him a pocketful of gold, and you will have instantaneous corruption. For unless gold is held in the hand, the hand cannot throw it away. And I say unto you, it is not *belief* in this new religion that builds the Christian ranks—for it can be shown, as I have demonstrated time and time again, that this religion is no more than a twisted mix of a number of time-honored parables—but rather the draw is the magnetic promise of corporeal safety and economic security for those who have never known stability or a proper education or upbringing. Fear brings people in also, and I could factually demonstrate to you that if you are a baptized member of the Christian church, even if you are completely impoverished, you will receive better protection from the church, even in wartime, than taxpaying Roman citizens will ever receive from the Roman army. There is something to be said for that!

It is not this simple, of course. Christianity fills a social and spiritual hole—it is like a lotus that grows out of the swamp that spawns it, do you see?—and yet it is dangerous. It fills a hole because the world is changing and people feel lost. Life seems almost nightmarish and Christianity offers "community"—a simple place for the mass soul to flee; simple associations. It offers people who have no access to schooling a sense of belonging, of inspiration and hope, through setting out a personalized god with whom the people can commune, a god whom the hierarchy insists is a *real* person. This might be well, except for the fact that Christians are led to believe that they are the agents of vast forces and that they are acting as the servants of this god, who happens to be fanatic and jealous, and, who, out of deep and abiding insecurity, cannot allow any opposition or tolerate any form of contradiction. Can you see how this erodes our civilization from below? Can you not see that the impetus is largely economic?

Oh, but with the changing mix of race and language, creed and culture, we have lost the underpinnings of thoughtful cohesion. We have lost respect for the rational process of democratic organization. We have sacrificed the elusive truth of relativity and tolerance—because the pursuit of relativity and tolerance takes *energy*, and, gods forbid, in some small measure, taxes the *brain*—and we have opened the way for unbridled plays of power, fallow ground for a Christian theocracy.

Christianity is accessible to *all*, they say, you need only "have faith." Not that the myth by which they organize themselves is not attractive and brilliantly devised, for it surely is attractive and brilliant. I am not so stupid as to miss that point. Clearly, the new myth ingeniously combines Greek philosophy and ethics, Jewish law, and Roman peace, and who would argue with that? It is beautifully magnetic, an exquisite amalgamation. Jesus, depicted as the master teacher, elaborates the ethics of Greek culture, reveals the Law to the Jews, and founds the Christian church synchronously with Emperor Augustus' foundation of "universal Roman peace." Perfect. Even I might be tempted to join.

What I fear, however, is the fanatic way they put the story across: persecution and death for those who speak against it, persecution and damnation for disbelievers, condemnation of the time-honored ancient wisdom traditions, destruction of the ancient temples.

Take two thousand deprived boys, take them to the Libyan desert where circumstances can be controlled, deprive them of all learning save for a few memorable phrases chanted over and over. Feed and clothe them scantily, keep them relatively dirty, but promise them rewards in heaven. Fill their heads with fearsome repetitive stories of turning on the spit in hell. Ply them with imaginative and graphic descriptions of their own young souls frying on Satan's grill. Can you smell the burning flesh? Then fill them up with a sense of belonging. Convince them that they are "The Chosen Ones." Build up their identity as *members*, and assure them again and again that those who are not among their ranks—especially those of the privileged class—are their enemies. Then promise them life-long protection: simple lodging, simple rations, health care, eternal brotherhood. Convince them that the study of letters, mathematics, history, time, space, culture, and philosophy is spurious and outmoded. Convince them, in fact, that this knowledge is not only useless, but dangerous. Convince them that it endangers the very continuation of their order as well as their on-going safety.

Scoop these boys up from poverty, structure their patterns of thought, and within short order, you will find you have produced a two thousand member army of treacherously ignorant, frightened, fanatic soldiers, poised to tear asunder every golden thread that weaves together the thing we call civilization. If I could only teach these boys. If I could only reach them, I would pass on to them what Socrates said: "I tell you that virtue is not given by money, but that from virtue comes money and every other good of man, public as well as private." I would teach them the real meaning of virtue, and what it means to take on the responsibility of citizenship.

Do you see, O Citizens of Alexandria, that this gruesome picture is exactly what is housed in the ruined Serapeum? Look amid the ruins, and you will find a violent army that calls itself an order of holy monks. You forget that it was not the Roman army, but Christian

monks, who destroyed the Serapeum before they came to live there—
either you forget or you blindly accept—but I, Hypatia, cannot forget.
I cannot forget how my mother died.

My humor has left me, and I wonder if ever there was a time I was
truly happy. It seems that all my life my family and my colleagues have
been at war with the Christian church.

I was 16, beautiful, filled with faith and innocence, looking forward to my future as professor and priestess in the Academy and Temple of Serapis when the Christian monks, powered by the edict of that
villian Theodosius, smashed the Library. Theodosius had threatened,
of course, but my parents did not think he would go through with it.
The Temple, with its Library and Academy, was one of the great wonders of antiquity, surely he would not go that far. But Theodosius was
ruthless. He sent in the monks from the desert.

My father Theon, who held the esteemed chairmanship of mathematics, somehow got wind of what was happening and helped to
smuggle out hundreds of books of ancient wisdom. These they sent to
Fez where now the adepts—the priests and priestesses of the ancient
mysteries—must meet in secret. What terrible times!

The monks came in—and these were our boys; most of them were
actually born in the shadow of the Temple—and they burned nearly six
hundred thousand scrolls. They smashed columns and statues. They
vandalized the beautiful sculptured figure of the God of the Sun, Serapis himself, and desecrated the pillars of time, broke down the very
foundation of our learned world.

My mother kept me inside where it seemed to be safe, but I heard
the devastation. They warred and screamed and bludgeoned in a mad
ecstasy that rocked the very ground. They screamed like animals. Their
screams filled the houses and streamed across the rooftops. My mother
sat, listening, like an unmoving statue, leaning against the roof wall by
the wind sail ventilator. She, too, was a priestess of Serapis, a scholar,
teacher, and student of the ancient mysteries, and, after the destruction
of her beloved books, she simply laid down on the floor and died of
heart failure. "Without freedom of thought," she said, "freedom to explore what has been and what is, knowing that the firm foundation of
knowledge has been eclipsed, I cannot live. My heart will not beat. It is
me, and everything I represent, that they smash asunder." These were
her final words: "I would rather die than see the soul of the world fall
into such wanton desecration."

My mother was a scholar, a woman of striking beauty, incompara-
ble brilliance, brought up in a family of scholars. I can remember her
lecturing in the hall in her white linen tunic and scholar's sash, her

black hair shining, her face radiant. She was quick to smile; her eyes were filled with laughter. Everyone was laughing.

Alexandria was the center of the world, the Serapeum was the center of Alexandria, and my mother was the center of the Serapeum. She epitomized the perfect elegance of the city. And she was only 32 when she died.

What really hurt her was this—on an impulse, her sister, who was also a Serapian priestess, joined the Christians. Perhaps she was afraid of what would happen to her if she did not. She sent her son, Marcus, into the Nitrian Monastery. But Marcus had lived in our home, and he was as close as a brother to me. It was as if he were my mother's son. I remember him toddling about the roof, my mother telling him stories—how Bast invented music, how Nut made the stars, how Hathor birthed the world—a thousand stories symbolizing the natural world and the role of humanity as the discoverers and guardians of that world. And I remember how she taught him mathematics and the fundamentals of Greek architecture as soon as he could hold a stylus steady on a wax tablet.

Marcus was a fast learner.

She took him into the Library of the Temple just as she had taken me a thousand times, and showed him the sacred scrolls, talking constantly of all the wonders that awaited him as he learned to read and understand more and more of the ancient wisdom. "The world opens up," she would say, "portal after portal." Marcus would become an initiate in the Serapian Temple. He would travel through every doorway of perception. She promised to take him to Athens to show him the teaching ground of the great Greek philosophers. Marcus was so excitable and he *was* excited.

Then the world changed; he was in a Christian monastery. We never saw Marcus again, but my mother knew somehow that it was Marcus who had raped and pillaged and brought to ruin her beloved world. Even now, I look back and ask: *What could make a child do this?*

I have asked many times: What is the role of destiny? Have we any free will? Did Marcus choose to be born into a wealthy and scholarly family? Did he choose to be sent to the monastery? Did he choose to destroy the most important Temple of all time? Could he begin to see a universal picture? They say we can look at our lot as a burden, a lesson or a gift. I wonder how Marcus viewed his fate, or if he even thought about it. It seems to me he was like an actor in a historical drama. Sometimes it all seems like theater, like we are all actors on a stage, playing out acts and scenes and bringing plots into moralistic resolutions.

And now, I, Hypatia, unwittingly, dance upon that world stage. The scene is a ship deck. The woman is dressed in men's clothing with a jeweled dagger tucked in her boot. The play is passionate. This is the dramatic climax where the persecuted but innocent priestess runs away from the death-dealing grip of the evil patriarchy. How will the story resolve? Playing the Priestess of Truth is by no means easy. The role is tortuous for the best of actresses. For me, Hypatia, it feels like a burden, but perhaps there is a lesson in it. I do not see at this point, however, how this destiny could possibly be a gift.

The sky lightens, becomes a pallid gray, but even as it lightens, I feel the chill. I pull the layers of cloaks closer about. The man's cloak is large and of fine quality. I wonder if it belongs to R. Even though I am 40 years old—a professor of philosophy—and, by most reckonings, beyond such silliness, I still feel a thrill in my body at the prospect of seeing him. It has been a long time. R travels. I teach. How wonderful of him to care for me still. How wonderful of him to protect me. I do feel alone sometimes, even when I am among hundreds of adoring faces, or rather, especially then. Incidently, R never married.

Another problem with Christianity: the emphasis on sexual abstinence. Even though I, myself, have not married, and therefore have been sexually continent, I feel myself as a sexual being. Naturally I have channeled sexual energies into my work, but it is exactly such energies that I feel Cyril recognizes and detests in me. No man has possessed me. No man can. There is no place for a free woman like me in the mythological landscape of the Christian worldview.

I pace the deck, wet with dew and sea water, and lean over the railing. The water is murky with waste from the cargo. Rotting fish entrails float on the surface. Would that I could read their message as priestesses did in days of old. A severed fish head, silver as the moon, gazes up at me with a sightless eye. Poor fish, it just takes one false move. But then, perhaps you gave yourself as a sacred offering that others might live. *Goddess of the sea, I thank Thee.*

A recurring dream have I had and it comes back to me now: I am dressed in white cotton. A full length Grecian chiton, the kind worn long ago, falls to the ground about my bare feet. Upon my head is a hood of white. My head is bowed. My hands and mind are praying. In meditation, I walk.

I pass beneath a lintel bearing the words "Know Thyself," following a path that leads to a sacrificial altar. Through a doorway, there is a temple, an inner sanctuary. Inside the sanctuary, which is inside a mountain, I sit by a cleft, a deep, dark abyss that cracks open the earth. An unpleasant sulphurous steam wafts from the opening, like the breath of some foul beast. My soul leaves my body and moves through this crack. I am not afraid, neither am I excited. Without emotion, I float. I am met by a gray wolf, my guide, who has one eye that shines like a polished gold stone tiger's eye. His other eye is blind, it sees inward for he is wise, he needs only one outer eye to see. He is Trota. I recognize him. He has run beside me through all time.

He takes me to the wise and ancient Earth Goddess in the deep, inner cave who stirs and stirs a mix in a great black stone pot. Her vessel is the womb of all creation and the funeral pithos of all that ends. The room smells of sage and is bathed in an otherworldly greenish light. She will not acknowledge me. I remove the cloak of my soul and my soul stands bare before her. She looks up.

"What have you brought me?" she says. I look around, feel my empty hands and realize I have brought nothing. Then I remember the golden ankh around my neck. I take off my necklace and, bowing my head, hold it toward her with both palms outstretched. "Fine," she says, "the golden ankh. You have worn it forever—womb of the goddess, emblem of eternal life, emblem of the pithos, the vessel of the world, caul from which all worldly life emits, tomb to which all worldly life returns, golden ankh, circle of all being, horizontal axis of matter, vertical axis of spirit, fulcrum of endless existence. See it as a key to open the temple door. And where is this temple? It is in the inner shrine in your heart of hearts, that place where you go to worship the sacred miracle, the deep miracle that needs no theatrics. In the inner shrine, your candle burns because you tend it. Your chalice is full because you fill it. Look in my vessel."

She motions me over. I walk closer, still holding the ankh and look over the edge into the bubbling fluid. It is silver and gold, green and brown, churning with precious stones, and now it sounds like water over stones, a fountain at a holy place. Somehow I know a prophesy will now be revealed. The old woman says, "This is the vessel of the world. In it is birth, joy, hope, wisdom, compassion, pain, suffering, old age, and death. In the mix is resurrection. It is for all time, like your ankh. There is one in the world who suffers now. Go to him, Priestess of Eternity, he calls you in his sleep. Call his immortal soul to enter the womb of this goddess to be born again and again, to inhabit every possible form. Call upon him to abandon his old bony shell. Long has he lived and much has he taught. He has learned well and his corpse has been of fine service. . ."

The dream ends. Who am I to go to, I wonder. It could not be R. Could it be Theon? But I do not think Theon calls me.

I reach for the ankh inside my cloak. Taking it in my hand it gives me comfort. I think of all the Christians wearing the cross of death prominently displayed on their clothing, their headpieces and around their necks. I saw a woman enter the Caesareum, dominion of the bishop, wearing a costume with crosses sewn all around the hem and a cloak entirely embroidered with rows and rows of crosses. Garish.

I cross the deck and resume my position in my chair, adjusting a bit, rearranging the implements stashed in my inner cloak: paper rolls, ink jar, pens, a few items of clothing, my book. Soon I will be able to put these things away.

Mist hangs over the harbor and smells of grilling fish and boiling grains fill the air. I am hungry—fish chowder would be heavenly—but I know this is no time to think about such trivial matters. I am sure we will eat soon enough.

Suddenly it hits me: The *ankh:* It is like a Christian cross with a circle at the top. The circle is the vessel of the ancient Earth Goddess herself, she who stirs the sacred vessel of Phthia. Where has she gone? Have they omitted her? Where is *She From Whom All Things Emit?* Where is *She To Whom All Things Return?*

The Christians say the god is the spirit and all matter—whether male or female—is essentially female. The church, as matter—as *people*—is female. The god fills the church with spiritual energy even as a man fills a woman's womb. The god fills men as well as women. Yes. This explains why they claim the mother of Jesus is no goddess. Mary is merely the receptive—and mortal—vessel for the god. That is why they insist upon collecting statues of the Great Goddess Isis holding her infant son Horus and renaming her Mary. The Great Goddess now becomes entirely mortal, the woman who contains the god. These men have thought of everything. Could it be they are systematically excluding from the pantheon the powers of the goddesses? All of matter, all that is physical, which is said to contain the spirit of the god, is seen as the feminine receptive force—*she who is powerless before him.* Why have I not seen this before? In denouncing matter in favor of spirit, all things physical are minimized and even demonized. All that is physical must be transcended, and the female half of humanity is seen as the living embodiment of physicality, much more so than the male, because what could call a man more powerfully into remembering his physical form than his own sexual response to a woman? I see now, very clearly. Woman represents the *profane.*

I represent the profane. That is why Cyril disdains me. He suffers from what I symbolize for him.

Cyril says the "reward" for all suffering and sacrifice on the physical plane is in heaven. That is the god's realm. There is no need for goddesses in heaven because the risen spirit, in abandoning the body, whether female or male, abandons the feminine. Rotting matter is left behind. I realize now that matter is the same word as Mother. Matter is abandoned as a broken pot or a womb that has carried a child but empties out and becomes useless. The woman carries the child and gives birth—we are all born into this "world of sorrow" of a mother—so the mother is responsible for the continuation of human pain. The idea of Christianity is to transcend matter, to transcend the mother, sexuality, procreation. Witness the zealots who hate or fear physical form so much, they would cut the head away from the torso, if they thought they could extricate spirit from that which contains it. They do not remember, for they have never been taught, about the sacred interweaving of life. The golden thread of life is fine, connecting inner and outer, below and above, spirit and nature, god and goddess, the supernals and humanity, the pattern for all structure and structure itself. The golden thread is thin, but it interlaces all, enwraps all, and all of life is interconnected. All is part of the plan, part of the web, part of the sacred cloth.

Truly, I have nothing against honest Christians, the honest followers of the "faith." My only problem is the leadership's rabid insistence that their way is the *only* way. It is *not* the only way—it is only a piece of the spiritual puzzle—and I will fight to the death to prove it, I think. All my life I have wrestled with the idea of "principle," "the principle of the thing." Is principle as important as life itself?

The principle in Alexandria involves freedom for all Christians and nonChristians alike. It is not about inventing answers, but about the freedom of inquiry. To conduct the search is the meaning of the word *philosophy*. *Philo*—love of; *sophy*—Sophia, the Goddess of Wisdom. Philosophy—the pursuit of wisdom. Of this I am sure: The issue is freedom to argue, freedom to worship in one's own temple, to serve one's own gods and goddesses, to speak, to act, to tap the great universal forces. Freedom is the great producer of self-constraint, not captivity. Socrates knew that. Socrates taught that. Freedom brings justice to the mind of humanity. How many times I have read his speeches.

He called himself a "gadfly." He said he was sent to remind people to walk a virtuous path. "If you kill me. . .," he said as he defended himself in court, for he was accused of corrupting the youth of Athens by causing them to *question* the values of the world in which they had been brought up, "If you kill me, you will not easily find another like me, who, if I may use such a ludicrous figure of speech, am a sort of gadfly, given to the State by God; and the State is like a great and noble steed who is tardy in his motions and growing to a very great size, and requires to be stirred into life. I am that gadfly which God has given to the State and all day long and in all places I am always fastening upon you, arousing and persuading and reproaching you. And as you will not easily find another like me, I would advise you to spare me." He was not spared, as history tells, for in *questioning* the way of things, his accusers believed, he created a milieu which led to destabilization of the social order. They condemned him to death.

The right to question is Alexandria's issue now, just as it was the issue in Socrates' Athens. To *quest-ion* means to "journey into." We are losing the right to seek knowledge, but Alexandrians tend to believe that the whole issue is taxation, and they feel the Catholic church would dispense money more wisely than the Roman government. People are angry. Everyone is tired of being taxed and taxed again, especially since the invasion of Rome three years ago, but to talk solely about taxation completely deflects attention away from the deeper issues. Of course, the deeper issues are too complex—too philosophical—for most people to grasp.

Socrates—how often I have taught his methods in the classroom. With what was he charged? Corrupting the youth, was it not? Corrupting the youth through developing the fine art of questioning. He entreated the youth to enter into the journey of consciousness: to question what constitutes knowledge, morality, culture, society, virtue. The keepers of the State were afraid he would create conditions which would chip away the foundation of the edifice they were struggling to preserve. Too much, they said, had been *questioned*, particularly when the very virtue of the statesmen themselves was alluded to. After a one day trial, the citizens voted on Socrates' fate. The vote was close, but "guilty" won by a slim margin of thirty. He had corrupted the youth, the future of Athens, and for that crime, he would pay with his life.

Would he choose exile? Would he buy freedom? For these two options were surely available—but as he said to his friend Crito in his cell the morning after the sentencing, he loved Athens, her citizens, even her laws. He had chosen to raise his own sons as Athenians, and he never had any curiosity to know other States or their laws. His affections did not take him beyond the city, except for a brief expedition or two, and he said he would rather die than leave his beloved home. The law he loved had found him guilty, so guilty he must be. He would not run away. He would even forgive his accusers, at least to a certain extent. "Wherefore, O judges," he said, "be of good cheer about death, and know this of a truth—that no evil can happen to a good man, either in life or after death. He and his are not neglected by the gods; nor has my own approaching end happened by mere chance. But I see clearly that to die and be released was better for me; and therefore the oracle gave no sign."

His oracle—a voice he had heard in his head throughout his entire life—stopped him from every wrong thought and action, but never commanded him. The oracle did not stop him from considering death. Therefore, he reasoned, death must be his fate.

"For which reason also," he continued, "I am not angry with my accusers, my condemners; they have done me no harm, although neither of them meant to do me any good; and for this I may gently blame them."

(Is this not uncannily like Jesus' words, spoken as he hung upon the cross: *Father, forgive them for they do not know what they are doing?*)

Death, Socrates felt, may be a great blessing. "I would rather die," he said, "than speak in your manner and live. . .The difficulty, my friends, is not in avoiding death, but in avoiding unrighteousness; for that runs faster than death. I am old and move slowly, and the slow runner has overtaken me, and my accusers are keen and quick, and the faster runner, who is unrighteousness, has overtaken them. . .Let us reflect in another way, and we shall see that there is great reason to hope that death is a good, for one of two things: either death is a state of nothingness and utter unconsciousness, or, as men say, there is a change and migration of the soul from this world to another. Now if you suppose that there is no consciousness, but a sleep like the sleep of him who is undisturbed even by the sight of dreams, death will be an unspeakable gain. For if a person were to select the night in which his sleep was undisturbed even by dreams, and were to compare with this the other days and nights of his life, and then were to tell us how many days and nights he had passed in the course of his life better and more pleasantly than this one, I think that any man, I will not say a private man, but even a great king, will not find many such days or nights, when compared with the others. Now if death is like this, I say that to die is to gain; for eternity is then only a single night. But if death is the journey to another place, and there, as men say, all the dead are, what good, O my friends and judges, can be greater than this? If indeed when the pilgrim arrives in the world below, he is delivered from the professors of justice in this world, and finds the true judges who are said to give judgment there. . .that pilgrimage will be well worth making. What would not a man give if he might converse with Orpheus and Musaeus and Hesiod and Homer? Nay, if this be true, let me die again and again."

I pondered Socrates' words. Death. . .Perhaps I would welcome it.

I still had the poison. I could use it. I studied my right hand. I wore the hollow ring on my first finger, the finger, they say, that points to your fate. My *fate*. Is this poison my fate, concealed as it is in the body of a carved lapis scarab? The scarab: the beetle who pushes the sun across the sky, the bringer of the dawn. Have I been that bringer—or the *holder* of the dawn—and shall I now fade into death's obscure darkness? *Or do I fade into darkness by running away?*

The sun is high now, it is warming as the year turns toward the ides of March. This feels like a fateful day for me. The eleventh day of the third month of the four hundred and fifteenth year, at least by current reckonings. I might rather choose to say this is the eight hundred and fourteenth year after Socrate's death. At any rate, by the calendar of contemporary times, today's numbers add to fifteen. Fifteen! Then, 1 + 5 = 6. Six! The day of the demons and the day of the lovers. What a paradox! Fifteen is the demons' number and, so be it, I am running from a demon. Six is the perfect balance of divine lovers, the god and the goddess, the six-pointed star with overlapping male and female triangles and I ask, *Do I run to the arms of my beloved?*

I remove my outer cloak, but my undercloak seems very feminine on board this ship, so I remove that and cover myself again in the big, dark cloak. I am so tired. I sit down on the floor of the deck, leaning up against the cabin, wadding my cloak behind me for comfort. I have been instructed to wait. I am waiting. Many of the men are out purchasing supplies necessary for the voyage and those who remain, readying the sails, filling the hold and so forth, have no idea, nor concern, as to my identity. They must believe I am one of R's boys. They are too busy to wonder anyway. Tomorrow, we sail for Delos, and upon that voyage, all intent is focused. Delos: that rocky place where the Goddess Leto bore Artemis of the Moon and her brother Apollo of the Sun, the place from which the ship would arrive on the day of Socrates' death. Is that not ironic? Socrates was told he would die when "the ship came in from Delos." He and Crito discussed this in his cell in the early light of morning after the death sentence had been pronounced. Socrates said, "I do not think that the ship will be here until tomorrow; this I gather from a vision which I had last night, or rather only just now, when you fortunately allowed me to sleep. . .There came to me the likeness of a woman, fair and comely, clothed in white raiment, who called to me and said: 'O Socrates—The third day hence, to Phthia shalt thou go.'"

Phthia, the vessel of the Earth Goddess, womb of all beginnings, funerary cauldron of all return.

I am so tired. It grows so warm now. My head aches with thinking. *Spinning dimensions of all that I have known and taught, leave me! Leave me here in this sun in peace. Leave me in peace. Let me go in peace.*

I feel my body slide down the wall a bit as a wave of sleep washes over me. Quickly, I snap myself awake. This is no time to sleep—or would it be all right, perhaps, to sleep for only a few minutes, just to sleep for a short while to renew myself so that I can think clearly and refresh my energies? No. But I remember that, as a child, when I was afraid, I could fall asleep in an instant. This was a special talent I had, I could fall instantly asleep as if to escape any harm. It was as if I were suddenly tumbling, as if I were standing at the top of a cliff with my arms outstretched and someone came up behind me and pushed me off and I tumbled, tumbled, tumbled into a deep abyss, tumbled ever downward into a deep, deep sleep. In a way it was a wonderful feeling, but my ability to sleep frightened me also, for I feared that I might fall into sleep at some point when I might desperately need to keep my wits about me. Uncanny.

I felt myself falling into sleep upon the deck. Drifting, drifting. And it was as if I could not control the process. The sun was so warm. My mind was so full and it longed to empty out, empty, empty...Then, it was as if the friend or foe, that one who had always been with me, rushed up and pushed me off the edge. I went sailing, sailing, tumbling, twirling, falling, falling, falling into the deep, deep abyss of sleep...

৫৯

When I awoke, I was sitting at my altar. The candle was still fresh, as if little time had passed. I was startled. How could I inhabit two worlds at once?

Riavek sat before me smiling tenderly. He did not speak, but sat calmly and lovingly as if waiting for me to collect myself.

I tried to focus, but my vision seemed blurred. "Take your time," he whispered. The thought came to me, *time is infinite.* Then, I thought, *there is no such thing as time.*

After awhile Riavek gently whispered, "Where are you?"

I answered softly, "In my room."

"Where were you?"

The memory came back, floating wispily. I could vaguely see the woman, concealed as she was in a patch of sunlight reflecting like a solar collector in a little opening amid stacks and stacks of wooden crates piled on the deck of a ship. She seemed almost enclosed, rather well hidden, even from the vantage point of the ship's deck itself.

"Study the scene," said Riavek. "What does Hypatia look like?"

I tried to attune my concentration. I don't know how I lost the thread. I tried to see. She was wearing a dark hooded cloak, black or blue. And beside her were boots. She had taken them off, probably because of the heat. These boots—I could not quite focus. They were red, then black, then red again. They seemed very large, much too large for her. I am certain they were not her boots. She had leather sandals also. They lay beside her on the deck along with a little collection of implements: an ink jar, the kind that scribes carry, the kind that fastens to your sash with a little handle. She had rolls of paper, a carved wood box holding fine reed pens. She had a copy of a book titled *Indigenous Origins of the Christian Allegory.* This seemed a strange collection of things to bring for a trip into political exile. And yet, it was clear, these were her highest priorities.

As I went deeper into the scene, it was clear that she was deep in sleep, and yet even in sleep she held clutched in her right hand a small silver dagger with a jeweled handle. The jewel-studded sheath lay upon the deck amid the disarray of writing implements.

Through the cloak opening at the neck, her gold ankh was barely visible. As the sun moved higher in the sky, the metal caught a ray of light, emitting a blinding spark of charged electric energy. It seemed to reach out to me across worlds and pull me further into the vision. . .

Her face was simple, peaceful, clear and open. What few lines were showing in her 40th year were lines of thought and reflection, sincerity. She looked as though she *believed* in humanity. I do not know how to describe this, but, although she was a social critic, there was no trace of cynicism in her being. It was as if she really believed if she could find the right words, strike just the right chord, she would be able to convince people to honor each other, to honor each others' wisdom traditions and to coexist in peace and charity.

For all her knowledge, she seemed incomparably naive, wrapped, as she was, in the rocking cradle of sleep.

"There is no time," Riavek whispered softly. He had not changed his position, but sat as before facing me, resting his hands gently on his knees, looking deep into my eyes. "Hours, days, years, centuries, *death,* none of these are terminal boundaries. None of these are uncrossable. No space separates one world from another, one life from the next. All is one. All consciousness emerges and returns to the sea of boundless perception. Attune to the vast—attune to the endless—the expanse of lands and seas, continents, worlds and universes is traversable in moments. Attune your thoughts to consciousness, *spirit,* eternal, deep, unending. Direct your mind toward awareness of the immense totality of thought, feeling, idea, impression. Attend to any dimension, and the key to that doorway will turn. Trust. Have faith. . ."

Riavek paused, as if to see if I were following. I was. They say the universe only delivers the lessons you are ready to learn.

"Trust. Have faith. There is no time, and yet there is. There is no space and yet there is. This is the key to the mystery of imagination. Imagination is the ability to shift perspective. This is the key of your current initiation. Inhabit your time. Inhabit your place. And yet know—" His voice broke off. He stopped for a moment, then he resumed very quietly, his voice so soft I had to still my breathing to hear.

"You will remember that you inhabit the deep realities that far transcend the supposed limitations of time and space. You will remember that the law of consciousness is the law of freedom and that images of limitation have no power. You will remember the source of your own creative imagination. And as you remember, you will understand your destiny. Memory is a gift, my sister, and as I have often said to you—as we both were taught—forgetting is also a gift in that it opens up the path of learning. This is not a contradiction. Even those with open eyes, the eyes to see all that has been, all that is, and all that ever shall be must see with the eyes of one who is learning, for the powers of the universe are vaster than even the greatest of visionaries can know."

He stopped speaking. I looked into the candle, now sparking like the sunlight on the necklace of Hypatia. I envisioned the spark on my mind's inner field, and began to tumble into the oblivion of the rapid journey through dimensions.

"We go now to he who calls you," Riavek called through the aether, "We go to him whom you have guided from the future from your place—our place—in the world beyond worlds."

❦

In an instant I stood in the cell of Socrates. Morning had not yet broken as the great master lay in innocent, deep, peaceful slumber. His face was very like hers, childlike, open, fair. Instantly, I knew my role. Trota was with me, he had never left. He stood guard in the corner in his wolfen form, sending me a sparking signal with the gold of his outward seeing eye. Instantly, I recognized the dream. Instantly, I knew my task.

I stood in Socrates' cell inhabiting Hypatia's slender form draped in an elegant long, white gown, goddess-like hood, golden ankh glistening about my neck, feet shod in shining gold leather. I had traversed the worlds to give him comfort, to guide him through the doorway of the Portal of Forever. The ancient one who stirred the verdant mix of earth had evoked my presence from Below. The endless one who traveled the stars' silver sheen had summoned my being from Above. Wolfen Trota had guided my entry, taken me to the honored task, leading me through Apollo's dark and open cave to the very heart of the center of all creation. Every road I had stepped upon had led me to this moment. I would midwife his precious soul beyond the edge of the River Styx to the place from which Sun and Moon spring forth, the passageway that links the seen and unseen worlds. It was I who hailed the ship from Delos, the *mythical* Delos of rapturous eternal beauty. And now I came to serve him as the Priestess of Death; I came to serve him as the Priestess of Life. He sensed my presence and awakened. Slowly, he opened his deep, piercing eyes, recognizing me at once: It was I who had loved him, was it not, and I who had been with him ever? His face alighted in a luminous smile of deep and rapturous acknowledgment.

I raised up my arms in a gesture of invocation. "Dearest Socrates!" I said.

He sat up, still smiling. His face filled with laughter and yet he spoke not. "O Socrates!" I continued, "The third day hence, to Phthia I invite thee! Back to the caul of she who stirs the mix of every sacred end and every sacred beginning. I invite thee back to the womb of she who heals and makes whole, that you may be reformed again."

Socrates face broke out in a wide grin and he looked as if he might burst out laughing. This I had not expected.

"Can we not rather on the Fortunate Isle stay?" he said, "That fabulous land of the mythical Delos? I have heard talk of this land where the employments of the blessed are splendid indeed. They say in this place the blessed are engaged in employments proper to the higher spiritual nature—tuning the sacred lyre of mystic piety to strains of ineffable delight, nourishing the higher intellect with banquets of the most fabulous spiritual food. . .Must we immediately away to that cauldron of rebirth?. . .For well I might enjoy a little retreat." Then he laughed heartily with sheer and unmitigated delight. "To Phthia, you say, must I race right back in? A wise one told me the ship was coming to take me to Delos, and here I envisioned that sacred realm of the blessed, that illumined isle of the soul, that shining rock raised above the sea just as I reasoned one might transcend the sea of humanity upon death. I envisioned a blessed isle where I might enjoy splendrous communion with truth and wisdom all flowing perfectly out of the Sun of Good for all time. And now you tell me I must go away to return again?"

He laughed with joy. "By the goddess Hera!" he said, "To Phthia! you say, Back to the womb! And, yes, did not the Pythian prophetess of the Oracle at Delphi say to my friend Chaerephon, who was so blatantly bold as to ask, that I, Socrates, am the wisest man living? Well, if I am so wise, I say it is to the Fortunate Isle to which I ought to go—or am I being punished for not doing penance at Eleusis; they tried for many a year to drag me out there—yet might I not go to Delos and let some other generation carry on the shepherd's work? What a task it is to always be returning the wayward to the path of virtue. . .Ha! What say you to that, emissary of the All-Knowing?" He laughed again, as if he were parrying with me.

"I say, O Socrates, that you, yourself said to the men of Athens, did you not, that if they put you to death, others like you would arise again and again? I say to you, O Socrates, that you have spoken truth. Indeed, you shall to Phthia go, dear 'gadfly.' You shall accompany me to the pithos of the Ancient One, for, as is your wish, you have need of remixing for you still have things to do in other forms. I am afraid, dear friend, your days of meddling in the world's affairs have not yet come to an end."

How he had laughed. Suddenly he stopped and listened, "Oh," he said, "but my friend Crito comes now. He will propose to buy freedom for this old and bony shell. Wait and see!" He laughed again, laid down, closed his eyes and breathed deeply, feigning the fathomless depths of peaceful slumber. His mouth, I saw, retained a smile.

With a quick glance, Trota signaled me onward, and we spirited ourselves away to return again with the ship from Delos. The last words we heard were spoken by Crito to Socrates: "Never did I see the like of the easy, cheerful way in which you bear this calamity, dear friend." Then we heard Socrates' responding laughter ringing merrily, echoing richly from the edges of endless time.

I awoke upon the deck of the ship—disoriented—soaked in perspiration, overheated from the brilliant sun. How long had I slept? And what was this dream? I was holding the dagger. I was going into exile; this was no dream. Socrates was laughing. I must have taken off the boots. I was Socrates' oracle. It was me, Hypatia, who invited him to Phthia. . .What prophesy this? It must be right, then, this ship sailing to Delos now—it must—for is this ship not returning to Delos, the Fortunate Isle, the birthplace of Sun and Moon; is this not the ship for which the master awaited long ago? No. . .But he was speaking metaphorically of a paradise beyond death. And I am not dead. No, I am very much alive.

I am so hot, I am not thinking clearly.

The sun has moved across the sky. Where is R? How long must I wait? The ninth hour must be upon us and I have had no food. And I need a bath. What will I do without water on the ship? I do not start this journey well, sitting in a puddle of my own perspiration. I shall be stinking soon. Aphrodite forbid!

Oh, but I believe R comes now. I hear movement and the sound of men's voices somewhere down the dock. Surely, he will find me a lodging place upon this boat. I wish that I did not have to see him in this deteriorated form—that I might greet him in a new white tribon, simple gold earrings and gold house sandals—and yet what does appearance matter in the face of a threat to my very life? Still, I wish these were other times, that this were another place, a cleaner place, more refined, where R and I might, in the late light of evening, raise our glasses to the gods and celebrate our accomplishments.

Before the Library was ruined, my nursemaid used to take me to the Roman baths. It was a fabulous experience. *I could not go to the baths now for fear of losing my life.* When my maid would take me, we would shower and she would scrub me down, then we would go into the hot room where steaming eucalyptus flooded the air. This was the healing room for the bloodstream they said, because eucalyptus opened the ears, head, nose, throat and lungs and then traveled through the blood into the brain and heart, clearing, cleaning, opening, and purifying. When that room became too hot, and we were as purified as we could possibly be, we plunged into the cool bath, where we sat and soaked and traded news and gossip with the voluptuous women who lounged like gorgeous nymphs in the water and on the marble slabs and benches all about the waters' edge.

Next, we went to the professional scrub woman. Oh, but it was heavenly. I laid upon a table where she threw warm soapy water upon me and scrubbed me head to toe, back and front with a stiff, porous plant from the sea. She said it took off the dead skin and renewed the skin's healthy glow, leaving the body supple and shining. This was the most sensuous experience I have ever had. She was so strong in arm and hand, and as she scrubbed my body, she stood naked, and rolls of her fat, wet, soapy flesh rolled over my form. Like an infant, I felt I was bathed by the Great Mother of all goddesses Herself. That joyous cleansing was followed by another shower and then, wrapped stylishly in a big white sheet, I was escorted to the massage woman. She, too, was *strong*. She rubbed my body up and down, front and back, working out knots in the muscles, stimulating the circulation of blood and oiling all my joints. She massaged knots out of the back of my neck. Heavenly. Then she massaged in gentle perfumes, expensive flower essences, absolutely wondrous to behold. She massaged my hair with lightly scented oil and brushed it down my back. After I was all finished, my maid dressed me in a clean white dress and decorated my hair with costly adornments. What days those were—before my family began to live in fear.

Fear! Some dark thought nags me. Why should Hypatia live in fear? What is the worst that could happen? Death? If death is a deep, dreamless sleep, so much the better—and if death, as they say, is a transmigration to a better world, a place of true justice, a radiant place where I may converse with the true and abiding judges of all time, Socrates, for example, would I not desire that?

"R! I have been lost in thought." Quickly, I rise to my feet as he bows.

"Come, Hypatia, to my room, where I shall explain what has happened."

No time is lost, no excess words, no measured greetings. He strides off down the deck and quickly I gather my things and follow. I follow him through an opening down a ladder, and enter into a tiny dank room that smells of mildew, where R turns up the wick of a low-burning oil lamp. I am not sure, but I believe a rat scurries across the floor. It is so dim. We sit on small wood stools. I can barely see his eyes. I can barely see the youth that I so well remember. Where has our happiness gone? R tells me that Cyril has decided to use me as an example. The bishop's message will be more effective if he singles out a woman, and most effective if he crucifies that evil temptress Hypatia, author of the most devilish works ever composed. The crucifixion of the blasphemous priestess is designed to horrify her students and dissipate her following, he tells me. Killing Hypatia, according to Cyril, he says, will be the death blow for Plato and the rest of the heretical Greeks, as well as for that devil Serapis and all his kith and kin, and Christianity will finally be able to rise up unobstructed to occupy its rightful position. "This I have learned from my man," R tells me, "who learned it from Peter the Reader who unwittingly divulged this information in an erroneous moment of misconstrued trust."

By the god Serapis! It is true then. Can I bear it? It is just that I am tired from fitful sleep and can barely think of what to do. I begin to weep.

I wept, and R wrapped his arm about me, purely a gesture of friendship and human compassion. These were not the arms of a lover. I felt like a dirty waif, dirty inside and dirty out. Why did I, who have never felt such feelings, feel so filthy?

I wept and felt my face streaking. I wiped my face with my hand and it became even dirtier. R pulled a damp cloth off the shelf and wiped my face tenderly. The cloth smelled of mold. I wept and R spoke no more. After a while he said he needed to go supervise the men. They were lowering cargo into the hold with a crane, and some of the merchandise was very delicate, especially the cages of living snakes. I blurted out, "What shall I do?"

"You will be safe in Delos. Do not fear, Hypatia." He disappeared up the ladder leaving me in the dark and moldy chamber, leaving me alone with the possibility of creeping vermin. I retched. There was a container on the floor, smelling of urine, and I vomited into this bowl. I vomited whatever was left from yesterday's meals, barley cakes, fish, wine, olives. . .and I thought, *yesterday will never come again.* I thought of Theon, probably very frightened, but nonetheless—with shaking hand—sipping an expensive imported wine. How I would love to join him now. R had made no mention of food, and I had been too stunned, or too unclear, to think of food in the moment I was with him. Should one mention wine and cakes when one's very life is in danger?

I stopped sniffling and wiped my face. I tried to clean myself up as well as I could given the circumstances. At 40, one ought to have dignity and demeanor and courage, no matter what the situation. I am afraid I have not acted very dignified. I must think and act clearly as befits a distinguished professor. I must write to my students and get the letter off the ship before we set sail for Delos.

My dream comes back. Socrates, how you laughed! How your laughter rang through the worlds!

I begin to retch again. *What is the matter with me? Am I so weak that I cannot stand up to this filthy ship?*

I acknowledge that this moment is not how I thought it would be, but something beyond that simple recognition is gnawing at me like a rodent gnawing at the back of my head. I am beginning to think I am very afraid of that thing that is trying to force its way up. I try to repress it, to push it back, but it insists on rising, and I vomit again.

Gods and goddesses, help me.

The message grows in breadth and girth, becoming louder and louder, clearer and clearer, playing like a demon across the screen of my conscience:

Hypatia, you are running away from your destiny.

Socrates was an actor—yes, that is why he dominates my thoughts and dreams—he was an actor crossing the great stage of humanity. I am no Socrates, and yet I am a professor of philosophy, and a priestess of the great god Serapis in the great city of Alexandria. Have I not sacrificed all else for the love of philosophy? I have given up all. Might I not also give my life as one final, clear and directed act? Or shall I fade quietly into obscurity as this ship fades quietly from the shoreline, crossing a cold and colorless sea. Might it not be better if I stay in the city I love and face Cyril? Perhaps I might find a way to continue. Perhaps I might even move him. I know Cyril was not always as ruthless or brutish as he seems to be now. I remember when he was young. He was an opportunist, yes, but he might have done any number of things. He might have been a priest of Serapis and a professor in the academy had the world turned in that direction.

It becomes clearer to me now. Hypatia is an actress on the stage of humanity. I never wanted to be a martyr, I would never choose to die for a principle, but what else is my fate? My mother died. My father died in his own way also, and perhaps it is right and just that Hypatia, too, should be crucified. And if I die, must Plato also die? Must Socrates die with him? But perhaps their light could grow stronger. *And yet, they shall certainly die if Hypatia embarks upon the voyage to Delos.*

It was not easy convincing R to take me home. He said I would surely die if I stayed in Alexandria, that it would be so much the better for me to go to Delos where I would be removed and protected, where I could write my books in peace. He said he would make me comfortable on the ship, and that once we arrived at our destination, his friend, Marina, would accommodate me in her beautiful white marble home on a clifftop overlooking the sparkling blue sea.

He was angry also, saying that, now that I was here, trying to get me back, once again under cover of nightfall, might endanger his men. Also he needed them. There was so much to do before departure and the ship was scheduled to leave in just a few hours.

I said I would walk away from the dock of my own accord and take my chances. I thanked him for all he had done, now and at all the various times throughout my life. I stood to take my leave, but then he would not hear of me going alone. He called his men and his men took me. R placed a gentle kiss upon my cheek and I knew, at that moment, I may never see him again.

Theon's doorman was happy to see me as I quietly entered. It seemed no one was watching the comings and goings from the house, and for this I was relieved. I will not pretend I was not frightened. I was shivering inside from the moment I left the ship until the moment I was in my bed in the home I had occupied since long before my mother died.

The pot had been righted on the table.

Before retiring, I went to Theon, explained what had happened, and I explained that I would be going to the lecture hall at the fourth hour as usual. I would meet my destiny, whatever that would be, face on. I would not turn my back on fate. Theon cried. He was old, and sad.

I felt old and sad also.

In my bed, I prayed that I had made the right decision, but received no confirmation. No god or goddess came. I called into empty space and this was not reassuring. I remembered an ancient prayer and recited it silently:

> *May the god who is unknown to me be pacified.*
> *May the goddess who is unknown to me be pacified.*
> *May the known and unknown god be pacified.*
> *May the known and unknown goddess be pacified.*
> *The sin which I have committed I know not.*
> *The misdeed which I have committed I know not.*
> *A gracious name may my god announce.*
> *A gracious name may my goddess announce.*
> *A gracious name may my known and unknown god announce.*
> *The sin which I have sinned, turn to mercy.*
> *The iniquity which I have committed, let the wind carry away.*
> *May my transgressions tear off like a garment.*
> *Forgive my sins and I will humble myself before thee.*

After what seemed an eternity had passed, the sweet release of sleep began to wash over me; strange rays of happiness began to radiate through my body. I stood on the edge of the cliff, raised up my arms, the unknown one pushed me over, and suddenly I began to tumble down, down, down into the deep, dark safety of night's sweet abyss. Wrapped as I was in soft and warm bedclothing, cuddled as I was in the familiar surroundings of childish securities, protected as I was by the white light of mystery I had learned to invoke in my training at the Temple of Serapis, I fell into a deep state of dreamlessness, a deep, deep, peaceful and dreamless sleep.

At first, when I awoke, everything seemed normal. It all seemed quiet and serene. But then the memories of the last thirty hours came flooding back and my heart flooded with doubt.

Why do I have to be so impetuous? I might have been on the ship with R, I might have been on my way to Delos, safely out of the way of harm. What kind of protection will I have now?

I got up and took off my poison ring. I began to wash with the fresh scented water my maid had already laid out for me. Oh, but the clean water did refresh. I washed my hands and face, then my whole body and even my hair. Rivulets of water streamed down my neck. Droplets of water splashed to the marble floor. And as I washed, I began to feel like a fish who has been hooked and pulled up on a dry dock, flipped around until all the fight is gone, and is, for some unknown reason, suddenly thrown back in the sea. Slowly, I began to come alive. I began to come into the full realization of the life and strength that surged inside me: *I am filled with life and I am free.*

As I washed in the cool scented water, I meditated. I meditated upon my lecture. And as I thought, going deeply inward, I began to overcome the physical sensations of fear through surrendering myself to love. I began to see that there is no point in creating a contest. There is no point in struggling. There is no point in fighting or running or hiding. I came to the world to speak truth. My power comes from my courage. My stamina shall come from my love of this very same world. Love shall be my guide. Love shall be my protection. I shall surrender myself to love and love shall form for me a shield that no sword could ever assail.

I shook out my hair and dried it with the bedclothes.

I found my most beautiful white dress and my golden sandals. I called my maid to fasten my hair in plaits upon my head. I asked her to find my most elegant white veil and my lipstick from Rome. She did not speak but raised her eyebrow almost imperceptibly. She helped me. It was as if she understood.

The driver came as usual, I said goodbye to Theon who began to cry again, and we traveled through the teeming streets without incident to the lecture hall. My students were waiting inside and out and the ones who were outside followed me in. All were awestruck by my appearance. They had not seen me as a woman, but as a teacher. Now they saw me as a woman.

I stepped to the front of the room and stood tall before them. "Thank you for coming today," I said. "Over the course of my career, I have taught many things. I have taught arithmetic, geometry—points, lines, surfaces, solids—the sacred equations to find weights, measures, volumes. Together we have studied the properties of the tetrahedron, the octahedron, the icosahedron, cube, sphere, pyramid, cone, and cylinder. We have studied circles, triangles, rectangles, squares, and we have asked, of these, which form is the most perfect and the most pleasing, the most useful, the most splendid? And some of you said the circle, for it is endless, and some said the triangle because three points create a plane and symbolize the law of dialecticians, and the square, you said, is elegant in its simplicity and stability and that is necessary also.

"We studied music, the sacred intervals. We asked what happens to tone when the string of the instrument is halved and halved again? When the size and weight of the gong is systematically varied? And we listened carefully and asked, which sound is better, the high or the low. And some said of you said high because high is clean, free and clear, and some said low because low carried you inward. We created chords and experimented with feeling.

"We did the same with the elements, studying the properties of fire, water, air and earth, searching for basic components, looking for the principles that make up matter.

"And the colors—we asked what are the basic colors of the world? What creates red and blue and yellow? We looked at wavelengths of light and divided these wavelengths the same way we had cut in half the strings of the lyre, and we experimented with correlating color and sound. And we asked which color is better, blue because it is pure? Or violet because it mixes the strengths of two pure colors?

"On all these levels, in all these ways, we experimented and examined our world. And, we discovered something about ourselves. Some of you are volatile and fiery. Some are as solid as earth, itself. Some are fat, some are thin. Some are partial to yellow and some to green. Some resonated with the lyre and some the flute. Some prefer sunset, others prefer dawn. We are all drawn in different ways, depending on what we have been taught and the basic constituents that make up our nature.

"Each of us has our own special calling.

"And, just as the world is formed of all types of solids, liquids, and aethers, all of us combine to create the sacred whole. One could not be called better than another for all are required to create shape and form and give rise to conscious awareness. If everything were red, we could not possibly know the essence of red-ness. Born of fire, water and air, a rainbow, so pleasing to the eye, is composed of a spectrum of separate hues. Beautiful harmonies cannot delight the ear if only one note is played, unless, of course, the mind *imagines* its own harmonies.

"I am but one woman, one player on the world's vast stage. All of us, together, like a choir, like a rainbow, combine at present as we have in the past and will in the future to produce the contrasting patterns and shapes that open our awareness and illuminate the grand brilliance that is life.

"And what, I ask you, do you believe unites the whole? What causes the colors of the rainbow to adhere to one another? What causes the planets to stay in their orbits? What causes the end of the circle to meet the beginning? And here I make a leap of logic I have never before made. It is, perhaps, a leap of faith, because, on this day, the twelfth day of March in the four hundred and fifteenth year of the Julian calendar, I, Hypatia, tell you that I have concluded that that adhering material is love. Love is the glue of the universe. Love binds colors, sounds, shapes and forms into beautiful arrangements. Love binds the seeker to the sought, the lover to the beloved, the student to the mysteries.

"Only one thing can hold you to your path eternally and that thing is not discipline, it is not perseverance, it is not even greed or anger or the thirst for power. It is love. All else shall pass. Love remains. Love is life's strength. Love is life's protection. All other forms of protection lead to desecration and to war.

"I ask you, on this special day, to look into your hearts and find love.

"Find tolerance, find charity, then go beyond tolerance and charity and find love. Let this feeling evolve. Let it grow. For love is our savior. Love is the only true freedom. Love and only love.

"And with that message, I, Hypatia, professor of philosophy, priestess of Serapis, one woman acting out life's sometimes perplexing script, leave you to your own thoughts and your own separate journeys. Long has this woman loved you, my friends, my students, you who have taught me more than you can ever know. Love binds me to you now and so it shall ever be."

With that I walked away from the podium.

All eyes in the room were turned upon me with shock, pity, adulation, and horror. All were still and all were silent. I walked down the aisle, out the door into the noisy street, bustling with people and animals, carts, hawkers and vendors, and quietly stepped into the waiting chariot. "Let us go home," I said to Trajan. He cracked the whip and the chariot rolled.

We edged through the mob.

We had only gone a short distance when I spied Peter the Reader in his monk's robes lurking in the shadow of a vending tent. He is so tall his head stands out above the crowd. He is watching me. I catch his eye and he quickly averts his gaze. Then I notice there are more monks about, many monks. From every direction, they are watching me from the safety of small huddled groups. As I look in their direction, they turn their heads away. Have I acquired the evil eye then? They seem to be as frightened of me as if I were Julian the Apostate himself. I hold my head high and look straight ahead. I am Hypatia and I will not be intimidated.

Directly in front of us a cart collides with a chariot. Ears of corn fall out of the cart's tattered wicker baskets and roll out into the street. The chariot, a beautiful new custom gilded cisium, is apparently damaged. The drivers leave their vehicles and begin to argue loudy in the street about who is at fault, about who will pay. Profanities are exchanged. The anger escalates. A crowd forms. All I want to do is get home. "I'll see what I can do," Trajan says and he disembarks to discourse with the drivers.

Tension mounts. There is more and more noise. Aggression builds. More screaming. More yelling. More people. People join in from all sides, pushing, shoving, clashing, crashing. The horse is jostled. She snorts and jumps. The energy is chaotic. Chaos boils into pure pandemonium. The horse raises her head, whinnies, rails and rears. I cannot see what has happened to Trajan.

Suddenly, monks are upon me, jerking me from the chariot. "Trajan! Trajan!" I scream as they tear at my veil and my gown, "Stop it! Stop! Trajan!"

The crowd of monks grows huge around me and they are yelling and screaming and tearing at my dress. "Blasphemer! Heretic! Temptress of Devils! Sorceress! She-Devil! Magdalene!" I hear all these things yelled out, and I hear "Kill her! Kill the She-Devil!"

They tear my clothes and knock me to the ground. I cover my face with my hands, but they tear my hands away, twist my fingers and hit my face with bricks and stones. So many are on me at once. I cannot see. I cannot even scream.

They tear my veil out of the pins. They hold back my arms and rip my dress from my breasts. Like a pack of wild animals, they rip my clothing off in shreds, all the time seething and screaming, swearing and slobbering. I try to pull in my arms and kick them off but I cannot fight them.

They are holding me down on the street, shredding my clothing, gripping me by the hair and pounding my head on the pavement. *By the goddess, they are crushing my head.* . .They are pulling at my legs and my feet and my naked breasts. They are hitting me with bricks. A hand tears away my golden ankh. The golden adornments fall from my hair. They are tearing out my hair. I am a mass of blood. I am going numb. I am bludgeoned with a huge club. . .My eye. . .My *eye*. . .Going numb. . .And then it comes to me, *Sleep Dear Hypatia. Sleep now, sleep well, sleep deep and dream of the jungle. The tiger. Dream of sacred fountains where pure waters flow.* . .

And I am standing at the cliff top. My arms are outstretched. I wait for the unknown one to come up from behind me and push me off, but instead she yells "Fly!" I leap and I fly! I am *flying*. I am flying, flying, free and beautiful, flying up, up, up over the lecture hall, the museum, the Temple, the Serapeum, our home, and I can look down in the street and see the monks bludgeoning the body of Hypatia and they have beat her to a bloody pulp and they are dragging her by the hair and limbs, dragging her through the street. Her left arm is nearly severed at the shoulder and still they use it to drag her. Trajan stands by struck dumb. Hundreds have gathered to watch; some follow and yell and and scream like monks, caught in the contagious frenzy. Hypatia's face is smashed. They have torn out her eyes and they drag her, lifeless, over the pavement, through the filth, screaming, "See! See O pious Christians? She is dead! The Devil is dead!"

They drag her to the Caesareum where Bishop Cyril stands by waiting. The screaming monks drag her body inside and ritualistically carry the bloody sacrifice to the altar.

Peter the Reader and the bishop exchange words at the doorway, "The Devil is dead," Peter says. "The holy bitch is nothing but a holy ghost now," says Cyril.

They throw the desecrated vessel of Hypatia on the altar. Hundreds pour from the street into the Cesareum to watch as the monks begin to hack what is left of Hypatia's worldly flesh away from her bones with oyster shells. *Oyster shells!*

I am somewhere in the room watching. I can see everything, hear everything. . .

Oyster shells—was that last night's dinner? Had they eaten of the aphrodisiac—with their sharp teeth gnawing the female genitalia out of the shell to which it clings—the very shells they now used to scrape away dear Hypatia's mortal being?

In the back of the room, a figure sits huddled against the wall shaking with waves of shock and struggling to suppress tears of horror. *Marcus.* Oh, my Marcus.

Although I know he cannot see me, cannot feel me, I go to him, hold him with my arms just as I had when he was a little boy, and I say, "Oh, my little brother, do not despair. The script is perplexing, but I shall be there to guide you when the ship from Delos finally arrives." He whispers, "Hypatia, my sister. . ."

I think he has, perhaps, heard me.

Then I hear a laugh coming from a nearby bench and the words, "The boy has heard you, and yet he has not. Of course, he is no boy now. . ." and then more laughter. "What an intriguing paradox! Is not the comedy divine?" Socrates stands to greet me, "Well now, by the goddess Hera, we meet again, do we not, fair one? And I believe it is I, this time, who have the honor of escorting you. Will you take my arm, dear lady? Shall we away to Phthia go? Ah, but your fair self there upon the altar lying is as good as ashes in the funeral jar now. Let the little monks have their fun, for they never meant to do you any harm, yet I tenderly say, they never meant to do you any good either. But as for what is left of you, your dear fairness, you are not yet finished talking, so let us back to the great womb go. For I understand some other child calls for you already and the boy Marcus has his own work to do."

"Socrates!"

"Come, let us go to the ship. We have lifetimes to share. And soon enough we will all arrive on Delos."

Smiling and inviting, he offered his arm. I rose and took it. What light shone from the eyes of the great teacher. I twined my arm through his, and in wondrous grace, we walked the aisle toward the blazing light of the Sun of Good. At the door I paused and stood before Cyril. I looked him directly in the face. "I am sure we will meet again, dear brother," I said, "for are we all not thespians in the same acclaimed company?" Socrates laughed heartily as a bead of perspiration formed itself on the bishop's furrowed brow.

ഐ

Riavek gazed at me lovingly. "They never meant to do you any harm," he said quietly, "Of course, they never meant to do you any good either, and for that you may gently blame them." He smiled softly.

I shook my head. *Hypatia*. . . I was born, in the incarnation of Pamela, on the day Hypatia died: the twelfth day of March. She died in her 40th year and this year, on my 40th birthday, I had the strangest experience. My friends and students arranged a party for me which would begin in the evening. I thought I would take the day for myself, sit on the beach, contemplate the ocean.

I have a little ritual I try to do on my birthday every year. I go to the beach and meditate upon the past and the future. If I am on the right track, the beach delivers to me a feather—seagull, cormorant, sandpiper or pelican—which I braid into my hair for the rest of the day.

I started to walk the path to the sea, when I noticed some boards in the field next to my home. *I'll just pick those up first,* I thought. They had been cast from the roof a month earlier when a workman was fixing our leaking chimney and now were overgrown by high weeds.

As I stepped through the wild radishes, a three inch carpenter's nail sticking out of a piece of wood hidden and secured by the vegetation went right through my shoe, and all the way through the middle of my left foot. In a reflex reaction, I put my right foot forward, shifted my weight and tried to pull my foot off the nail. To my surprise and horror, another nail suddenly punctured the sole of my right shoe and went through the middle of my other foot. I was completely impaled. I had to sit down in the weeds and pry the boards off.

What are the chances of this happening? Carpenter's nails through *both* feet—what are the chances of being impaled by nails on your *40th birthday* three months before your *ordination?* I never made it to the beach that day—it seems my birthday ritual was enacted closer to home—but, after fearing I might not be able to walk, I ended up dancing many a dance that night upon those wounded feet. It is amazing what the body will stand up to. (I got the tetanus shot later.)

I doubt if I will ever feel the same about the date of my birth, about my spiritual path, about my ordination, about the purpose of my incarnation, and now, the feeling is intensified. The message I receive is this: The path is fraught with difficulty, even when you think it is "your day." You must *purify yourself from undue hopes and fears, unnecessary attachments.* You must *walk the path as a beginner, and your inner eye will begin to exercise its clear and solemn vision.*

I asked myself: What is the purest form of clear and solemn vision?

Cyril was made a saint by the Catholic Church in 1882 for developing the idea of the "Holy Trinity": the Father, the Son, and the Holy Ghost. Goddesses, mothers, and daughters must have invisibly occupied the third angle of the holy triangle, that elusive realm of the Holy Ghost, and, taken together, the feminine, possibly, even today, may comprise one-third of the sacred formula.

Is seeing the truth of this equation, and the imbalance thereof, an exalted projection of clear and solemn vision? Or, is even this revelation something to be apprehended, digested, and eventually discarded as one moves along the path of initiation into ever-greater understanding?

How many lifetimes, I wonder, have I struggled with the Church? And how odd this spiritual dissonance. We are all on the same spiritual path, are we not? Cyril, Hypatia, Marcus? Why should there be any conflict? The words come back to me: *As a woman, you certainly had your go-arounds with the Roman Catholic Church.* My teacher had spoken these words only a few days ago but they seemed to have so much more meaning now.

Riavek interrupted my thoughts. "That is enough to remember for today, dear one. Go to the beach and refresh yourself. Find a feather to twine in your hair, but take care, dear sister, not to hurt your feet as you walk down the path."

Again, he smiled his soft and gentle smile.

I laughed, shook my head, and blew out the candle.

CHAPTER 10

BITTEN-BY-THE-WOLF
THE DARK AGES

Friesland, 735 C.E.

Day Six: I light the candle.

The days stretch out like aeons. Each day, a piece of the world is created. Day One, mystery awakens. Day Two, initiation deepens. Day Three, love begets life. Day Four, life contains death. Day Five, there are killers in the road.

The candle flickers. The day is dark, misty. Low fog rolls over the blufftops, lodging in droplets on anise and yarrow. The ocean lolls and crashes, a heavy gray metallic mass, rolling at the bottom of the cliffs. I can see no seal or dolphin. A raven croaks from a high wire calling to me to pay attention.

The wind is still but there is a curious movement in the air. I whisper silently, "Riavek, are you there?" For a moment I do not know if I want to go on. I do not know if I can go on or if I should. How deep will this journey take me? Must I open this channel? What price will I pay for knowing?

"What price will you pay for remaining ignorant?" Riavek addresses me softly, but directly.

"Riavek!"

"We will not go much longer," he says, "We are skimming, skipping. But there is so much more, so much in between. It is like your writing, a few black scratchings on a white page—you choose a few thoughts to record—but most of the page lies empty, fallow. The emptiness is the space between: the births, deaths, and resurrections of eternal cycling, seeds dormant in the winter field. An eternity passes between Day One and Day Two, between Day Two and Day Three. The black scratchings illumine fragments of creation, but you will soon understand, if you do not already, that the creator is larger than her art. The soul is far vaster than a few selected recollections.

"It is Day Six. Day Six is the day of repose, not because we are finished, not because you have seen everything you need to see, but because Six is regeneration and Seven is fraught with difficulty. Rest awhile on this day and experience the wisdom and gratitude that is in you."

Three scenes flash quickly before my mind. I am twenty-something, walking—limping—down a narrow walking path lined with plantain and I see, in a rut, a mummified cat head. It is shocking. But that seems way ahead of the story. . .Then I see Mar-Emma, much younger than when she died, walking the same path with a hand cart on the way to Coldwater. Then I see Mar-Emma in the cottage.

Mar-Emma is a strong Friesian woman, tall, lean, keen, a clear light in the forest. She has a mind of her own. You can see it shining out of her deep set midnight-blue eyes. The sisters of the tribe call her to the village to help them and to cure them, but they seem to be afraid of her at the same time. They do not befriend her. She was the one who could not be tamed. She is not like them. At the same time, Mar-Emma is the one the spirits picked to understand the ways of life and death. She has the power of wortcunning. She knows all there is to know about the nine sacred herbs and this she has taught to me—just as the forester's grandmother taught her.

I see Mar-Emma in the cottage and I am there with her and she is telling me a story. This is how it begins:

"It was a long, long time ago. The forester was still alive then. He was a much younger man and still had the fire of the forest in him. He was a wild one, he was—he had fire in his eyes—and this is exactly what drew me. He and I, dear Wolfje, were birds of a feather, we were. I was mad with the entrapment of the village, like an animal caged by conformity, houses with open doors, clean new thatch, neatly stacked wood piles, yellow klampjes uniformly click-clacking down the hardbeaten road, stored-up bags of corn flour. Of course, this sounds perfect, but it is not perfect for a wild-hearted Wolf girl. Was I to spend my whole life making cheese? I had the fire in me and it was the fire of the wildland. Not of the village. Not of the farm. I did not know then that it takes the fire of the wildland to brave birth and death also. I would learn that later. When I was a girl, dear Wolfje, I could only think of flying away, raise my wings up and fly like a marsh heron in the spring. I had no idea how strong I was."

Mar-Emma always told stories about her life. This is how we passed the days in our little cottage in the midst of the Crescent Forest not too far outside of the village of Coldwater.

I looked around the inside of the cottage. Two rooms and a thatched roof. Rafters hung with cook pots and dried herbs. Fresh straw on the floor. A lovely warm fire. Pea soup with fat carrots bubbling in the pot. Little breads—broodjes—on the table. I loved the broodjes. They were a special treat from Coldwater. Mar-Emma was paid for her healing services in many different ways. Little tiger breads were my favorite. The way the crust cracked in the oven—it came out looking just like a tiger's fur is supposed to look. Naturally, I had never seen a tiger, but I had seen many cats and Mar-Emma had many stories. We even had a black and white spotted cat called Little Bread once, a small version, Mar-Emma said, of the mother beast.

I had never seen an oven either. Mar-Emma did not have one, and although I was born in the village, I had not been back since my birth.

As I looked around I saw a part of the house at the corner was crumbling. Some of the mud and small stones that filled space between the wood had melted or collapsed. This worried me a little—sometimes I worried since the forester died—but Mar-Emma said we would repair it in the spring. She said, "Just now the ground is frozen so our repair work is frozen as well." She had the hole stuffed up with rags. She said that was fine.

Mar-Emma helped the village women. She was there when they gave birth, there when they did not choose to give birth, there when the children were sick—plying them with herb teas—there when they died, and she even helped the men in spite of the fact that they envied her time and relationship with the women. Mar-Emma was loved, venerated, and ridiculed all at once. She was called the Woman of the Forest, the Forester's Wife, Mevrouw Coldwater, Madame de Fries, Midwife and Lady of Herbs. Very few knew her as Mar-Emma. Perhaps the forester and I were the only ones.

"The forester was a bright-eyed boy," she said, "I knew him when he was a child and I knew how the frogs sang to him, how the herons swooped down and fanned him with their wings, how wild boars rubbed against his legs, how the roe ate grasses from his hand. What other Frieslander was like the forester? What other Fries would help the mother wolf birth her pups?

"The forester was magic. When he entered the sacred grove, the hunebed filled with light. The mound of Earth Mother shuddered and the world was born anew. His power was as strong as the power of Wolf Spirit."

I interrupted her. "Tell me about my mother," I demanded. I had heard about the forester over and over. I lived with him for eight years but I don't remember so much magic. I don't remember the hunebed lighting up. He seemed a tired old man to me, not so different from others I had seen. I would rather hear about my mother, even though the story made me sad in my heart. Mar-Emma would never tell me my mother's name. I believed my mother was still in Coldwater.

"Your mother," Mar-Emma began, "was young. You were not her first. There were four others before you. I attended at each birth. You were the fifth child to come and you came in the fifth year. I had a special connection with all your mother's children—all were my spirit children—but none of these connections could rival the one I have with you."

Mar-Emma was my spiritual mother. She raised me from a kit in a basket.

"Your mother called me to her house and I went as I had done four times before. She was big and strong and built for having babies. We expected no problems. She had taken the motherwort all through the gestation to keep away evil spirits. She had drunk strawberry tea and the labor was good and strong. But when you came out your little foot was tucked under. It was clubbed and twisted and you were completely covered with little strawberries like a strawberry patch at mid-summer."

(All my strawberries are gone now. I wonder what I looked like when I was covered with strawberries. Mar-Emma said they disappeared shortly after my birth. I had never seen one on anybody's body. Of course, I had never seen anybody's body except Mar-Emma and the forester.)

"Your mother would not look at you. She said, 'It is Bitten-By-The-Wolf Spirit. The child is cursed. The Wolf has got its foot and I cannot suffer it to live. Take it away. It cannot help with the planting, nor can it help with the harvest. Take it away—and I will give you extra.'

"She promised to make me a warm blanket of sheep's wool to ward off the ice cold winter if I would take you away, and take you away I did. I gave you syrup of poppy to stun you into quietude and I took you in a basket to the frozen stream. I could hear the water swirling and hissing under the ice. I broke the edge with a rock, pounding until the rock cracked the surface and I could break out a hole and I was just about to push you through the hole, basket and all, when the River Spirit spoke. She spoke like a gentle woman. 'Do not put this child through the hole,' she said, 'Let her sleep the night in the hunebed and if she lives, she will be yours. If she dies, I will dissolve her in the current.'

"I was astonished because I had not heard the voice of the river before. I went to the grove of the hunebed and by now it was late afternoon and dark and cold. I walked down the thin-blanketed snow path through the woods in the misty semi-darkness of a February's eve. The Full Moon was already up and shone through layers of silvery clouds, and she lit my way, though dimly, because it was that time when it is not all light but not dark either, the kind of wintry darkness you have a few hours after noon. I came to the oval mound in the midst of the Crescent Forest, the mound where I had communed with the Earth Mother many times before. In the dark, against the dusting of snow, the uncovered rocks of the hunebed looked pitch black, huge dark forms, and they were full of life, filled with death also, the births, illnesses, struggles, and deaths, of the ancient ones of whom we do not speak. The shapes of the stones looked like an animal, like an animal's legs, and in the dark they seemed to crawl like a strange night creature on the Earth Mother's belly. I was frightened. There was so much movement in the stillness. Who had taken shelter here? What footsteps, now silenced, had moved through these woods to this sacrificial grove?

"Hidden in the deep twilight cloak of the bare hazelnuts and oaks, I paused at the edge of the circle and hid. I knew there was no-one there—how could there be on a wintry night such as this one?—and yet I had to be sure. There was a feeling in the air, a strange hush. I felt I was being watched. But who could be watching? I felt queasy in my stomach. My hair stood on end with chill bumps that raced down my legs and crawled over the top of my head. My knees were shaking. There must be spirits about. Perhaps the Wolf Spirit.

"I noted the position of each stone—those stones I knew in daylight like the fingers of my own hand. I noted the position, checked the placements east to west, and waited in absolute stillness just to make sure they were not moving. Every time I looked away and looked back, they seemed to have changed positions.

"I wanted to go home to the forester's fire, drink some steaming ewrten soup, warm my hands and nose and feet, but there was no escape. I must face my task.

"I watched. I counted the stones I could see—thirty-nine—and counted them again. I waited.

"White wisps of lace and frozen beaded ice hung on the dried plant skeletons and spider webs near my feet. I could see them better and better as the full mother moon rose higher.

"An owl shrieked in the darkness. I jumped and almost dropped the basket. You had not made a peep and I thought you may be dead already but I dared not look. I dared not move my eyes from the vision of the hunebed. Those black stones rising in the clearing, they seemed three times their normal size and so very, very black.

"Stepping very lightly I approached the outer ring of stones and paused. My feelings were heightened. I could feel the spirits. I could feel movement. The back of my neck bristled and the inside of my head felt lightning. I could see the open doorway on the side of the hunebed. A strange light seemed to shine out from the covered area at the end where the slabs were still across the top, and the earth was still piled atop the roof, providing a hiding place or shelter, a site for secret meeting. I knew that the most secret place, the most sacred of sacreds, was the place where I must go.

"In terror, for it was terror I felt now, though I could not understand why, I stepped close to the door. I was afraid the spirits would pull me in the ground or trap me in a stone. I looked in the door, saw nothing but a strange light at the far end. The light came from nowhere, just floated in the darkness. I shivered, my shoulders shuddered. Then something brushed my face. I gasped. I looked behind me. Nothing. Beside me. Nothing.

"I ducked down and scooted into the hunebed, pushing the basket before me. It was dry and dusty on the floor and with my eyes accustomed as they were to the dark I could see the shapes of dried oak leaves and old acorns. In the open places, moonlight speared through like icecicling shafts of silver light.

"I pulled up my cloak and half-walked, half-crawled, pushing the basket to the end, terrified that the spirits would push a stone before the door and I would be trapped inside forever with a dead clubfooted baby, a spirit child, that had been Bitten-By-The-Wolf.

"As fast as I could, then, I pushed the basket against the big stone in the end room and hastily backed out, scooted backward through the door and as deftly as possible, I spun around to face the outer circle. My heart was pounding.

"All was silent. Hushed. An eery hush. Then the owl shrieked again. I screamed and my own scream frightened me more than anything before. I began to run and I ran through the woods. Something was chasing me. I ran from my own fate. I ran from Death. Death was chasing me. Death: I must run *faster*. I felt a pain in my chest and still I ran faster. On and on I ran. Fear was strong. Fear was stronger than Death."

Mar-Emma thought for a second. Then she added: "Even stronger than the thought of breaking my ankle in the dark.

"I ran as fast as I could to the forester's house, and when it came into view, how grateful I was to see the frosted thatch, the cozy yellow light shimmering around the edges of the door, smoke from the little fire curling toward the moon. I ran through the cabbage patch. Boerenkool still stood on frosted stalks. It is strange what you remember. I remember hoary white frost dangling about the edges of the wrinkled leaves.

"I ran to the door and banged. When the forester realized it was me knocking and banging, he unbolted the door and I can remember how he stared at me with fear in his eyes. He was nearly as frightened as I was since he thought I was staying in the village. He was frightened by the disturbance, frightened by my appearance. I told him I had decided to walk home but was caught by early nightfall and had to run. It was that kind of night. An eery feeling was in the ether.

"I sat before the fire. My feet were numb but I had not noticed. The forester melted snow in a pot and I dangled my feet in the tepid water until I could feel them again. He gave me soup and tea and I warmed up, but I could not sleep.

"All night I heard the cries of owls, the shriek of night herons. Why were they not sleeping on such a cold night as this? Something scratched on the door and I heard sniffing. Someone rattled the bolts. Spirits were about. Spirits were about. Surely."

Now Mar-Emma was coming to my favorite part of the story. I liked this part because it raised my hackles. I knew something happened there in the hunebed that night, but my memory is only partial, like a memory seen through a thick forest mist on a no-moon night.

I remember going back and forth between dreams and waking that night. I was just born, so I would not have said that then, but now that is the way I would say it. First I was rocking in a gray misty sea, rocking and turning, then I felt my head and shoulders being crushed. Then I remember frosty silver spears. Then I remember a big black warm body. The main thing I remember is a huge black tail fanning over my face.

All these memories are glimpses and all my life I have tried in dreams and waking to remember that night in the hunebed.

Mar-Emma told stories late into the night. I loved the ones that frightened me. Now I know that is because I felt protected by Mar-Emma. . .Almost. . .She chased a tiny mouse across the floor once, yelling frantically at me to get my feet up. She chased it and smashed it and smashed it and smashed it with a giant broom. This took away some of my feeling of safety. Mar-Emma was like a madwoman chasing after that mouse. It was almost like she was taken by spirits. Remembering now, I think she was afraid of something I did not know about, and that made me afraid, also, but I was not afraid of mice. Or at least I did not think I was. Some things in life are hard to understand.

"In the morning when I could see—morning came late in the mid-winter—," Mar-Emma continued, "I bundled up in my blue cloak, heavy socks and wood shoes and walked back through the Crescent Forest to the hunebed.

"As I neared the grove, I held my breath. The mists of morning still swirled about the ground but it was warming up a bit and the hoarfrost was beginning to melt. At first glimpse everything looked different than it had in the night and I wondered if my own fantasy had tricked me. The hunebed stones were pale brown and friendly, not at all black, and they were a little bit green, a little bit mossy, not all cold, not all dead as I thought. Sunlight bent through the trees and light shadows fell across the mound. It seemed inviting and friendly, but I knew my task was neither inviting nor friendly. My task was a cruel one. I expected to find a dead baby, perhaps half eaten by the forest's night creatures, perhaps stolen away and dragged to some hungry lair for a steaming winter breakfast.

"Gingerly I approached the mound. Gingerly I approached the doorway. I crouched down and looked inside. At first my eyes could not see. I squinted in the dark. I could vaguely see the basket, but it became more and more clear. I crawled down the corridor, dragging my hind legs as if I were crawling down the inside of a petrified beast—now I was sure the beast was sleeping—and I crawled to the place where I had laid the basket and what I saw there caused my jaw to drop open. All around were scratchings in the dirt and piled leaves pushed up around the basket. The place was warm, too warm, and smelled of dog. I sniffed the still air. No it did not smell of dog. It smelled of Wolf. Someone had definitely been here. There was a clump of black hair in the leaves and this I picked up and placed carefully in my satchel. Mustering my courage, I looked inside the basket and you looked happily up at me and cooed. You were warm and snuggled up into the blankets.

"I said, 'My babe, you are bitten by the Wolf Spirit and by the Wolf Spirit you are saved. You must be a Spirit Child sent to me to learn Earth Mother's ways. Yes, you are Bitten-By-The-Wolf. . .'

"You were so sweet in your little bed, little pink face and blue eyes, little fat cheeks. What a pretty baby, I thought. You seemed to be glowing. I was glad I had not put you in the river.

"You raised your arm and pointed a finger at me and I took this as a sign that I was to raise you up. The forester and I had no children, only the animals of the wood, so you would be our child. I knew the forester would not mind.

"I called you Bitten-By-The-Wolf. . .

"Once I named you Gerdje—The Protected. That was years later when someone came around from the village and saw you limping and I was afraid the word might travel that there was a lame girl here, that a baby who was supposed to be born dead had somehow lived. But the name didn't take. Of course, no one could have known you were not mine. Only your mother knew about your foot. Not a single other soul saw you. And there was no way your mother would ever say anything even if she knew.

"So that is the story of how you came to be my girl. You were saved by the River Spirit. Wolf Spirit kept you warm. Goat gave you milk and so you grew to be a woman."

Mar-Emma had taken that wolf hair and carved a little hazelwood box with a sliding top for it. She carved a picture of a wolf on top of it. She kept the box in a special place in the rafters and brought it down to use for charms and incantations to heal babies with strawberries and others with afflictions of the blood, hair and skin. She let me touch the hair. She said it would put the power of healing in my hands. It was softer than you would think. Always I wondered why Wolf Spirit had not eaten me.

I was a happy girl. As soon as I was big enough and strong enough, probably when I was about thirty moons old, Mar-Emma carved an oak stick and I began to walk with it. She carved a wolf head at the top of the stick because I was Bitten-By-The-Wolf, and this is one of my first memories, walking the path with that stick in the summer sun, gathering roots and tubers in the forest with Mar-Emma. Wild boar rooted and snorted with us and every now and then, the forester speared a boar or a deer or squirrel and we had meat in the pot.

As I grew, Mar-Emma taught me all the plants of the forest, grove, and field, and how to use them. Weybroed was for sore eyes, loose bowels, bloot-spitting and piles. Ellhorn buds were for skin eruptions, for cleansing wounds, to grow hair, and to dye the hair black. Mar-Emma stuffed ellhorn leaves in the nostrils to purge the brain and to stop the fever. At mid-winter, we made a circle of ellhorn berries at the hunebed. We stood in the middle to generate strength. Banewort, which only came in some summers in the Crescent Wood, was boiled in goat's milk to open breathing and to help with the falling sickness. Extract of hazelnut berries soothed the throat. A boiled concoction of goat's beard roots dissolved bile, cured burning in the chest, watery stomach, and pains in the side. Slippery root tea also helped loose bowels and internal bleeding.

The nine sacred herbs are mugwort, plantain, stime, cock's spur grass, mayweed, wergulu, apple, thyme, and fennel. I learned their sacred rhymes:

> *This is the herb which is called Wergulu*
> *The seal sent this over the back of the ocean*
> *To heal the hurt of other poison.*

We gathered with the left hand by night or by day, depending on the plant, by the full moon and sometimes in certain seasons, like the misletoe we gathered on mid-summer night. We never let the herb touch the ground, as that might drain out the potencies, but we placed them carefully in a basket or a carefully folded cloth. Year to year the patches were always the same, sometimes thicker, sometimes thinner, and Mar-Emma tried to keep her stores fresh within each year saying the plants would lose their cures if they hung in the rafters for long.

Mar-Emma ran away from Coldwater to go with the forester when she was a young girl, and it was the forester's grandmother, called by the same names that Mar-Emma came to inhabit—Wise Woman, Midwife, Healing Woman, and so on—who taught Mar-Emma about wildcrafting, wortcunning, and curing. When Mar-Emma first came, the forester's grandmother still lived in the cottage. Grandfather was the first forester.

We always asked the patch spirits for permission to cut, crop, chop, and gather as Grandmother had taught Mar-Emma, and Mar-Emma had taught me. Mar-Emma taught me many rhymes to use for the asking:

> *Banewort, Banewort*
> *how do you grow?*
> *And now may I dig up*
> *just one little row?*

And there were rhymes for curing:

> *Banewort, Banewort*
> *in the milk of the goat*
> *for breath and for life*
> *open this throat.*

Then the Banewort would be drunk and if the spirits willed, the child would be able to breathe.

Mar-Emma taught me everything, and as I grew she carved me bigger and bigger sticks. I had a collection of walking sticks with wolf heads, each one taller than the last, leaning in the corner. This was the record of my growth.

Since we lived so far back in the Crescent Forest, we had few visitors. Sometimes runners or men came from the village to call Mar-Emma to a sickbed or a motherbed. I always hid when these runners came, so I never spoke to anyone except Mar-Emma and the forester. I never went to the village because my foot would not walk me.

When the forester died, Mar-Emma and I buried him ourselves, digging a hole and making a mound of stones over him. Mar-Emma said it was lucky it was summer or she did not know how we could have done it, old as she was getting, and me with my twisted hip and foot.

I grew old in the cottage—Mar-Emma said she was so happy with me, that our lives together were so cozy, so gezellig—and, as I grew old, Mar-Emma grew even older.

Mar-Emma had often been paid in rags for her services, and she and I sewed sackdresses and quilts and doekjes for the new babies. We sewed and talked, and she told story after story of how she had run away to live with the forester, how magical the forester was, how she had left the stifling village and run away to the woods, how they did not even try to find her, how she and the forester had passed a stick three times through the fire at mid-summer in the presence of the grandmother to make a marriage, and how when she returned to the village to attend the mothers and children, they did not even acknowledge she was the same girl who had run away. Once she attended her own mother and her mother did not know her.

Old as she grew, she always took care of me.

One day Mar-Emma did not return from gathering. It grew dark and still she did not return. I called out into the night: "Mar-Emma! Mar-Emma!" but she did not answer. I tried to walk with my stick to find her in the night, but I could not see, and I stumbled and fell. All night I sat burning a candle and praying to the wood spirits to protect Mar-Emma. After a while I cried.

I banged the rafters with my stick in the middle of the night and knocked down the Wolf hair. I opened the box and it seemed all light inside. It brought me comfort. I touched the hair:

> *Wolf Spirit, Wolf Spirit flying free*
> *bring Mar-Emma home to me.*
> *Wolf Spirit, Wolf Spirit flying free*
> *bring Mar-Emma home to me.*

I whispered over and over into the flame, but the more I whispered the more I knew Mar-Emma would not be coming back.

In the day I searched for Mar-Emma, looking at all the blooming patches. And I searched the next day and the next and the next. My good leg became very tired and my hips ached and I fell and hurt myself and had a hard time getting up.

Then I realized the only way I would find Mar-Emma is to sit in the deep silence, inside the hunebed at the center of the stone circle, and let the spirit of Earth Mother tell me where she was.

The next morning, I put on Mar-Emma's long blue cloak, pulled the hood over my head, and began upon the walking path, moving very slowly, lumbering past the gearwe, the yarrow, winding past the sourgrass, thumping my stick in the dirt thinking:

Stick, Stick, Wolf Head Stick
Get me there and make it quick.

It seemed the faster I wanted to go, the slower I went until all time slowed into a few deep breaths, and then into one breath at a time, one step at a time. It was then I looked down and saw the cat's head.

It was right in the middle of the path, but had I not been moving so slowly I would never have seen it. It looked just like a clod of dirt. It was the color of summer dirt, and the shape and texture of summer dirt also, but there was something about it that made me look closer. Balancing on my stick I leaned over and picked it up. It was a completely dry and furless cat head with the skin stretched over it like thin worked leather. I had never seen such a thing before. The ears were bent down on the sides and the mouth was open slightly with the sharp little teeth perfectly white and bared. It was not frightening, but it was strange. I had a feeling I should move it aside so it would not be smashed in the path—I had a momentary feeling it was the Little Bread of so many years ago, but I am sure it could not have been. Still, I do not know what became of Little Bread; she disappeared just like Mar-Emma. Anyway, no one really used this road but Mar-Emma and me. No one had visited for months, so there was no way the head would be harmed. I don't know why I was worried. I put it back. I put the cat head down exactly where I found it.

I walked deeper and deeper into the Crescent Wood. The sun was high to guide me as I followed the path to the earth mound of the hunebed.

When I reached the mound in the clearing of the sacred grove, I stepped inside the outlying stone circle and walked around the hunebed three times. I stood at the place where we had made the ellhorn berry circle. This was as Mar-Emma had taught me to do when seeking guidance from the spirits. Then I went to the place where Mar-Emma had first laid my basket when I was a baby. I crawled deep inside the hunebed, crawling through rays of sunlight that shone through the open stones, stones no longer covered with Earth Mother's deep protection, until I entered the inner room. That room was still covered.

Far in the back end my eyes began to adjust to the light until I could see the inside of the stone hunebed. I saw a tiny carving near the bottom of the end stone that looked like a wolf. I thought that must be a sign.

> *Wolf Spirit, Wolf Spirit*
> *help me see*
> *where in the wood*
> *Mar-Emma be.*

> *Wolf Spirit, Wolf Spirit*
> *help me see*
> *where in the wood*
> *Mar-Emma be.*

I repeated this over and over, over and over, falling into a deep trance until a picture was revealed to me. I saw Mar-Emma clutch her breast and fall dead by the river. I saw the River Spirit rise and claim her empty body. I saw her soul fly up from her body, fly to our cottage and enter the little carved box of Wolf hair she kept in the rafters.

I saw this and then the Wolf Spirit was before me. The Wolf Spirit was before me, a big, black She-Wolf. Her eyes glinted yellow in the semi-dark of the enclosed daylight. I was not afraid. She looked me in the eye, raised her black tail, and suddenly the entire memory of the first night of my life returned.

She said, "I bit you when you were still in the womb, twisted your foot and slowed you down so you could have a life of rest. You were weary of living even before you were born. Wolf Spirit Child, I called to the River Spirit to send you to the Sacred Mound. I warmed and suckled you in your nest. I gave you the Wolfen Magic of Protection, the Wolfen Magic of Invisibility, and I called the Wise Woman to come and get you. I come now to tell you you shall go to live the rest of your days protected and revered: You shall become Visible. You shall be known for what the Wise Woman taught you. You shall be born again as quiet wisdom for the ignorant. Your path will be a gentle one. You will find great happiness and I shall come again to guide you when it is time for your soul to depart. You are my child, Wolfen One. I have been with you from the beginning. From the start I have guided you and I will be with you for all time."

She disappeared then, leaving me containing a strange mystery, and I knew there was no more to be said. I knew that there was no point in searching for Mar-Emma's body. I would find her soul at home.

Slowly I crawled from the hunebed feeling the big black She-Wolf Spirit beside me. I felt her walking beside me as I retraced my steps, pausing in the ellhorn circle, three circles around the mound, and then I walked the path home.

So slowly did I move that life seemed to pass in the tiniest increments. Every plant called out to me and I called out "Hallo!" and I recited in my mind the magical curative properties and incantations for each patch. With every step I felt Wolf Spirit beside me.

Spirit Stick, Spirit Stick
guide me home
I know that I am
not alone.

I repeated the rhyme as I walked, and when I came to the neck of the woods near where the cottage was, something strange happened. Again, I beheld the cat head on the path and part of it was *crushed*. Only one side, not as if it had been crushed by a footstep, for anyone, man, woman, or beast would realize instantly if they had stepped upon such a fragile skull, but it was more like it had been crushed by a *wheel*. My first thought was to worry for the head, and I felt sorrow for not having moved it in the first place. I picked it up and placed it behind a clump of fennel, but then something else struck me. The plants were bent down, strangely crushed as if they had been greatly disturbed.

Something very big had come down the path. Something very, very big. I was not sure how to feel. Mar-Emma was gone and could not protect me. Mar-Emma could not hide me. I continued on slowly, thinking, lumbering. I thought about what to do and then the voice of the Wolf Spirit spoke beside me:

Wolf Child, Wolf Child
go straight home
You will find that you are
not alone.

Wolf Child, Wolf Child
go straight home
You will find that you are
not alone.

Outside the cottage I could see what had happened. There stood a wagon and a huge four-legged black beast, the likes of which I had never seen. I supposed this was a horse, but though I had heard horses came and went all up and down the rivers to the north and the south that led out to the sea, the Crescent Forest stood between rivers where no routes went, and since I could not walk fast enough to leave the wood, only forest animals had I seen.

The horse was sleek and beautiful. The wagon was awesome to behold. Smoke was curling from the smokehole and I smelled cooking barley. Someone had opened up the barley stores!

I stopped in the path. Wolf Spirit spoke, urging me on:

> *Wolf Child, Wolf Child*
> *go straight home*
> *you will find that you*
> *are*
> *not*
> *alone.*

I stepped briskly to the door, banged it open with my stick and boldly walked through.

The man that sat at the table screamed, then was silent. He shook with fear or exhaustion or wonder as he sat looking at me. He made a magic sign with his hand on his head and heart and could not take his eyes off of me.

As I stood in the midst of that room I realized I had spoken to no one in all my life but Mar-Emma and the forester.

Time stood still. I stood in silence as the sun moved across the sky.

The one sat at the table dressed in a rough brown robe tied with a crude rope, his mouth gaping open. The other one laid upon the floor, face as pale as snow on a winter day. He was as white as Death. Clearly, they had come to Mar-Emma for healing.

I did not move, but waited.

I did not know that the one at the table had been struck dumb because he believed me to be the angel or the mother of his god. I did not know that when the one on the floor opened his eyes at last, he would be instantly healed by the sight of my eyes alone. How could I know that I stood in an aureole of light? That my eyes glowed like lightning? That my staff shone like a torch? That my blue cloak was the image of the cloak of his goddess?

The man at the table breathed, "Mar-ee-ah."

I said, "Mar-Emma."

He shook his head in affirmation and whispered, "Mar-ee-ah."

I fed them. I sewed their tattered clothing. I cared for the men-children as Mar-Emma had cared for me. I gave them soups full with healing herbs that restored the dead one to life. I lit the candle for them, knelt when they knelt and whispered when they whispered.

The one at the table I learned was called Brother Jan. The other—the one who rose up from death—was Father Wynfryth. They were from a far-off tribe. Father Wynfryth's words were twisted, but some of them I could understand.

I understood they felt the spirits were with me—that they had been magically led to me—and so they had. The Wolf Spirit *was* with me. I was Bitten-By-The-Wolf, but I did not tell them this. They called me Mar-ee-ah.

I understood they wanted me to go away with them, that they would take me to a kind man who would take care of me forever in exchange for what I had done for them. They had friends waiting at the edge of the Crescent Forest, who could take care of the cottage and if I ever wanted to come back, I could easily come.

Over and over they said the words *Me Phi Bo Sheth, Me Phi Bo Sheth* as if I would finally understand their meaning. I never understood, but I remembered the words. Wynfryth pointed to bird tracks bound in leaves that he carried in his robe when he said these words. I nodded and smiled. Wynfryth nodded and smiled.

I decided to go. My heart trilled with excitement. I must have felt like Mar-Emma had felt when she left Coldwater for the freedom of the forest. I would leave the Crescent Forest for the freedom of the world.

The men were so kind.

I bundled my precious plants, sewed the soul of Mar-Emma into her blue cloak which I kept ever close to me and began the long ride in the grand wagon to the city at the center of the world.

At the edge of the forest, we met a large band of men and here we left Father Wynfryth, who was, by now, completely cured. Some of the men were on their way to Saxony, some to Upper Frisia. Some went into the Crescent Forest to live in the cottage. They were telling the people all around about their Church. Brother Jan stayed with me, and accompanied by almost thirty men in caravan, we wound through the countryside, by hill and dale, raging river, village after village on our way to the Great City of Utrecht.

They called me Sister Mar-ee-ah.

I was transported into the most sacred of inner circles.

The *music!* Harmonies moved against the stone walls and circled back around the empty room raising the hair on the back of my arms and hands. Bells rang. Brothers and Sisters sang, and the singing echoed like nothing you have ever heard. Wolf Spirit howled in my heart. The howl moved into my throat and came out my mouth and I was singing. I was *singing.* I was *singing!*

I sang and sang and sang, my own heart making a sound that split like one color into many like a lily bursting open in the spring. The flower opened, and closed again and it went on this way song after song, chant after chant. And I was transported into holiness. My life became a holy life.

They draped me in robes. Clean, beautiful. And these robes I sewed for the Brothers and Sisters.

With great joy and in great beauty, I sang and I sewed. I sewed vestments for the Brothers and Sisters. I sewed vestments for the Fathers. I sewed stoles for the Fathers.

I prayed with the Sisters and ate with the Sisters and little by little I learned one word, then another, then another, and all the Sisters were kind to me and they were loving.

And I lived in that great enclosure in true and utter happiness, cooking soups with the healing plants which I taught the young girls to gather by the stream.

Father Wynfryth came to visit once. Everyone whispered about him and called him by the name of Father Boniface.

For Father Clement, I sewed the most beautiful stole you have ever seen. It glittered with amethyst, garnets, rubies, diamonds, golden lace and beads. Such riches! Such beauty! Such elegance.

And inside each stole I made, I sewed in a hair of the Wolf Spirit from the clump in the hunebed that Mar-Emma found the day after my first night. I sewed in this bit of Mar-Emma's soul so that the Fathers might be empowered by the spirit of the Wolf Mother of the Crescent Forest as they went out on their missions to heal the sick and redeem the wayward heathens.

ᘒ

"It is not all one way," said Riavek tenderly. "There are many lives and many guises."

The candle burned low. I looked into the crystal sphere.

I sighed.

More and more missionaries went to Friesland, to Saxony, and to Frisia, radiating out from Rome to the ends of the earth.

The English Church, especially because of its strategic position in relationship to Northern Europe, was controlled by the papacy more than any other church outside of Italy. Englanders were delighted with their high status within the hierarchy of church, and when the English missionaries went out on missions, their first act was to go to Italy to seek the blessing of the Pope himself. Willibrord and Wynfryth, young English noblemen anxious to succeed, went to Rome to seek the Pope's blessing and support. Wynfryth began in 718. His lifelong goal was to convert all of Frisia. He divided Hesse, Bavaria, and Thuringia into dioceses. He founded a string of Benedictine monasteries. Wynfryth was so successful in Northern Europe that Pope Gregory blessed him with a new name, Boniface, and eventually made him the archbishop of Mainz. Willibrord, blessed by the Pope with the name of Clement, became the archbishop of Utrecht.

It was Father Clement for whom I sewed.

Father Boniface was working under Father Clement when he claimed Coldwater. It is told in the Catholic Church that it was Father Boniface, later to become St. Boniface, who was shown the miracle of the Christmas tree. While working to convert the northern heathens, he intruded upon a group of worshipers in a sacred grove making a sacrifice to the god Thor. He stopped the sacrifice, said to be a little prince, and cut down the giant sacred oak at the head of the grove. He called this tree the "blood oak." As the oak fell, the story goes, a fir tree appeared. The new tree, he said, was the Tree of Life, the Tree of Christ, that would now replace the blood oak throughout all of Europe.

In 742, the law of Northern Europe became papal law. All marriages were to be public. All Christians—*and now all people were Christian by law*—must tithe to the Church. In 747, bishops of Northern Europe declared they would "maintain the Catholic faith and unity and subjection to the Roman Church till the end of their lives." In 772, Irminsul, the most sacred oak tree in all of Saxony was felled. This symbolized a major victory for the Church. In 768, Charlemagne became King of the Franks and in 785 he decreed that if the Saxons, who he had violently conquered along with the Frieslanders, refused to be baptised or in any other way insulted Christianity, they would suffer the death penalty. All pagan customs were outlawed. Violators were savagely punished by Charlemagne's army. Thus, on pain of death, all of Northern Europe was finally "converted."

The lands Charlemagne conquered, all lands and tribes of Northern Europe, were brought to order, it was said, in accordance with God's will. Strict canon law was enforced, complete conformity was demanded in monasteries and correct Christian living was required throughout the kingdom. To this end, manuals for effective preaching were created and schools were established for the clergy and the people so the Bible could be more correctly comprehended. During the reign of Charlemagne, Church and State completely united so as to bring Christianity to all, Christianity under strict control. On Christmas Day in the year 800, Pope Leo III crowned Charlemagne "Emperor of the Romans."

The northern tribes resisted—in 754 Boniface was slain by Frisians who were called by the Church "a band of pirates"—but the power of the Church combined with the power of the Frankish army was as strong as it was ruthless. By the end of the eighth century, Europe had been effectively Christianized, organized and totally subdued.

"Lifting the veil of ignorance you learn that there is no one angle, no one right way," Riavek said sadly. "The soul grows through the accumulation of experience. It pushes out its boundaries, becomes compassionate, becomes wise. It opens to encompass all that exists, to embrace life and all of life's creatures. The heart opens, broadens, deepens, and makes room for all. This is the way of love. Love is the path of your soul, Pamela. Open to love and receive your calling."

I thought about all of this as I opened the carved wood box of wolf hair given to me by my friend at that 40th birthday celebration when I danced all night on punctured feet. Now I understood the meaning of the strange gift.

I took out a piece of wolf hair and carefully sewed it into my minister's stole—the purple and white stole I had recently finished making and in which I would soon be ordained—and, as I sewed, I remembered my roots as a member of the Wolf clan. Somehow, I thought, as a minister I must remain *open*. I carefully stitched on deep red garnets to remind me of my womanhood and as I stitched, I had the very strong memory that, since the beginning of the Dark Ages, every priest's garment I had made I had made as a woman in servitude.

Still, I had loved the priests. Still, I had loved the Church. Still, I had loved the *music*.

Do not judge, I thought to myself, there is innocence and guilt in every direction.

CHAPTER 11

DIANA BROSSEAU
THE REFORMATION

Paris, 1541 C.E.

T oward the end of the Dark Ages and even through the flowering of the Renaissance, thought and education were governed by the Roman Catholic Church. In all of Western history, there has been no other period of time in which culture was so exclusively dominated by one institution. The clergy controlled all schools, libraries, and books. All ideas were subject to the scrutiny—and judgment—of ecclesiastical authority.

The Inquisition was established in the 13th century by a series of papal bulls, edicts issued by the popes. Pope Innocent IV issued *Ad extirpanda* in 1252, which authorized imprisonment, torture, and death for those accused and convicted of heresy; that is, having religious beliefs opposed to the orthodox doctrines of the Church. During the procedure of processing the accused, her property was confiscated, partly to pay for the expenses of her trial, imprisonment, torture and execution and partly because those convicted of heresy lost all rights to ownership. Seizure of property was viewed by the Church as a major weapon against heresy in that it deterred others from taking the "wayward path" while simultaneously generating healthy revenues for the holy purse. Being financially sound helped the Church tremendously in carrying out God's work.

Pope Innocent's 1252 decree placed "inquisitors," those responsible for finding and questioning suspects, above the law. Rulers and citizens alike were expected to assist these inquisitors in their work or face excommunication, fines and the charge of complicity with heretics. In 1257 torture was officially sanctioned, and, the methods used were so effective that heretics, when tortured, tended not only to confess, but to supply the names of many others who were also guilty.

Thus, the Inquisition grew. The Church collected more and more goods, more and more funds, more and more property.

The Inquisition targeted Jews, Gypsies, women, and some men—those who appeared to be witches, hags, fairies, stick-riders, herb-gatherers, screech owls, spirit wolves, wise women, night-monsters, card readers, workers of charms, keepers of potients, diviners, wise-sayers, and others who were called hermeticists, astrologers, cabalists, magicians, alchemists, and anyone who possessed a "superior knowledge of the natural sciences."

In 1215, the Fourth Lateran Council of the Church decreed that Jews, who had been granted immunity from persecution earlier in the Christian era, must wear a yellow cap or patch. Throughout Europe strict laws were passed confining Jews to ghettos, usually the least desirable quarter of any given town or city. The persecution of Jews became epidemic. The *Talmud* was seized and burned on the grounds that its contents were offensive to Christ, and ultimately, all Jews who refused conversion were expelled from England in 1290, Germany in 1298, France in 1306 and Spain in 1492. The Jews became homeless wanders subject to continuous intimidation, humiliation, and blatant massacres that would last for centuries.

All sorts of problems were blamed on Jews and "witches," and almost any kind of activity could be interpreted as witchcraft. Naturally, the practice of witchcraft was imagined to be the worst form of heresy. The "Witch of Newbury" in England, for example, was killed for surfing on a river. "To and fro she fleeted on the board standing firm bolt upright. . .turning and winding it which way she pleased, making it pastime to her, as little thinking who perceived her tricks, or that she did imagine that they were the last she ever should show." Witches were killed for decorating tables, wearing laurels, taking omens, observing pagan holidays, speaking out, and engaging in politics. Witches were frequently clan, tribe, or community leaders. A woman could be accused of witchcraft simply because she was old. Or young. Mary Spencer was accused of witchcraft in 1634 because she started her bucket rolling down a hill, ran in front of it, and playfully called it to follow her.

The *Malleus Maleficarum,* known as *The Hammer of Witches,* written by Dominican priests Heinrich Kramer and James Sprenger, was one of the first books published after the invention of the printing press. Six editions were published by 1500, another thirteen by 1520, sixteen more by 1669. It was translated into German, French, Italian, and English. This book, a manual for witch-hunting, specifically attacked women as witches. "When a woman thinks alone, she thinks evil," it said. The *Malleus Maleficarum* instructed inquisitors in methods of extracting confessions. The suggested torture was brutal. For light questioning, hanging by the thumbs or by the hands with the wrists tied together behind the back so as to dislocate the shoulders was recommended. For more serious questioning, prodding, pinching, or removing lumps of flesh with red hot irons or pincers was considered to be effective, as was the insertion of body parts into boiling liquid. All the time, the woman was asked repeatedly if she had copulated with devils, whether she had ever impeded or prevented procreation, whether she had changed her body into another form, such as that of a beast, whether she had offered children to devils, or injured cattle. Under torture she confessed. Eventually she confessed to each and every charge. After torture, she freely confessed, thus, it was said she confessed of her own accord, when she was in her right mind, and not solely under the conditions of torture. After conviction, she was most likely burned alive.

This went on, waxing and waning and waxing again, for almost six hundred years until torture was finally abolished by Pope Pius VII in 1816.

Diana called to me through the thin veils of place and time and I did not want to hear her. It was as if she called, "My name is Diana. . . My name is Diana. . .," and I could hear her thin cry faintly, but my rational mind wanted to be someplace else at some later date. Still she would not stop calling. I was not meditating when at first I heard her call, nor do I know if my Guide was in attendance. I was doing ordinary things—washing clothes, answering correspondence, walking the dog—when her name reached me, echoing through the light and shadows of the aeons.

I was on the blufftop. The wind blew through my hair. The ocean cascaded and eddied, breaking in white swirls around the cliffbase. I was walking past the wind-bent cypress trees which were leaning over landward and the overgrown lupin and sage. Everywhere cottontails were jumping and Skipper, my white Lab, was bounding and rooting in the pseudo-pampas grass in a frenzy frightening and toying with the small game. That is when I heard her. At first it was fuzzy—I was not even listening—but then it came clearer and clearer until the name was absolutely unmistakable: *Diana*.

As it came in clearer and clearer, as I, in fact, began to turn my attention in her direction, I began to get a nauseated feeling in the pit of my stomach. It was like being torn in two directions at once, the sick feeling of a classical psychological double bind: damned if you listen, damned if you don't. . .

I felt like I wanted to help her or at least bear witness to her suffering, but I felt also like I just wanted to go on with my life. *Don't look! Don't look!* one angel called. *Don't look and remain at peace. . .*And the other angel called, *Look, because you must. Look and become wise, become compassionate, become feeling, because we are all, every one of us, interchangeable, and this you must know if you would feign to conduct your ministry in truth.*

And I listened to the warring angels and my mind went this way and that, but my heart kept hearing the call, and the call grew louder and louder. It was as if Diana, herself, would not let me be. She wanted me to see her face, her eyes, her condition. She wanted me to hear her plea, to know she had cried, and that her tears has been real, not just saliva she smeared upon her cheeks to attest to her innocence. I felt all these things and still I did not want to look because I had a vague, gnawing feeling about what might be entailed and the instinct of every cell in my body said, *Turn your head away, or you will be in her story.*

And there I am, chronically helpful, chronically curious, and before I could even analyze what I was doing, I was asking, *Where are you? Where are you? Where are you calling from?* because there was absolutely no mistake; this Diana was crying for me. . .right there on the California blufftops. . .centuries and systems and endless fashions later.

At first it seemed like she was calling from the North and my mind flitted about thinking Holland? England? Germany? Ireland? Austria? My mind went in circle after circle, circling inward geographically until my sense of place was honed. I halted, fixed, focused, and the place was unmistakably Paris. Then it was *When? When?* My rational mind wanted to go to the French Revolution—I kicked a rock out of the dirt road—I had always been interested in the Revolution, but Diana herself pulled me back, back, back in time, back to an earlier era, and in that earlier time and place, I suddenly saw her, I saw her distinctly, and there she was manacled in black chains in a dungeon.

Her hair, about six inches long, was filthy and matted and half gone as if she had some disease of the scalp. Her colorless eyes, sunk back in her head in death-like holes were half-closed, as if she were dazed and glazed with insensibility. She was dressed in a filthy tattered rag that may have been white at some point and it covered her only to the thighs. It looked as if that was all she had on amid those frigid gray stone walls. Her bare arms and legs were covered with scars and indentations, as if flesh had been removed in chunks, and everywhere I could see open sores that were festering. Her right foot, nail-less, was gray with gangrene. Her lips were so pale, she looked as if all the blood had drained out of her body. She was as thin as a skeleton. She had urinated upon herself, and what little urine there was, was tinged with dark red streaks. The place smelled of old urine and human decay. There was evidence that others had been chained up also.

The sight of her made my breath catch. It made my teeth ache.

It was as if my own body felt suddenly suspended in helplessness—or in horror—as if there was absolutely nothing that could be done, absolutely nothing. It was like watching a hawk fly far overhead with a squirming baby bunny in its talons. All you can do is glance up and look away.

This feeling was partially fear, partially paralysis, partially the kind of inner sickness that results from witnessing some kind of hidden knowledge, something the eyes see that forever alters the course of one's life, and yet that thing is somehow too painful to be spoken of, even though it is with one constantly, even though one talks around it always, never exactly addressing it, like one of those deep secrets of the soul, that, if someone asked you, as in an interview, "What incidents, would you say, helped shape you as the person you are today?" you would talk of everything else, but never mention that one thing, which, all the time, was sitting in full view right up front like the first thought on your mind in the morning. This kind of thing twists the pit of your stomach, contracts your solar plexus, stills and wrings your heart, strangles you like a wad of wet linen jammed down your throat, pounds in your head like a jackhammer and causes your limbs to shake. It leaves one single question upon your lips and that question is *Why?*

My consciousness did not want to go into the crumpled body of Diana Brosseau.

They say the universe does not deliver challenges that we are not prepared to meet. I wonder if this is so. This kind of thing, I kept thinking, is unbearable, too unbearable to look at. Still, my subconscious mind kept returning me, returning me, to the dungeon where Diana laid rotting. My heart was saying, *You must see the world for what it is. To do anything other is to live a falsehood. You must look. You must see.* And my heart kept saying, *Will you live a lie?*

I went home and lit the candle.

Riavek said, "You cannot understand the situation of Madame Brosseau—and why she was sentenced by the rules of the *Hammer of Witches* in the 'sixth manner' which happens in the case of one who is 'gravely suspected of practicing witchcraft.' You cannot understand why she was sentenced to die, burning at the stake, after serving one year in the squalor of prison, being tortured and examined very often, especially on Holy Days, unless you can understand Madame Brosseau's marriage."

Pictures began to open up.

Jacques-Thomas Brosseau was a good man, ethical in business dealings, caring to his family, intelligent. He was responsible for quite a few people. He was successful, too, for all practical purposes. From the king, he leased a wonderful free-standing brick house with a tall pointed roof on the Rue de la Seine, wherein lived his mother and father, one of his brothers, his brother's wife, his brother's three children, and his wife Diana Marie Brosseau.

Jacques-Thomas was what we would call a contractor. He and his brothers were excellent stonemasons who worked with high integrity. Jacques-Thomas organized a crew of masons from the guild and they were rarely without work. The economy of Paris was booming, or at least it certainly seemed that way, judging from the king's oppulence, the games—*tennis anyone?*—the tournaments, the flourishing arts and the twice-weekly balls the king held for the Paris aristocracy at the Louvre. That seemed good to Jacques. In the early days, he believed that money flowing into Paris would flow in the direction of the arts, the trades, the merchants. Everyone would benefit. Masons, in particular, would benefit greatly from all the new construction. In the place where the mason's guild met, Jacques-Thomas preached endlessly about the virtues of the healthy economy until eventually some of the masons began to joke when they saw him coming, *Hey Brosseau, played tennis with King Francis lately?* And they would all laugh because they knew he would never in a million years play tennis with the king, yet Jacques-Thomas Brosseau insisted upon thinking himself the king's foremost supporter.

Jacques could remember distinctly, how, when he was only 14, Francis was anointed as king. The pageantry was unbelievable—Jacques loved to tell the story. He thought King Francis was the most impressive man he had ever seen and, at times, when people mocked the king, especially when they poked fun at the king's unusually long nose, Jacques-Thomas would always rise to the king's defense. Here is how it was: Francis was anointed and immediately thereafter he gathered together twenty thousand Swiss mercenaries—the most fearsome fighting men in Europe—and they marched on Milan with pikes, axes, and spiked clubs. How fabulous it would be to take Milan, then the King of France would hold the Pope like a squawking chick in the palm of his hand. The canon roared—Jacques-Thomas could almost hear the screaming—Francis' allies rushed in to help, and in the very first battle, the King of France triumphed. The whole plan worked. Pope Leo could not have been more frightened, at least that's what the placards posted around Paris proclaimed, and, as a concession, the Pope gave Francis the right to nominate bishops. That meant France was freed from some of the tyrannical power of the Church.

King Francis was daring and audacious. Jacques-Thomas was in awe of his courage. And shortly after Francis had been made king—Jacques-Thomas could remember so well, he had been right there watching—Francis had boldly entered Paris with his entourage. (Diana had been there, too, watching the procession with her father. She was 11 years old. Jacques-Thomas was 14. They were unacquainted at the time. Paris was not so small as all that. . .) Jacques-Thomas had never seen the houses so fabulously decorated. Brilliant tapestries hung from all the balconies and eaves. Paris was awash with vibrant color. And what a *parade*. First there came group after group of royal musicians, trumpeters, drummers, one leg red and one leg white—you should have seen them march, first all red legs forward, then all white. What a display! There were even bagpipe players from foreign lands wearing the plaid of their clan, or so it was said. A man stood by Jacques and explained the significance of all the people passing. There were court jesters in funny pointed caps dancing this way and that waving little batons, sometimes imitating the drum major who never responded or even changed expression. There were royal pages, some of them Jacques' age, all dressed in white velvet from head to toe with beautiful white velvet hats. Then there came the smart-looking officers of the king's house followed by the king's own Scottish Guard, all the vogue among the kings in Europe. What incredible *whiteness*. So much white velvet. How pure. How perfect. Even the streets of Paris seemed cleaner. . .

Finally, King Francis, himself, came and he was not carried under a canopy as kings had forever been—and this is what impressed Jacques-Thomas the most—the king was riding his own horse. He was dancing his spirited steed this way and that, doing little zig-zags and circles, and the horse was going from right to left and left to right in perfect little dances, raising up her front hooves and striking them on the ground, and Jacques-Thomas would swear to all his friends later that he actually saw sparks fly between hoof and stone pavement. Then there was King Francis, himself, atop that phenomenal mount. You should have seen him glittering, all in silver with his jaunty white velvet bonnet all a-sparkle with glistening gemstones of every kind. The wealth! The *riches*. The power. It was thrilling.

But that was before Jacques-Thomas was a contractor. *Long* before.

It is easy to impress a boy with the glories of war, a good joust, strong biceps, some wrestling acumen, a jaunty hat, precise horsemanship. . .

What Jacques-Thomas learned was this: It is one thing to be a nobleman—where some of those things might actually be in reach—and entirely another to be a member of that great supporting caste we refer to as the *bourgeoisie*. About 1530, when Jacques-Thomas was about 29 years old, he began to get angry. Very angry. At first he only whispered in low tones in the bedroom to his trusted, intelligent, and loving wife Diana Marie; it was as if he were compling a list of complaints and figuring out how to articulate them. And, after a period of about two years of quiet late night discussions, Jacques-Thomas was fuming. It came to him how it was. The *king* is the problem, King Francis. Francis, Jacques said, is amassing too much power. He keeps reducing the powers of the public courts, raising taxes, creating new tax bases, raising rents, shifting internal alliances, toying with other countries. You cannot discern where he stands. Watching him maneuver is like watching a stick on the bottom of the Seine; with the movement of the water and the way things look through it, you can hardly judge its location. You can reach in to grab and not even be close. One minute the king is liberal, the next he is stamping out all attempts to reform, executing anybody he wishes. His sovereignty is maddening. How could anyone, even a *king*, be above all laws?

Jacques-Thomas solidified his arguments. Increasing rents on the king's property (and how did *he* come to own so much of Paris?). Increasing customs duties. Ten percent taxation on commercial transactions. Rising sales tax on meat, wine, cloth, and a hundred other items. The salt tax, which means each house has to buy a fixed minimum of salt each year from the government warehouse—and the salt, of course, is sold at huge profits to the *king*. Beyond that, as if *that* were not enough, what about the increasing monopolization of power and justice? Not only that the *king* is above the laws—limited only, as the *king* says, by divine and natural law—but that the *king* regularly sells public offices and who can afford those but the richest men? Worse, then, *worse*, those offices can be *inherited!* Passed on from father to son. Where will it end? Jacques-Thomas fretted enormously. Everything is wrong. One power after another is being removed from the *parlements* and what other recourse for grievances might there be for a member of the *bourgeoisie?* The parlements seem to be the only possible check for the royal will and they are going, going. What right does he have, even if he is *king*, to replace all the courts with courts composed only of the royal council? There is no way you can fight it. Do you remember, Jacques-Thomas would say to his brother masons, in 1527 when the president of the highest court in France assured Francis that "we do not wish to dispute or minimize your power; that would be a sacrilege, and we know very well that you are above the laws." *Do you remember?*, Jacques-Thomas would ask, and the more Jacques-Thomas talked, the more his blood boiled.

Then in 1528, what happened. . .The Church councils of Sens and Bourges requested "action" against heresy; the Church became more and more violent.

Further, the educational system fully supported the Church—and the Church's violence—and the Sorbonne, well-known as the most eminent school in Europe, gained the highest recognition as the professors systematically, with the most rigorous scholarship of the day, scientifically proved and justified Church doctrine and thereby bolstered the powers of the Inquisition. All powers—religious, educational and governmental—consolidated and conspired under the reign of King Francis. And what was their goal? *Power and Wealth.*

Jacques-Thomas could see all of this clearly. He was constantly trying to explain this to people who seemed to think only of themselves, whether they had work in the moment, or the immediate comfort of their own families. It is a real curse, Jacques often thought, to be born with eyes to see.

And yet, Jacques-Thomas Brosseau was not the only mason in the guild who could see the problems to some extent or another. They were all beginning to notice that it seemed they lived on less and less while the king lived on more and more. Not just the king, but the nobles, the ones who went to the king's parties. And the nobles, of course, were exempt from all this taxation. In fact, they were the ones who collected the money from the likes of Jacques-Thomas Brosseau.

Jacques-Thomas was a good story-teller, a good speaker, a natural-born leader, and, seeing no-one around who might take the reins, he began to organize the members of the guild into an "underground" fraternity. They met, at night, sworn to secrecy, in the parlour at the home of Mr. Brosseau, where they discussed the issues and tried to determine whether there was anything that could possibly be done. Meetings had to be conducted in secret because now anyone could be accused of treason, heresy, or even *witchcraft,* just because they had gathered with others.

The problems multiplied. In 1533, King Francis agreed to publish a papal bull against heresy which was backed by the Sorbonne professors, and the Inquisition was fully launched in Paris. Books were banned and burned in the towns and at border crossings. Dissenters were beheaded or burned at the stake. The people, it was said, were being saved from *perdition*—loss of the soul, damnation and Hell—and the Holy Roman Church was being saved from dissolution.

There was a little reprieve in 1534 when the king was disappointed in his dealings with Rome and backed off a little, allowing some freedom for Lutherans (and now everybody who was not extremely visibly Catholic was called a Lutheran). But one morning, after Paris along with Rouen, Orleans, and several other cities awoke to find their walls plastered with placards denouncing the orthodox doctrine of the Catholic mass and eucharist—a specific series of prayers and ceremonies that reinforced certain patterns of thinking—King Francis cracked down. They had even posted a placard on the door of the room where Francis slept, and this infuriated him. He brought an immediate halt to all attempts to relax or reform the regulations and rituals of the Church. The consequences for anyone caught trying to instigate change after that were severe. Offenders were handed over to inquisitors from the Church and these men were highly trained and skilled in systematic, swift and efficient arrest, torture, trial, conviction, and execution of "heretics" and "witches."

The final straw: King Francis got wind that the trade guilds were organizing "secret fraternities" against him and, in 1539, he passed an edict to eradicate all fraternities and craft guilds. The masons were instantly legally dispersed. The guild house was no longer.

This was the background and there you have it.

But politics, edicts, bulls, laws, and power struggles are not the only things that life is made of. There are layers and layers and layers of being, and over the years Diana Marie Brosseau had a number of things to think about.

The year is 1525, and this is where we begin with Diana. At 21, she had already been married four years, and not a single child had she been able to carry to term. Her sister-in-law, Jeannine, lived in the same house, was younger than Diana, and already had three and another on the way. Of course Diana loved her neices and nephew; sweeter children could never be, but that was not the point.

She tried and tried and tried to get pregnant. She had miscarried early in three pregnancies, but never told anyone. It was so early each time, even she was not sure herself whether she had lost a child or only some big clots of blood. Only Jacques-Thomas knew about these things, Jacques and Jeanne-Marie.

Jeanne-Marie de St. Germain was Diana's dearest friend and companion, and she knew about Diana's miscarriages because she was a midwife. She knew all about plants and how taking certain teas might help one conceive or mis-conceive.

∞

I was in the middle of looking at the form of Jeanne-Marie—sandy-blond hair, a happy disposition, lots of energy, a pretty blue dress with a long white apron—when Riavek interupted my reverie. He said, "Move into the life of Diana Brosseau. Explore that life from the inside, feel it, feel it acutely, then you will better understand. . .Imagine yourself moving into her body at 21. Take up space there. Remember how it feels to be her."

Hesitantly, because I had glimpsed the end of her life and did not want to face it, I moved into her body. I felt her body and it did not feel ill. It felt, rather, very healthy, very youthful and healthy, and, at that moment, very excited.

⟨⟩

The rain was pouring off and on in torrents that night, but Jeanne-Marie and I would not be daunted.

"Jeanne-Marie," I had said, "I do not know why I cannot keep a baby," and she had said, "Let us petition Our Lady. You are a good woman and she will bring a baby to you." Everything about that seemed right.

It was afternoon and winter when it darkens early, and it was cold, but we would go no matter what.

Both of us bundled up, layer upon layer, and collecting our rosary beads, we left for the Isle. When we finally reached the Cathedral of Notre Dame; we were wet, but we were there. It was a special night. We walked slowly around the building, feeling the energy of those powerful stone walls, preparing ourselves with our prayers. The gargoyles were defiant. We could see them at the top of the cathedral. Yes, they would keep out evil. Yes, they would let in good. Our thoughts soared heavenward, winging in hope and expectation. We felt full with divine passion, full with divine grace.

With the hundreds of other worshipers, we slipped inside the massive carved wood doors that were open on their hinges and moved into the middle of the magnificent edifice. My eyes lit upon the round blue window fading quickly from view as what was left of the outdoor light flattened into darkness. My ears attuned to the mass, only a little of which I tried to understand. It was more like I wanted to be imbued with the *feeling*. It was the *feeling* that was important. There was a word, a phrase, a gesture, and the hair-raising echo of the choir swelling as one swirling voice in praises of Almighty God. Thunderbolts flew from the organ loft, hit the far wall and returned upon themselves. The effect was piercing. Penetrating. Breathtaking. The Blessed Virgin looked on with babe at breast and I believed she was looking right at me. I could see her eyes. The Blessed Virgin was smiling on me. A little gray mouse scampered over my foot and scuttled and scavenged about near the post beside me, looking for a crumb or something, and, for a moment, I was afraid someone would step on her, so full was the cathedral with masses and masses of people. But then she disappeared from my sight and I returned my attention to the Blessed Virgin who was watching me, waiting, listening, wanting me to ask her. Her eyes were looking right at me. She was all illumined by hundreds of white candles, bending with the heat, burning, burning, in that she might grant the request if the candle should long enough burn.

Jeanne-Marie and I went forward and took communion, the body and the blood, and it was as if God entered me as he had done to the Blessed Virgin and I felt again as if I were with child. Hands clasped, eyes down, I walked back through the singing, back through the throng of devoted worshipers, stood, then kneeled, praying, praying, praying to the Blessed Virgin for a child, praying, praying for a child who would live.

Rain beat upon the windows.

The priest raised up his arms—the effect was magnificent; it was as if Father, himself, were a god—and we all rose up as one single body. We kneeled as one body and we bent our heads and we prayed. *Blessed Virgin, a child. . .A child. . .*

I glanced at the confessionals. In private, just then, I confessed that I had not been able to carry a child. I prayed for a child. Please. . . Please. . .

At the end, I put money in the box. *Please. . .Please. . .*I lit a white candle and knelt at the little side sanctuary with my rosary beads whispering, "Please, Blessed Virgin. Please send me a blessed child." Jeanne-Marie lit a candle and knelt with me and we prayed. We prayed to Our Lady for a child.

The Blessed Virgin heard me. She looked straight at me and smiled just as I glanced up. I squealed out loud, accidentally, of course, and Jeanne-Marie raised up her head, crossed herself, and looked at me with wonder. One look at my face and she knew. She knew Our Lady had answered my prayer.

That very night I did conceive a child.

The day was hot. It was summer, June, and it was the middle of the afternoon when I first felt something like a strange pressure in my abdomen. I did not know if this meant I was going to have the baby. This went on into the evening. I went to my bed and I sent my nephew to fetch Jeanne-Marie.

Her face was radiant when she entered the room. She was all aglow with pure happiness. She knew it was time, and I knew it was time when I saw her.

After a while Jacques-Thomas came home, and he, too, entered the room like a radiant being. They looked like angels to me, even Jeannine, my sister-in-law. Jeannine was more beautiful than I had ever noticed in all these years, and, as I looked at her, I saw the perfect mother. She, herself, was the image of Our Lady and, as I labored in birthing, I saw this for the first time.

The women scurried Jacques away and he winked at me and smiled as he left. Now he would be a father. Jeannine called in Ursula, her oldest girl, and these three attended me.

In the late evening, my belly began to contract at regular intervals and Jeanne-Marie said this is exactly the way it should be. Jeannine nodded in affirmation and I trusted them both. Jeanne-Marie had assisted at fifteen births already, Jeannine had four babies herself, one very recently. As the hours passed, Gilles, Jeannine's second girl, brought in little Marie-Anna for Jeannine to nurse every so often, and the sight of the little baby, only two months old, with her tiny hands and feet, brought me a sense of serenity and hope and made the contractions much more bearable.

Jeanne-Marie had me get up and walk around the room. She said this would make the baby come down, and when I sat down on the bed, she leaned over my belly and sang a little birth song to coax the baby out:

> Sweet Little Baby, come along home
> Your mama is waiting, she's waiting alone
> So much does she love you, so much does she care
> Come into her arms and you'll always stay there.

I cried when I heard this song. It seemed as if everything was affecting me more than usual. Even the room seemed to be bathed in a holy light. The light from the candles shining on the red quilt was soft and yellow. Everything seemed golden, rich, and the ladies were like angels, coming and going with cool wet cloths for my face, hot cloths—which they had warmed at the brazier—for my belly. They had wrapped up a little baby blanket and it was warming by the fire.

The hours seemed to pass although I was not aware of time. Things quieted in the street. Things quieted in the house. All the children, one by one, were put to bed and Jacques-Thomas and Georges had gone out to pass the time with some of their friends. Jacques' mother had come in, but then even she had retired. She said her old heart could not take another birth and we all laughed. She had retired and so had her husband and all was quiet. All was still.

I was very quiet, just breathing loudly when I felt the contraction coming, and Jeanne-Marie said she had never seen anybody so quiet. Normally I had so much to say, but I was concentrating.

There was a time I began to shake. My whole body began to shake, my legs were shivering—all a'quiver—and I could not stop them. My teeth began to chatter. Jeanne-Marie and Jeannine looked at each other and began to push rags under me, then they layered me with covers and on the very top was a beautiful red and purple shawl my mother had woven when she was a girl. This was so special to me. I shook and breathed and then I got some sharp pains. I yelped and Jeanne-Marie, Jeannine, and Ursula quickly gathered around my head, holding my hands next to my face and whispered words of encouragement. When the contraction was over, Jeanne-Marie gently pulled back the covers and they noticed that the bed was wet and Jeanne-Marie said that the bag of waters that held the baby had broken. That was a good sign. Really it was soaking and it seemed like the water just kept gushing out of me. They changed the rags and put a rag between my legs which they kept changing as soon as it would be drenched. I was afraid with all this water, but Jeanne-Marie said, "Do not be afraid, Diana, be of brave heart, for all is well. All is well." They laughed and sang a little, and during each contraction, we all huddled together and breathed.

I kept shaking and shaking and the water kept pouring out of me. I squeezed their hands and squeezed my eyes, and Jeanne-Marie said, "Relax your face, Diana, relax your face," and I did. I instantly relaxed, so much did I trust my friend. Between contractions, the light seemed ever softer, ever more golden. This was a secret and sacred chamber, the place where life begins. I felt myself connecting with the spirit of my mother, long dead, and her mother, and hers, and hers, and hers. It was as if my mother came and said, "I love you, little girl. All is well. All is well."

At one point I cried out *Mama!* And Jeannine said, "Yes, so soon, you will be a Mama." And Jeanne-Marie whispered, "She is calling for her mother."

I went deep inside myself, deep inside.

I went deep inside the pain and I felt my whole abdomen, the circumference, the heighth, the breadth, the depth, contract in a pain that seemed as endless as all eternity. I screamed.

Jeanne-Marie said, "Shhh, Diana, shhh. . .Relax your face, Diana. Open your eyes and look at me. Open your eyes and look at me and relax your face." She repeated over and over, "Relax. . .relax. . .relax. . ." I tried. I tried. When the contraction was over, Jeanne-Marie said to me, "Look at me Diana. Look at me. Open your eyes, Diana." I opened my eyes and looked into her eyes. She was holding my hand, and her face was only inches from mine. I loved her. I loved her for being in my life. She was like my only sister. "Diana, pain is not a *thing*. It is a process. It is moving." She said, "How do you feel right now? Right *now?*" I said, "I feel fine." She said, "Good. Now I want you to remember that pain is a fleeting thing. It comes and goes. It does not stay with—" She could not finish the sentence because another pain came. I clenched my eyes and teeth against it, but it was so severe I screamed. I began to shake my head and scream and cry and talk gibberish. I breathed harder and harder.

Jeanne-Marie became very stern then. "Stop, Diana, *stop*. Open your eyes. Listen to me." The pain had passed and I opened my eyes and looked at her. She said, "Diana, next time the pain comes, imagine that you are in the most beautiful place you have ever seen. Imagine that it is peaceful and quiet and heavenly—"

Again, the pain came. They were coming so fast. It was like the inside of me was a'swirl with screaming pain. Pain. Pain. *Pain*. I screamed. I screamed. *The world was ending*. Wails came from my deepest insides and I could not stop them because I was not myself. I was possessed by a devil. *Possessed*.

The pain subsided and it was over then and I was fine. I knew the pain was over because I opened my eyes and looked right at Jeanne-Marie, and she was looking in my eyes, and she held my hand and said, "There is no pain now," and she was right. It was like I was going in and out of myself. Then she said, "Think of a beautiful place, a heavenly place," and immediately I saw Heaven. I was in Heaven and it was all bathed in golden light and the angels were there, and they were playing harps and trumpets, and they were singing and it was like the singing in Notre Dame only more beautiful still, and then suddenly the singing got louder and louder and I was chanting, long, loud high notes, and I was singing with the angels and the singing was fabulous, and we all sang louder and louder, and the trumpets played and the trumpets blasted, and the entire holy chorus moved into one uncontrollable and glorious crescendo, and it was so fantastic, so brilliant, so beautiful, so awesome, and slowly, then, slowly it got softer and the song ended, and everybody in the room softened and smiled.

The song came and went three more times and I felt myself floating on clouds, singing with the angels, but all of a sudden it was like a wolf came inside of me and I began to growl, deep and low, growling and growling, and Jeanne-Marie said, "Sing low songs, sing low," and I remembered and tried to make the growls into low tones, but this hurricane inside of me swelled down and I was pushing and pushing and I had nothing to do with it. The wolf was pushing. The body pushed.

The pushing came and went. Then, all was still, all was silent and Jeanne-Marie and Jeannine kept saying, "Good. Good. We'll have a baby soon, Diana. Good. Good. . ."

And I think they were getting things, maybe water to wash the baby, maybe the baby's blanket, maybe more rags or more candles. I think I saw Ursula's eyes and I think they were as big as saucers. Jeannine held my hand and sang low notes with me. Jeanne-Marie removed the covers and pulled up my nightdress. I barely noticed. I only could feel the inside of my body. I remember noticing gray light outside the window. Could morning be upon us?

Then the low growls, low notes. It was like my body was opening from the inside, so huge, so huge, I was exploding. I was exploding, my hips separating, my legs separating, and I felt the angels there; one was holding my hand, and the other was holding my other hand, and they were filling the room with the sound of harps and trumpets, and I was a swirling hurricane and it was the end of the earth. *The end of the earth.*

Jeanne-Marie said, "I can see the hair, black hair, one more push, Diana. Just push a little." And I said, "But it is all still now, there are no trumpets," and she said, "That's all right, push anyway, push now," and I tried, but it was so hard when there were no trumpets and then the trumpets came again, and she felt the movement and said, *"Push! Push!"* and I did push, but it was not me pushing and she seemed to have her hand inside of me, and then she said, "The baby's head is almost out."

I opened my eyes a little and tried to sit up to see, but the room was dark and the baby's face was down and the head was part out, just suspended, and then the trumpets came again and I pushed and pushed and pushed and pushed. Jeanne-Marie said, "Good. Good." And I saw her struggling quickly and she said to Jeannine, "Get the knife quick." Jeannine dropped my hand. And then I was pushing again, pushing and pushing and it was the wolf pushing, it was not me, and Jeanne-Marie said, "Don't push, Diana. *Don't push!"* But I had to push because it was not me and I pushed and pushed and she was struggling against me and I pushed and pushed and the baby did not move out of me.

Then the pushing was over and Jeanne-Marie said, "This is very important Diana, *listen.* Next time you get a pain, do not push. I am trying to free the baby. The cord is three times around the neck, do you *hear?* It is too tight to slip over the baby's head and I have to cut to free the baby so I can bring it to life. *Don't push."*

I did not understand, but the trumpets and the wolf were there again and I was growling and singing and pushing and crying out and with a huge swoosh, I felt the whole baby come flying out of me and I vaguely saw Jeanne-Marie pull it up in her arms, put it down on the bed and begin to hit it and hit it and blow and blow and blow into its mouth. Jeannine began to scream and cry and she yelled at Ursula and told her to leave the room. *"Now!"*

I was confused. I don't know how much time passed. "Is it a boy or a girl?" I asked. Jeannine wailed. I said, "Is my baby all right?" I sat up and saw the baby for the first time. It was blue, lying all alone and naked on the bed, completely blue. Obviously dead.

Then I began to scream and scream and scream and I screamed and screamed and suddenly Our Lady stood before me all dressed in her flowing veils, blue and white and purple, standing before me in a golden glow. She came forward and held me and rocked me like I was her child, and her eyes were kind and she said to me, "Diana, I know your pain, for my son, too, was taken."

And together the Blessed Virgin and I screamed and cried and prayed, and together we shared the deepest sorrow that ever was or could be, *ever*, on the face of the earth in the whole wide world.

Oh, my *son*. . .

France was not so different from other parts of Europe, except perhaps that King Francis was less tolerant religiously than other kings. He had taken that reformist placard posted on his bedroom door as a personal insult. Francis never had been recognized for his sense of humor.

Then there was King Charles V who inherited all the Danubian lands, Luxembourg, the Netherlands, Spain, Sardinia, Naples, Sicily, and won the overlordship of Germany and Northern Italy. King Francis was surrounded, and between Kings Charles V and Henry VIII in England, Francis had his hands full with negotiations and sundry dealings. Not to mention continually negotiating with Rome, trying to marry his children off wisely and so on and so forth.

Humanistic and religious reform movements were springing up everywhere. The kings, compelled to protect their own interests, were constantly suppressing the uprisings, by whatever means possible.

Jacques-Thomas found a number of ways to communicate with like-minded people inside and outside of Paris, and in the underground movement, he gained recognition and a modicum of power.

I organized a wonderful charitable organization called Baskets for Mothers. All the girls—my neices—worked with me, Ursula, Gilles, and even Marie-Anna as she got a little older, and we gathered food and presents from the mason's wives and other women who could afford to give a little away, and all this we delivered to the new mothers in our quarter. Jeanne-Marie always knew where the mothers could be found and, as we discovered, they always welcomed our help.

This was immensely satisfying to me. I held all the little babies and cooed in their faces. They were always so soft. I sang songs to them, and, in a way, I became a kind of assistant for Jeanne-Marie.

I tried never to think about my little Timothy-Jean, born the 16th day of June in the year of Our Lord 1525, who was dead when he was born, and whom we had buried under a tree. I tried not to think about how I had to give birth to the afterbirth after I knew he was dead, or about how my milk came in, and how it hurt so much and I just had to let it dry up because to become a wet nurse for another baby—even to nurse Marie-Anna to take away some of the torment—would have been just too painful.

I tried not to think of him on the 16th day of June in the year of Our Lord 1530 when Marie-Anna was 5 years old. I tried not to think of him on the 16th day of June in 1541 when I was rotting in prison halfway through my sentence and he would have been 16 years old.

Jacques-Thomas found ways to travel in and out of Paris. He said he had to do what he had to do, whatever the consequences might be.

Jacques-Thomas was not in Paris when the king's men came to get him that November in the year of Our Lord 1540. I am grateful to God he was not there and that they took me instead. I am grateful to God that I had no children of my own that could be taken.

Jacques-Thomas and I and everyone in our home knew how to read. Jacques had been to the Church school when he was young, and had been taught to read so that he could read the Bible. He taught all of us how to read and it was if a wonderful door had opened. We could read and we read many books as individuals and together as a family, but the problem was that books of interest were getting harder and harder to obtain. Books from Mainz were stopped at the border, ship-ments were searched and many, many volumes of precious books were burned. Books were considered to be subversive material. Even know-ing how to read became suspect.

At the same time, the art of mass block printing was very much in vogue and sets of wonderful story-telling cards were being produced in Mainz and other places as well.

In the autumn of the year of Our Lord 1540, when Jacques-Thomas returned from a brief journey to the east, he returned with a set of won-derful cards printed in red, blue, yellow, and green. These cards, called *Les Sortes,* were said to be created in Venice or somewhere in that vicinity.

It all seemed very romantic to me; I had never been outside of Paris.

The game of *Les Sortes* was about placing qualities in certain arrangements. It was about recognizing certain associations that would spontaneously arise as a result of the game. It was said that drawing cards could answer questions.

There were four divisions or suits called Swords, Batons, Cups, and Coins, with ten cards each. There were four court cards after the ten cards in each suit and these were called King, Queen, Knight, and Page. So there was a King of Swords and a King of Batons and a King of Cups and a King of Coins. These were supposed to represent the types of kings in existence and also certain qualities of that type of king within each person. Beyond that there were twenty-two other cards that were individual people, conditions, virtues, and follies. These cards were the Fool, the Juggler, the Empress, the Emperor, the Popess, the Pope, Temperance, the Chariot, Love, Courage, the Wheel, the Old Man, the Hanged Man, Death, the Devil, Fire, the Star, the Moon, the Sun, the Angel, Justice, and the World. The idea of the game was to ask a question, mix the cards up and then place them in a certain order to answer your question. Or sometimes, people would pick a card, Jacques-Thomas said, and then have to think of someone they knew who was like the card and act out his or her qualities. Sometimes people bet money on the different games you could play.

Les Sortes was illegal in Paris. Jacques-Thomas thought the card game was harmless enough—and it had been given to him by brother masons—so he had hidden it in his bag and brought it home from his travels. I was afraid though. It was clear that Jacques-Thomas' activities had now become known to the authorities and I thought we did not need extra trouble. Also, I was worried that perhaps this card game was about divination and that divination was a form of sorcery or witchcraft that went against the rules of God.

Jacques-Thomas said that was silly.

I said, "Remember Jacques-Thomas," and I quoted from the Bible, "Now a man or woman who is a medium or a spiritist shall surely be put to death. They shall be stoned with stones, their blood guiltiness is upon them." Jacques-Thomas said that was not in the Bible, that I had made it up. Jacques-Thomas refused to read the Bible and he never went to Church. I crossed myself.

"It is just a game," he said.

Jacques-Thomas and I retired to the room where Timothy-Jean had been born and we made a little place to play in private with *Les Sortes.* Jacques-Thomas sat on the bed and I pulled the trunk up next to the bed to sit on and I pulled the sideboard close with the candelabra burning brightly as he mixed up the cards. Our idea was to follow the instructions and see what we could come up with.

There were complicated diagrams in the instructions, so we just picked one to begin with. Jacques-Thomas asked, "Is it possible to dethrone the king? How? What would happen? Could it be worse than it is now?"

I said, "Jacques, do not ask such questions. Let us ask about something happy. Do we always have to talk about politics?"

Jacques laughed, but he was already laying the cards down as the instructions said. He put out six cards, face down, and as he was setting the deck down, a seventh card fell out face down. He raised his eyebrows and looked at me and smiled, silently placing that card with the others.

He turned the cards over one at a time.

Card One was supposed to be the major issue. It was the Knight of Batons and the instructions said the Knight of Batons meant "departure, journey, advancement into the unknown, altercation, flight, absence, and change of residence." Jacques laughed and said, yes, he would very much like it if the king changed residence.

Card Two was supposed to be something that stood in the way of progress. Jacques turned the card over and it was the Seven of Batons. He looked it up in the instructions and it said, "anxiety, hesitancy causing losses, uncertainty, perplexity."

"This doesn't make any sense," Jacques said, "It doesn't have anything to do with the question." I agreed. "Let's just look at the rest of the cards," I said.

Card Three was supposed to be about material gains and losses. The card was the Four of Swords which said "exile, retreat, seclusion." Jacques-Thomas said, "Maybe this means the king will go into exile. That would be a nice way to get rid of him." I laughed.

The instructions said Card Four referred to the intellectual position of the player. Jacques turned over the Six of Swords and it was upside-down. When the cards were upside-down, the meaning was different. He read "stalemate, unwanted proposal, no immediate solution, confession." He commented, "I don't think I like this game. It is totally negative."

Then he turned over the next card which was the player's spiritual disposition and the card was Fire. Fire meant "continued oppression, inability to affect worthwhile change, entrapment, imprisonment." I felt a bolt of fear move through my body. Jacques-Thomas felt it, too. I could tell because he stopped joking. He turned over the next card, the player's emotional state, and it was the Two of Cups, "love and friendship." "That is so sweet," he said, "It is about you my Diana Marie. You have always been my true love and my best friend." I knew that was true. I smiled. I know he did not see the tear that ran down my cheek. He was busy trying to find the meaning of the card that had fallen out. It was the Four of Coins and the description said simply "usury." "Yes!" he nearly yelled, "Usury, that is the issue. That has always been the issue. Excessive taxation. Ridiculous interest rates. . .But this thing is confusing, Diana. Let us just pick out one card and see what happens. I'll put them all back, hold the whole deck and fan it out, you pick the card and we'll see what we can do."

"All right."

He mixed up the cards and fanned them. I picked the Page of Cups and the description said "reflect." "Fine," he said, "Then what should Jacques-Thomas Brosseau do? What in particular? What exactly?" He was shuffling the cards, mixing them around and fanning them out again. He held them up for me to pick one. I did and it was again the Knight of Batons. It said "departure, journey, advancement into the unknown, altercation, flight, absence, and change of residence." I started to cry. I could not help myself. I said "Jacques, the cards were answering about what you should do, not about the king. It was about you and Jacques, you have to leave. You must leave. Oh, Jacques, I am so afraid. I fear your life is in danger."

His face looked like I had never seen it before. He was pale and afraid. "How has it come to this?" he said, "How?. . .We were so young and innocent. All we wanted was to be free. . .All we wanted was a chance. . ."

I was crying now and I could not hide my tears.

Jacques put the cards on the bed and asked, "What will happen if I stay here?" The Eight of Swords: "crisis, calamity, censure, criticism, imprisonment."

"When should I leave?" The Eight of Batons: "swift action, sudden movement, speed, hasty decision."

Suddenly we were both very, very afraid. "What about me?" I asked and I grabbed a card out of the pile. The Seven of Batons upside-down: "anxiety, hesitancy causing losses, uncertainty, perplexity." The cards were repeating themselves!

"What should I do?" The Knight of Cups: "appeal."

"Jacques, the cards are saying you should go and I should stay here and appeal your case. Jacques, you must go immediately." Then I asked, "What is going to happen to me?" and I drew The Pope: "ritualism, religious leadership, a person with historical importance." "Jacques, maybe that means the Church will help us. I will pray Jacques. You must leave. You must leave here right away."

"Oh, holy God," said Jacques, "I never thought it would come to this."

"Let's ask another question," I said, "Is there anything else we should know?" We mixed the cards all around on the bed, both of us mixing and mixing, both of us hoping for some solace. He said, "You pick." And I said, "No, you." He waved his hand over the cards as if he were feeling for temperature and finally settled on a general location and dug down underneath for just the right card. He pulled up the card and turned it over. It was blank. There was nothing there. We did not know there was a blank card in the game and we were shocked. "There's nothing more," he said. "We must hide the cards," said I. I crossed myself.

Jacques-Tomas Brosseau was packed and gone before daylight.

All that autumn, during the months of September, October, and November, I studied *Les Sortes*. I hid the cards under a loose floorboard where Jacques-Thomas and I kept the secret money. I told no one in the house about them, not even Jeannine. Not even Ursula. Ursula was 20 now and engaged to be married to a young mason, the son of a member of the guild. (Of course, the king had officially disbanded the guilds, but it is not as simple as the king might think to disband something as strong as a guild.) Ursula was as dear to me as if she were my own daughter and she always came to me, especially when she had complaints about her mother. I was a perfect resolver because I knew and loved them both. How fond we had all become of one another over the years, especially since Jacques' mother and father had died. We had moved into the position of the oldest generation and this changes so many things.

At night I would get the cards out and arrange them according to the diagrams. I did this behind the quilt so I could quickly cover them if anyone should wish to enter my room. Usually I asked questions about Jacques-Thomas. *Is he safe? Is he well? Will he ever come back?* And all the time, night after night, I drew the Two of Cups, love and friendship. This was our card. Two cups held high as if at a wedding. We were toasting each other, toasting our marriage. Whereas some are not happy with their husbands, this was not true for me. I had always loved Jacques-Thomas. He had never mistreated me and he had felt nothing but sadness for me when I could not bear a child. His parents, too, had loved me as they would have loved their own daughter. I would say our household was unusually happy compared to households I have known, except that now Jacques-Thomas and Georges also, were potentially in great peril.

Exactly what I loved about Jacques-Thomas was exactly what I despised—only because of the present circumstances. I thought of this irony all the time. I had loved his courage, his strength, his sense of justice, but it was his courage, his strength and his sense of justice that had ruined our lives. When I drew a card to explain this to myself—the meaning of this—over and over I drew Fire: "inability to effect worthwhile change, entrapment, imprisonment."

As I studied the cards and the strange way they repeated themselves, I could not help but realize that *Les Sortes* was much more than a game. While the instructions were worded as a game might be worded, the sequence of cards seemed to describe the state of the world and what might happen to you if you did not support the existing power structure. This is what I mean: with the picture cards, the first six were powers that were above or outside of the laws of the kingdom and the Church. These were the Emperor, the Empress, the Pope, the Popess—who was described in the instruction book as Pope Joanna (I wondered who she was and the idea of a Popess became an incredible curiosity to me)—and then the Juggler and the Fool, who were allowed into the king's court as entertainers. They were not subjected to the rules of the court in the same way that the knights and pages (and even queens) were. Then the Chariot and the Wheel represented the continual movement and change of power and wealth. One day a king has power, the next day he does not. Then there was the influence of astrological forces, the Star, the Sun, and the Moon, and these are forces over which people have no control. Then there were the virtues, Temperance, Love, Justice, and Courage, and it became clearer to me that virtuous behavior is a choice on the part of every living person whether they are in positions of power or not, regardless of whether or not they are subject to the laws. The virtues are forces over which people have control. Then there was the Old Man—Father Time—who shows death will come to all, whether in power or not, whether virtuous or not. But then there was the Hanged Man, who was a traitor—and anyone could be seen as a traitor depending on who is in power at the moment. The Hanged Man was being tortured by being tied up and hung upside-down. Then there was Fire, which showed a prison tower, and there was Death. The last card was The World. All this misery existed in the world. That I could see. And there was the force of evil which was The Devil, and the force of good which was The Angel, and both of these existed within the world as well as beyond it.

As I asked questions and combined these cards over and over, I learned more and more about power and men's use of power to acquire wealth. I understood why *Les Sortes* had been banned. If everyone had these cards, there would surely be massive revolt. *Les Sortes* was far more than just a game.

I have to say something about The Devil. This card frightened me tremendously. I was afraid a devil would come in my room if I looked at the card. Especially at night, I saw his eyes leering out from the card. It was as if they glowed in the candlelight. When I looked up the meaning of The Devil in the instruction book it said: "subordination, ravage, bondage, black magic, violence, fatality, temptation to evil." One night I got the idea to ask the cards to give me another card that would better explain The Devil's true meaning, because, I felt, somehow, there was something more I needed to know. I drew the Three of Batons and it said: "practical knowledge, business acumen, trade, commerce." After thinking about this for a long time—I mean over a few weeks—I began to see how useful the idea of devils was in "business." I suddenly realized that the persecution of traitors, heretics, and witches was like a *business*. It transferred wealth from one group to another, even from one class of people to another, and I realized this is exactly what the game of *Les Sortes* was trying to point out. It was all in *code*. I was shocked. I was so shocked. Everything was just as Jacques-Thomas had said. *Things are not as they seem.* If the nobles had the cards, they would learn how to effectively retain their power. If the bourgeoisie had the cards, they would learn something about breaking out of existing structures.

On the 21st day of November in the year of Our Lord 1540, Georges rushed in the house in mid-afternoon and said, "Clear out all of Jacques' writings, papers, everything, burn them, do whatever you can. Hurry. They are searching the masons' houses."

All of us together went through the house inch by inch and found everything we could that might be at all incriminating, and all this we hurriedly burned in the fire. Jacques left very little, as he kept most of his ideas in his head, but everything I could find, I burned. But I did not want to burn *Les Sortes*. I would have to find a hiding place for the cards.

While they were still scurrying about, I quietly dressed in my brown dress, my stockings, my leather shoes and my cape, pinned up my hair and put my hat on. I tucked the cards deep down in my bodice. I would take them to Jeanne-Marie. She would know what to do.

Afternoon, 21st November 1540. I am halfway down our street. Turning back to look, beyond the people and the vehicles engaged in the business of the day, I can see our chimney smoking. I do not know why I look back, but as I glance, I note the dormer window, the window of the room where Jacques-Thomas Brosseau and I made our marriage.

The day is dark. Low, dark clouds. It smells like rain. I must get back before it rains. I turn and hurry on.

Just as I am rounding the corner, I am approached by a man in a green velvet doublet with a lace collar, white leggings, a white cap, and red shoes. He seems very friendly. "Madame Brosseau?" "Yes," I say.

"I am pleased to make your acquaintance. I am Mr. Rainnier, a friend of your husband. Might I find him at home?"

I was considering how to answer when a group of men emerged from the house of the Durands. Mr. Durand was in the midst of them. They immediately came walking swiftly in our direction. Mr. Rainnier turned to them and signaled as if to stop them, but they did not respond. When they arrived, he introduced me as Madame Brosseau.

"Accompany us if you please, dear Madame," one of the men said. I was about to protest when he added briskly, "You are being taken for questioning by the orders of King Francis the First of France." And then I saw, to my horror, parked along the side of the street, along with several other vehicles, was a prison car with bars, and there were people inside of it. Suddenly I could not breathe and I fainted in the street.

Yes, they put me in the prison wagon. Yes, all of us, Mr. Durand and two other men, two women, and one child, were taken to a stone house we had never before seen in a far quarter. I kept thinking, *This cannot be. This cannot be.*

One of the men began to cry.

In the house, I was led into a room with the women and the child. We were asked to sit down—there were comfortable chairs there—and we were told not to speak to each other or to attempt to leave. They left us sitting there, alone. We were extremely nervous. The child cried.

Once I whispered to one of the women, "What is happening?" and the door, which was not closed all the way immediately opened and a man came in and said, "Do not speak or the punishment could be severe."

Then another man came in and sat down with some papers. He was writing on the papers and watching us. Hours must have passed. I felt a desperate need to urinate but I fought it. I would wait. Perhaps I would be home soon. No one else said anything.

Eventually we were asked our names, which the man wrote on the papers. We were also asked the names of our husbands and the names of all of our children. I said my only son had died at birth. He wrote that on the paper as well. One of the women seemed to be Mr. Durand's grown-up daughter. She seemed even older than Ursula.

Finally a woman arrived. She was introduced as a midwife, and she led the group of us down some stairs and into another room where she asked us, once again, to sit. Two men came in and stood by the wall. She asked one woman to accompany her down the hall into another room. We heard nothing more. Then she came for the second woman and the child who was clinging to her. Finally, she came for me.

She took me into a dark stone room with raw stone walls. I told her I needed to use the water closet and she pointed to a pot. She stood there watching me. I realized I was truly a prisoner. This felt extremely humiliating. But my natural need was strong. I moved out my dress and squatted over the pot, but nothing happened. It was as if my body had completely frozen up. Then she was convinced I was hiding something. My heart stopped.

"Take off your dress," she said.

"No."

"Take it off. You must be searched before you are questioned."

"No."

"Guard!" she called and the door immediately opened. He raised a baton threateningly. "Take off your dress," she said. It was then I noticed the clothing of the other women piled in the corner of the room. I saw the stone floor was wet. I saw buckets of water. There was a hole for drainage in a place where the floor sloped. There was a vent on the wall with iron bars. "Take off your dress!"

I began to take my cape off very slowly. She said, "Hurry."

I took off my cape. She said, "Your shoes."

I took off my shoes and she picked up each one and felt inside. My hands began to shake so that I began to fumble with the fastening. Perhaps I could take my dress off in such a way that I could fold the cards into the fabric. "Hurry up!"

I was removing the dress from my shoulders when the cards spilled out onto the floor. I gasped.

The midwife said, "Hah!" and then, "Pick them up."

I stood there shaking. "Guard!" she called. He immediately opened the door and stood there poised to beat me. "Pick them up," she said.

I stooped down and gathered them together, my fingers shaking, my hands shaking, my knees knocking, my heart pounding. She said, "Put them down there," and she pointed to a table. I put them down and again she called, "Guard!"

When the other guard came in, she said, "Watch her," and she picked up the cards and walked out the door. I just stood there, half-dressed, and the two guards stood by the door watching me. It seemed at least an hour passed. When I started to sit, one yelled, "Don't move!" I felt frozen. We were silent. I could hear scratching behind the wall. I began to pray. I just closed my eyes and prayed. All the time, the guards were staring at me.

After a long time, a man came in holding some papers and said to one of the guards, "This one is being transferred to the Church." *Oh, thank you, thank you,* I thought. I crossed myself.

Two men came in and one said, "This way."

I said, "Wait, my shoes. My cape."

The other one laughed and said, "You won't need any shoes where you're going," and he grabbed my arm and pulled me, just as I was, down the hall, out a back door and into a waiting prison car. They took off my hat, tossed it on the ground, blindfolded me and shoved me inside.

That was how the ordeal began.

They handled me roughly, took me to another stone building, still blindfolded, put me in a room with some women who stripped me naked. As I stood there naked, they pulled the pins from my hair, threw buckets of water over me, threw water on me until I was so frightened, I urinated upon myself. They made sounds of disgust, and one said, "Go get another bucket." Again, I stood in silence. I heard the door open and suddenly water splashed down my legs. I was soaking wet and they put some kind of short, light gown over me and called, "Guard!" The door opened, someone came in—a man—roughly grabbed my arms and clasped my wrists behind my back and tied them with what felt like a leather thong. Then they began to cut off my hair. "Oh, *Mother of God*, No! No! My *hair*. . ." I screamed and yelled, "*What are you doing?*" and I fought and tried to push them away, but more came in and they held me and tied me and gagged me so I could not scream, and they cut off all my hair. Then they shaved my head, shaving around the blindfold, then moving it up a little, and oh my dear Lord, they shaved the hair under my arms and my *pubic hair*.

They said they were looking for witch's signs and they said I should tell now if I had anything magical sewn into my clothing. They took off the gag and I said, "Oh, my God. . .Oh, my God. . ."

Finally, I could not hold back the tears and I began to cry uncontrollably.

I was left in a cell for days. There was a bucket in which to urinate. There was a dirty tattered blanket in which I had to stay wrapped to keep warm. They brought in old bread, some scraps of food, and a little water twice a day. I asked the food person over and over what was happening, when someone could see me, when I could contact my family, but he did not know. That was not his job. I sank more and more into a deep state of anxiety.

Then I was told by a man who came in, and who seemed official, that I would be questioned soon.

More days passed.

I was given no information.

One day the guards came to get me and they said I was being taken for questioning. They tied my hands behind me, blindfolded me, and took me down the hall into another room. I stood with bare feet on a cold stone floor. I had on only that thin gown with nothing at all underneath. They would not take off the blindfold. There were at least three men there; I could hear them. They made me sit on a stool. They asked me who my husband was. I said Jacques-Thomas Brosseau. They asked me what kind of work he did. I said he was a mason. They asked me where he was. I said I did not know. They asked me if I had children. I said my only child had died at birth. They asked me who the midwife was. I said Jeanne-Marie de St. Germain. They asked me if the child was baptised. I said yes. They asked me if I was baptised. I said yes. Then they asked me if I had had the game *Les Sortes* when I was brought in for questioning. I said, "Yes, but—" and I started to explain something but they cut me off. "Just answer yes or no." They asked me if the game had a picture of a devil. I said, "Yes, but—" "Yes or *no.*" They asked me if I had been carrying a picture of a devil when I was brought in for questioning. I said, "Yes, but—" "Stop, Madame Brosseau," a man said, and his voice sounded very kind. "You must only answer yes or no." "Yes," I said. I was asked if I had used the cards for divination. I hesitated, and here I lied, "No." Then I was asked if I had copulated with a devil. I was so shocked, I laughed. The men laughed, too, but then the one asked the question again, "Did you copulate with a devil?" "No," I said, and he continued quickly as if he were reading the question, "Did you bear a child for a devil?" "What is this about?" I asked, "Why am I being held?" There was a pause. "You are charged with practicing witchcraft," the one who had been talking said. "There are strong and grave indications which render you gravely suspect of this heresy against the Church. Now you must speak no more, only answer the questions, yes or no."

I was shocked.

"Did you bear a child for a devil?"

"No!"

"Did Jeanne-Marie de St. Germain offer your child to a devil?"

"No!" *Oh, Blessed Mother, Jeanne-Marie! What is happening. . .?*

"Did you bewitch your husband?"

"No!"

"Take off her blindfold." A man took off my blindfold and I saw a small, stone room with a plain wood table. Two men were sitting at the table, one was apparently recording what I was saying. He looked at me sympathetically.

There were some ropes and devices about the room.

Another man stood behind me.

The man who was talking said, "We just want you to tell the truth, Madame Brosseau. It will be so much easier for you and for your husband and for us if you do tell the truth. You are a God-fearing Catholic, are you not?" "Yes," I said, "Then let us get this over with quickly, Madame." He asked me the set of questions again and I slowly answered yes or no to each one. Then he nodded to the man behind me. The one who was writing protested, but the man behind me ignored him, and started doing something with a rope that was hanging on a pulley from the ceiling.

"Madame Brosseau," the man who did most of the talking said, "We would rather not use the devices that are allowed us by the Church to encourage you to tell the truth. Please do not make us have to go through this."

"But what I have told you is true."

I heard a wheel creaking as if the man behind me were turning a crank.

"Please let me talk with her," said the man who was writing.

"Go ahead, if you think you can get through to her."

He stood up and came to me. He took me to the other side of the room. "Madame," he said, "They will hurt you. They will make you tell the truth. In the name of God, just make your confession now. I cannot bear to see you go through this. It is inhuman. Please. . ."

"But I have done nothing," I whispered.

"Please, Madame." His eyes were so kind, but how could I confess what I did not do? Worse, how could I confess what I *had* done?

He led me back and sat me on the stool again.

"I will ask you one more time," the first man said. "Did you use the devil's cards for divination?" "No." "Did you copulate with a devil?" "No." "Did you bear a child for a devil?" "No." "Did Jeanne-Marie de St. Germain offer your baby to a devil?" "No." "Did you bewitch your husband?" "No."

The machine creaked. The man who was writing looked at me and shook his head sadly. The man behind me came forward, blindfolded me, lifted me off the stool by the arm and took me near the wall. He hooked the rope hanging from the ceiling onto my wrists where they were tied together behind me and began to crank the rope upward. When it was about as high as my shoulder blades, and my arms were straight out behind me, and my body was bending over forward, he asked me the questions again. Again, I answered "no" to each one. The machine began to creak. I felt my arms being lifted, lifted. I felt a tearing surge of pain shoot through my back, and then the man who had been writing said, "Please, let her down, let her down." And the other said, "Well, perhaps she will tell the truth tomorrow."

Suddenly, they let me down and took me back to the cell. They did not come for me the next day, nor the next, nor the next.

I do not know how many days passed and every day, I would hear footsteps in the hall and my whole body would begin to sweat and shake. My palms would perspire and I realized how afraid I was.

One day they came. They tied my hands and blindfolded me and led me back to that room. They placed me on the stool and they began. "Have you thought about the questions that were asked of you, Madame?" This sounded like the same man as before. "Yes," I said. "Fine, we will go over them again. Answer simply. When possible, just answer yes or no, if you please. Do you understand?"

"Yes, I do."

"Just answer with a simple 'yes.'"

"Yes." I tried to appear cooperative.

"Who is your husband?"

"Jacques-Thomas Brosseau."

"What kind of work does he do?"

"He is a mason."

"Do you know where he is?"

"No."

"That is not a problem, Madame Brosseau. We do know where he is." I thought, *He is lying to me. Jacques is safe.*

"Do you have children?"

"My only child died at birth."

"Who was the midwife?"

"Jeanne-Marie de St. Germain."

"Was the child baptised?"

"Yes."

"By whom?"

"Father Paul of St. Mary's."

"Were you baptised?"

"Yes."

"By whom?"

"Father Paul."

"Did you have the game *Les Sortes* with you when you were brought in for questioning?"

"Yes."

"Were you carrying a picture of a devil?"

"Yes."

"Did you use these cards for divination?"

"No." (I had gone over this answer a thousand times until I could say it perfectly and emphatically.)

"Did you copulate with a devil?"

I sighed.

"Did you copulate with a devil? Note on your paper, Monsieur, that I had to ask the question twice."

"No."

"Did you bear a child for a devil?"

"No."

"Did Jeanne-Marie de St. Germain offer your child to a devil?"

"No."

"Did you bewitch your husband?"

"No."

The room was silent. Then I heard that creaking.

What happened after that should not happen in a holy organization. What happened after that should never happen in the world.

The man asked, "Did you use the devil's cards for divination?" "No." "Did you copulate with a devil?" I was silent. I heard that creaking and I was thinking. Louder he said, "Did you copulate with a devil?" I was silent. Suddenly someone slapped me hard across the face. I was stunned. "Did you copulate with a devil?" I was silent. I was slappped again, so hard that it knocked me to the floor where I hit my head. Two men grabbed me by the arms and lifted me back on the stool. My cheek burned. I believed my head was cut. "Did you copulate with a devil?" I began to cry. As well as I could, I said, "No." The man said, "Make a note that she is crying."

One of the men made a joke about my husband being the devil, himself, and they discussed among themselves just how much I *had* copulated; they all laughed. I cannot repeat what they said.

He asked me if I had borne a child for a devil. I said no.

He asked me if Jeanne-Marie de St. Germain had offered the child to a devil. I said no.

He asked me if I had bewitched my husband. I said no.

Then the man said, "We are just going to ask you those last few questions again. We want you to tell the truth. It will be better for you and better for your husband if you tell the truth."

"Did you use the devil's cards for divination?" "No."

"Did you copulate with a devil?" "No."

"Did you bear a child for a devil?" "No."

"Did Jeanne-Marie de St. Germain offer the child to a devil?" "No."

"Did you bewitch your husband?" "No."

One of the men said, "She is lying."

Roughly they picked me up off the stool, moved me across the room and I heard the wheel creak. They fastened the rope to my

wrists—still tied behind my back—and I heard the turning sound begin. The one said again, "We are just going to ask you once more. If you
tell the truth, it will be much easier for you."

I felt my arms being pulled up behind me. They pulled them up
with the rope until they were about shoulder height and would not go
anymore. It forced me to bend over forward as I had experienced before. The creaking sound continued. They were pulling my arms up,
up, toward the ceiling. When I was standing on the tips of my toes, the
man asked, "Did you use the devil's cards for divination?" "No." "Did
you copulate with a devil?" "No." "Did you bear a child for a devil?"
"No." "Did Jeanne-Marie de St. Germain take the child for a devil?"
"No." "Did you bewitch your husband?" "*No.*"

The cranking continued. I felt my feet leave the ground. My shoulders felt like they were coming apart. I began to scream. "Shut up!" one
of them yelled. I screamed and screamed. Again I felt a slap across my
face, *hard*. My whole body swung. My cheek was aflame. I cried and
screamed and began to beg for mercy. "*Please. Please. . .What do you
want from me?*"

"We just want you to tell the truth. That is all. No more. That is all.
It is very simple."

"I am telling the truth!" Again I heard the cranking. I was using all
my will to try to hold my body in one piece. It felt like my shoulders
were going to give way and my arms were going to fall out of the sockets. All my muscles were concentrating on trying to hold my body in
place.

"Let's try it again," the man said. And again, he asked: "Did you
copulate with a devil?" I was whimpering, "*Please. . .Please. . .*" and I
could not answer. And, once again, "You do carry a picture of a devil,
do you not?" I whimpered. Again, louder, "Do you copulate with a
devil? Do you? Do you? Have you copulated with a devil?" The rope
that was holding me suddenly jolted up and down, jerking my arms in
their sockets—the pain was searing—horrendous—excruciating—and
I screamed. Louder still he spoke, "Did you copulate with a devil?" I
screamed. "Shut up," a man said. "Have mercy, *please. . .,*" I cried,
"*Please.*"

"Answer yes or no or we will gag you. Do you understand?" I
stopped screaming. Now, very quietly, "Did you copulate with a devil?" I yelled as loud as I could "*No-o-o-o.*"

They dropped me down to the floor, roughly stuffed a rag in my
mouth and tied a gag around my mouth and raised me up again. They
jolted the machine so it bounced my body up and down. My arms were
slowly breaking out of the sockets. I could feel the sockets loosening. I
screamed and screamed, but the screams were catching in my throat
and strangling me.

Then they dropped me on the floor, ripped the gag off. I choked out the rag, and they raised me up again. I could only whimper. The man whispered, "Do you copulate with a devil?" I was lying in a heap, my arms were broken, and I whispered, *"Yes."*

Sometime between the 21st day of November and the 24th day of December, I was tortured twelve times. I cannot say what else they did to me. I will never, ever say it. Never. It is too terrible.

I was chained in a stone dungeon.

I was humiliated in every way.

I confessed. I confessed to every accusation. I confessed under torture. I confessed when I was not under torture. I confessed to everything I was charged with and more. I named my family. I named my neighbors. I named the men in the guild. I had copulated with the devil. The devil had impregnated me. I named Jeanne-Marie as my accomplice. Together, we had conspired to produce a child for the devil. I had bewitched my husband. That is why he was plotting against the king.

Whenever they took me for questioning, I was blindfolded. I learned this is because they were afraid I would give them the evil eye.

On the 24th day of December in the year of Our Lord 1540, I was taken into a courtroom walking backward so I could not give the judge the evil eye, still wearing that same prison gown. A guard held each of my arms. They were walking correctly, of course. My arms were dislocated and hanging down uselessly, but my hands were still tied behind my back in case I might attempt to get away.

They forced me to drink holy water. Then a judge came up behind me, placed his hands on my head and said, "I conjure you by the bitter tears shed on the Cross by our Savior the Lord Jesus Christ for the salvation of the world, and by the burning tears poured in the evening hour over His wounds by the most glorious Virgin Mary, His Mother, and by all the tears which have been shed in this world by the Saints and Elect of God, from whose eyes He has now wiped away all tears, that if you be innocent you do now shed tears, but if you be guilty that you shall by no means do so. In the name of the Father, and of the Son, and of the Holy Ghost, Amen."

The whole court waited for me to cry to prove my innocence, but I could not cry. The torturing had taken all the tears away from me.

I was found guilty on all counts. I was found guilty as charged by the inquisitors of the Church. I was guilty of practicing witchcraft, guilty of worshiping the devil, guilty of copulating with the devil, guilty of being impregnated by the devil, guilty of offering the child to the devil, guilty of conspiring with Jeanne-Marie de St. Germain, guilty of bewitching my husband into plotting against the King of France.

I was sentenced to death—by yet another court, a criminal court, I believe—by burning at the stake. But first I must spend exactly a year in the squalor of prison, being tortured very often, but more especially on holy days. Then I would die by burning, but since the date of my execution, according to my sentence, would fall on Christmas, and executions are not carried out on Christmas Day, I would be granted one extra day to live and be executed on the 26th day of December in the year of Our Lord 1541.

"The guilt of this witch, Madame Diana Marie Brosseau, wife of Jacques-Thomas Brosseau," the judge had stated, "is hereby determined fully according to the rules and regulations of the Holy Roman Catholic Church and sanctioned by the grace of God, in the name of the Father, and of the Son, and of the Holy Ghost. Amen."

The days came and went in darkness. This darkness is difficult to describe. It was a dim-lit grayness, a nothingness, like an abyss of complete suspension. Hell could have been no worse, and yet I settled into it as if I were dead already.

At first I tried to think about Jacques-Thomas. I concentrated on sending him love in my prayers. I tried to sense whether or not he was safe. *Jacques-Thomas*, I would call in my mind, *Jacques-Thomas*. I thought about Jeanne-Marie and Ursula. I worried for their safety. At first I thought about all of them, trying to remember their tender voices, their sweet faces, as the days passed, one by one.

At first I thought about my hair. My beautiful hair, long and thick and brown and curling, and I was filled with anger—the anger that comes from feeling helpless—when I thought, over and over, over and over, about how they had torn the pins from my hair and how I was worried that I would not be presentable.

I replayed every event, every sentence—at first. At first I thought I would be rescued, that Jacques-Thomas or Georges would use their influence to have me freed. At first, I even thought they may raise the money and buy my freedom from prison.

I waited. At first, I waited. *This cannot go on,* I thought, *I will be rescued.*

When I could reach it, as best I could since I was hurting, I wrapped myself in the dirty blanket.

I had a wood bucket for my excretions and that is all. There was no way to wash, and, at first, I worried about this. I could not comb my hair when it began to grow out, and I remember the horror I felt in the beginning when I first felt the lice crawling. There was nothing I could do.

I was alone. I saw no one. I was allowed to speak to no one. Even the food man was sickened, after a bit, by the sight and smell of me. At first *I* was sickened by how I knew I must have appeared, but after a time I became a dead animal and I did not care.

In the beginning, when they tortured me, I screamed. I screamed and sweated, and felt myself coming in pieces, and I struggled in my mind to hold my body together. I screamed and screamed and screamed for my mother, "*Mama!. . .Mama!. . .*" At first, I cried. How the tears came after I realized they had pulled out my fingernail.

And when they broke my finger by crushing it, I suddenly remembered Jeanne-Marie's voice, and her face right up against mine saying, "Pain is a process, Diana. Do not grab onto it, but let it flow through you and be gone like a river. Let it flow through you and then be gone." And, at first, for a few times, when they took off pieces of my thigh with burning hot pincers, I could let the pain flood through me and be gone. I could go through it with my eyes closed, thinking of Heaven, thinking of the angels singing, thinking of the clouds.

At first I screamed and cried, and then I became silent. I became more and more silent until I was dead inside. I was dead inside and I could not speak. I could not even think. One day passed into the other. I could not distinguish the Holy Days, but sometimes I heard footsteps and I would awaken a little, knowing it must be a Holy Day and they would hurt me more.

After a while, there was no passage of time, only that infinite dull grayness like the grayness that must be like the place where unbaptised babies go. *Babies, babies. . .Marie-Anna. . .*One time I remembered the trumpets of the angels, and the blasting of these trumpets, and I began to sing. I began to sing loudly as if I were singing with the angels. I sang and sang and I felt a moment of joy with the singing. But as I was singing—I don't know if I sang for minutes or hours or days—I realized that my voice was going into nothingness, I remembered only that empty gray nothingness, and I felt like I was disintegrating. I was becoming the grayness.

After a time, I did not use the blanket. I did not try to hold myself in one piece when they applied the instruments of torture. I did not eat the stale bread. I was dead. Already dead.

All the tears dried. No more tears. I was dead. Already dead.

I did not eat the food. I did not eat, so they put a tube down my throat and poured water into my belly and my belly got bigger and bigger and they said if I did not eat, they would make me fat like this and when they did that I had thought I was dead, but I gagged and cried and vomited, and felt like I was dying over and over and over again.

One day I laid dead like a rotting animal, as cold and dead as the stone floor. One day, I laid unseeing, discerning nothing, feeling nothing, thinking nothing. The Angel of *Les Sortes* appeared before me and said, "I shall take you to Heaven and there, waiting for you, is someone who was called away from you so he would not be hurt." And then my son appeared to me, my son, my Timothy-Jean, and he was a young man, and he was 16 and it was his birthday, and he said, "Mother, I am waiting to meet you in Heaven and you and Father and I will meet, and there we will live forever in Heavenly Paradise." And Timothy-Jean, he was so beautiful, looking just as his father had looked as a young man, dashing, and he had my eyes, and it was like I was looking into the eyes of my own soul, but I was looking into the eyes of my child, and I knew it was right that he did not live. It is better to die than suffer the living Hell that life makes. And I said, "Happy Sixteenth Birthday, Timothy-Jean."

Then he was gone and I died again, and again, and again.

On the 26th day of December in the Year of Our Lord 1541, they woke me by shaking and shaking me out of unconsciousness. I could not stay awake, I could not stand up. I did not care that my head was hastily shorn by some attendants, that these attendants were revolted and disgusted by me. I did not care that they brought in water and threw it on me as if to clean me as I laid there. I did not care that they were shaking me, and only briefly did the thought cross my mind that they would take more pieces out of my leg or my belly with the instrument. But even this could not move me. I was dead already. Already dead.

I tried to stand when they pulled me up, but I fainted, then I was awake, then I fainted again.

Then my body was being rolled on a cart through the grayness, rolling on a cart, and I fainted.

Suddenly, I awakened. Our Lady was holding me. The Blessed Virgin Mother was holding me and she was like the sky. Her robes were flowing like the sky, and the sky was blue and white and lavendar and glorious, and her eyes were like the sky, and they sparkled with stars, and the stars were like glistening tears, and she was holding me and holding me and holding me. And the breast of the Blessed Virgin Mother was warm and my limp form melted into her breast, and I disintegrated in the sky and I was wrapped in the sky, and her arms wrapped around me like the sky, and her arms became tighter and her precious hands were about my throat, and she held me lovingly and looked into my eyes, Her eyes were like the sky and the tears inside them were like the stars, and she spoke to me, and she cried in deep, deep pain, and her lips spoke and I heard her voice like the wind blowing out of her mouth, and she wailed like a storm, *"First my son, then my daughter!"* But she held me and I was not afraid, and her hands got tighter, and I felt peace in her loving hands and her voice issued from her lips like a summer breeze, and it smelled of sweet star jasmine and oranges from Spain, and she whispered, "Sleep, my daughter, sleep, then awaken from your dream." And she was holding me and her hands were tight about my neck, and then I could not breathe and I floated, floated, floated into a deep and dreamless sleep.

I was dead when they burned me, strangled in the cart on the way to the stake for mercy.

∞

My breasts ached. My breasts ached and I felt sick to my stomach. I had seen. I had forced myself to look. I had forced myself to look; I wanted the story to be over, but I knew it did not end there. I knew that in that same century, countless numbers of women would be burned as witches. The still extant records of documented witch trials show that over time there were 2,000 witches executed in Bavaria, over 1,000 in Trier, over 400 in Nassau, over 800 in Westphalia, at least 274 in Eichstätt, over 200 in Walbeck and Schaumburg, 430 in Lippe, 1,000 in Kurmainz, 1,602 in Bamberg and Würzburg, 700 in Fulda, 1,000 in Bohemia, 1,500 in Austria, over 5,000 in Alsace, over 3,000 in Lorraine, 55 in Montbéliard, 90 in Vaud, 141 in Geneva, 214 in Neuchâtel, 328 in Zurich and Lucerne, 355 in Luxembourg, 144 in Namur, 238 in the Netherlands, over 5,000 in France, over 2,500 in the British Isles, 35 in New England, 1,800 in Scandanavia, 65 in Estonia, more than 15,000 in Poland, 462 in the Balkans, unknown totals in Italy and Spain. Estimates by the most conservative historians, basing counts only on documents that are in existence in some cities today, place the number at well over 100,000. Even this count is horrendous when weighed against the size of the 16th-century population in general. Some estimates of the numbers of people executed as witches, however, place the count over the centuries of the Inquisition as high as nine million. Whatever the actual number, at least 85 percent of those executed were women.

There is more. I knew as I came out of meditation on the seventh day of my meditations in preparation for ordination, that the people of the 16th century would continue to organize. I knew that, by the end of the century, *Les Sortes*, which would be called by the names of *Tarocchi* and *Tarot* would be all over Europe, and that all over Europe, it would be illegal because it was a coded book that called those who were oppressed into revolution. It showed people the way out. I knew that the cards and other systems were known and held by the underground crafts guilds and others involved in the various social movements directed at religious reform. I knew that the Inquisition would shortly begin to "unceremoniously roast" hundreds of male Rosicrucians, Freemasons, and others accused of possessing magic, consorting with the Devil and holding the keys to the Ancient Mysteries.

Even as late as 1738, an anti-Masonic papal bull, called *In Emenenti Apostolatus Specula,* was issued by Pope Clement VII. By this decree, Freemasons were condemned and excommunicated together with those who promoted their cause.

In part, their cause was simply to develop a fraternity to explore and educate in accordance with the intellectual development of the day. But, intellectual activity was considered to be subversive, as was the fact that all over Europe, the Freemasons were concerned with religious freedom *and* not only were they beginning to reawaken the supressed teachings of the ancient Mystery Schools, they were also beginning to admit women to their lodges. All of this activity was considered suspect by the Church, *highly* suspect. It threatened to overturn the way things were organized. It threatened to undermine the positions and roles of male and female. It threatened to dissolve the very pillars of society.

In the year of Pope Clement's anti-Masonic bull, Freemasonry was suppressed in many countries, however in many, many more, new Masonic lodges were established.

In the following year, 1739, alarmed by the organizational activity of the crafts guilds, Pope Clement issued a still more vigorous edict in which Freemasons were made liable to the death penalty, confiscation of goods and "exclusion from future grace or mercy."

In the meantime, freedom of religion had become a battlecry throughout Europe as well as in the New World. The New World was on the brink of revolution, and, in 1752, only thirteen years after Pope Clement's bull sanctioning the execution of Freemasons, George Washington was initiated as a Freemason in the state of Virginia. In 1776, the year of the American Revolution, George Washington was the Grand Master of the Alexandria Lodge of Alexandria, Virginia and on April 30, 1789, he was inaugurated as the first president of the United States. Other prominant revolutionaries who were Freemasons were Benjamin Franklin and Paul Revere, along with most of the signers of the Declaration of Independence. Four out of the five cornerstone layers of the Capital of the United States in 1793 were Free- masons. A major issue of the American revolution was the right to religious freedom and the separation of church and state.

I felt very upset. I cried for Diana. I cried for her even as my rational mind fought my tears, saying to me, "Diana Marie Brosseau is fiction, a product of your imagination."

And yet I kept thinking of when I had gone to San Salvador in the middle of the Salvadorean War in 1985 as a delegate of the Third U.S. Public Health Commission to El Salvador to study the effects of war on health. The Commission was composed of fourteen doctors and nurses, one journalist, and me, the only social scientist. At the time I went I was employed as a Public Policy Analyst by the School of Public Health at UCLA in a research position that was funded by the Department of Health Services of the State of California and, at the same time I held a position as an Affiliated Scholar at Stanford University (although I did not go to El Salvador as a representative of either institution). With my Ph.D. and my background in health and healing, I thought I had a fairly good understanding of how things might be. But, what I saw in El Salvador should never, ever happen in the world—the torture, the pain, the suffering.

I remember how a woman in San Salvador sighed behind me as she tied about my neck a black crucifix for death and a red crucifix for blood. Both crosses—fashioned of wire wrapped with thread—were made by incarcerated political prisoners who somehow had the crosses spirited out of jail. I remember how this woman told how she cried and screamed as men came to arrest her 17 year-old daughter in the middle of the night. "There was a knock on the door," the woman said, "then another, and when I ran to open the door, the room filled up with hacienda police who said they were doing a 'clean-up operation in the barrio.' They asked 'Who are you?' 'What is the name of your family?' and then they ran to the bed and pulled Christina up by the hair and said, 'It's *you* we're looking for.' I said, 'Please respect her, she has a baby.'"(Christina, she said, had been sound asleep with her three-month-old.) "But the policeman picked up the baby by the foot and threw it across the room onto another bed and pointed to me and said, '*You're* still young enough to take care of the baby.' And I said, 'Wait, let her get her shoes,' but they said, 'Where she's going, she doesn't need shoes.' Then they tied a cloth around her eyes and put her in a tank. All the time I kept pleading, 'Why are you taking her?. . .Why are you taking her?. . .' And Christina only yelled at me, 'Mama, I'll come back to you. Take care of my baby.'"

Three days later her daughter reappeared—dead by the side of the road with two of her girlfriends from school. One eye had been torn out of its socket, her face had been destroyed, and one of her arms and one of her legs and the whole left side of her body had been burned. Christina was too mangled to be prepared for burial.

In El Salvador, I sat in a room with seventeen mothers of children who had been taken away. They told me that some of their children had been found—all of them dead—but most had never been found. They told me they had an organization, the Mothers of the Disappeared, and that there were 550 Salvadorean mothers involved. They said, "We need psychologists, not bullets." They said, "We know no Communism. We know no Democracy. All we know is pain and suffering." They said, "We have lost mothers through reprisal and some were tortured, but we will still be here on every street corner, in every cafe, and in every church, carrying out our work. Just like blades of grass, we will rise up again and again." The mothers said to me, "We won't be silenced. We have left our fear. We left our fear in the garbage cans where we found the dead bodies of our children. We left our fear in the clandestine cemeteries where we know the bodies of our dead children must be. We don't cry now," they said, "We are beyond tears. We struggle for human rights, for the human right to dignity."

Then I remember how one woman began to cry. Then another. Then another. Then the cries of all seventeen women rose up and began to comingle into one long terrible and continuous wail. They cried and cried and cried. And Sandra and Nate and I—three naive children from Los Angeles and San Francisco—wailed and wailed and wailed until Sandra finally spoke and all she could say was, "Your pain is our pain."

We are *never* beyond tears.

And what about the other 20th-century tragedies? Germany, Korea, Vietnam, Nicaragua, Lebanon, Chile, Cambodia, Bosnia, Uganda, Iraq, Nagasaki, Hiroshima, Angola, Afghanistan, Rwanda. Even *Ireland*. The list is endless. You could expand it and expand it.

Throughout the world, Christina is dragged out of bed. Throughout the world, her little tiny baby is tossed across the room. Throughout the world, Christina is raped. She is tortured. She is killed.

In every country Diana Marie lies rotting in prison.

How can we go on?

"My sister," said Riavek—he was sitting in my room meditating with me, he had never left me—"You have been schooled in the Earth World. You are beginning to comprehend the great transitions of five millenia. For more than two hundred and fifty generations, you have walked upon the Earth, and, as Sandra said, you are beginning to understand that all the pain of the world resides in your own heart. All the world's joy resides in your heart also. My dearest sister, that is why you will now begin to teach. You are remembering everything. You are forcing yourself to see. You are blocking nothing out. And, as your sorrow grows, so does your compassion. You have something to say. And now, dear one, twin of mine, you will begin to put forth spiritual values, values that integrate, values that include, values that honor and sacralize, values of freedom and justice. You will speak. You will teach. You will write. And your speaking and teaching and writing will be far beyond what you thought it would be. It will be far beyond the nature of what you thought of as good speaking, good teaching and good writing when you were fully engaged in the Earth World's universities. Your time has come. The time is now."

I sat before the candle in awe.

"And it is not as you thought it would be," said Riavek. "It is not as simple as any of us thought. None of us knew how deep the experience would be. When you left for Earth, Silver Reed, you were so uncomprehending. You were like the Pamela of latter 20th-century Earth who went to El Salvador with the wisdom of a newborn lamb. And then you awakened. Then you remembered. So many times, dear sister, I have rejoiced that I was not walking in your shoes, but still, just as you could not block out the cries of Diana Brosseau, I could not bar your experience from my consciousness. And so many times, my love, I have wanted to fill your shoes, so that it might be me who suffered, not you. Nonetheless, I knew if it were me suffering, you would suffer nonetheless, because whatever is in my consciousness is in yours also. Our consciousness is interchangeable, just as you are Diana Brosseau, and Bitten-By-The-Wolf, and Pamela, and even Christina. I, too, reside in Universal Soul. Our consciousness is one, dear sister, and when one suffers, all suffer. When one single being suffers on Earth, the whole of the universe quivers with pain."

I held my solar plexus and rocked.

"It's all right," Riavek whispered gently, "We are ready for the task."

CHAPTER 12

PAMELA
THE SECOND REFORMATION

California Coast, End of the Second Millenium C.E.

Some say the labyrinth is a prison from which only the brilliant, creative or extremely resourceful can escape. Some say this prison harbors in its deep interior spaces the monster of the moon—the Minotaur—representative of the frightful unknown, who, at any turn, around any bend, in any instant, may devour the innocent wanderer. The Minotaur, they say, *must* be appeased.

The challenge of the labyrinth, therefore, is to willingly become a sacrificial victim: to enter the precarious maze strong and without flinching, to consciously navigate the dark passages of inner fear—to turn the power of fear into faith and strength—and to creatively slaughter the beast with the simple weapon of your own ingenuity. That is how, they say, you will come to understand the true meaning of freedom.

Some say the labyrinth is a birth canal, that through the twining labyrinthine passage we wind our way into life. *Labyr* is Latin after the Greek for "labor." *Inth* has the same meaning as "into." Through a difficult and laborious process, all of us—all sentient beings—spiral into the condition of form and substance. Through the intense process of parturition—the labor which molds and carves the primordial forces and forms of the universe into patterns and shapes—we *become*.

They say, too—those who have thought about it—that the labyrinth is the intricate passageway into death. At the center, they say, is the tomb, the womb at the end of the journey that opens to receive us. To die, they say, is to travel to the Under- world, the unknown Abyss, that deep and chilly place where every Sun King must come to rest in the cradling folds of winter.

They say, too, we can navigate the Abyss without dying.

A human-made, architecturally designed labyrinth—symbolic of the passage of the soul through life—is a patterned walkway, a building or underground tunnel system, a maze, often constructed with confusing entries and exits and convoluted hallways, that stop abruptly and just as abruptly open onto other hallways so as to confound the journeyer's rational or intuitive sense of direction. Such mazes—oriented on the Earth as to honor the course of planets and stars, sun and moon—were built by Egyptians, Greeks, and Europeans of yore. It is told that adepts in the highest degree, great hierophants and priestesses, entered the meandering passages of these labyrinths with secret guidance to the inner chamber—the holy of holies at the labyrinth's heart—where the most fabulous initiations in freedom, compassion, wisdom and possibility were known to magically unfold.

There is lesson after lesson upon the labyrinth's path.

The labyrinth I have walked in this life has not been fraught with dead ends or spiraling maelstroms from which there was no return, but rather, it has been as if I place my foot upon the path and the one-way road opens miraculously in front of me showing me the way at every bend.

I have learned that I travel protected.

Sometimes I get wonderful glimmers of insight. It is as if I can sometimes see through windows in the labyrinth's walls straight into the ceremonial chamber where the holiest acts occur. These windows, like thick-framed, rectangular glassless openings in baked mud-brick masonry, are ancient altars lit with candles, set with holy objects, to remind you of your ultimate destination, to remind you of what is truly important, especially when you get distracted or frightened by the worldly ebb and flow.

I have been inside the ceremonial chamber of the labyrinth also. I have been inside and back out again and time after time, entirely new pathways are revealed.

I light the candle to celebrate the eighth day of my ruminations.

"The power of the priestess is the power to remember," Riavek says, "You are remembering. You are remembering all that has ever been so that you can understand what is. Through remembering what has been, you shall know what is to become. You shall break every pattern and mold, and your service to the Earth World shall be thoughtful. You are preparing for your ministry by activating the memory of what has gone before, and with this memory activated, you are preparing to remember the depth of who you are and the sacred form of the future.

You are remembering that you are limitless. You are remembering your sacred dance, that the dance is universal, that the whole of the universe is the sacred temple for the dancer who is awakened."

The power of the priestess is memory. The priestess remembers all that has been, all that is and all that ever shall be. She blocks nothing out, denies nothing. She opens her inner vision and sees all. All knowledge—all that seems dark and light alike—stands revealed. The priestess is keenly sensitive, highly aware. She realizes that every experience contains a message. She learns. She grows. She finds omens. She heals. She teaches. She learns.

This is her Mystery: *Through the dark collective memory of all that was, is and shall become, the one light of knowledge is revealed. Truth shines through the collective memory of darkness. There is light in this darkness. We know this to be true, and yet the source of our faith remains a mystery.*

The priestess carries male in one hand, female in the other. She is yang as well as yin, light as well as dark, positive as well as negative, action as well as reception, initiative as well as response. In her hands she holds the Akasha, the sacred records of all that has been and all that is yet to come.

She stands at the conjunction of the Eternal Father and the Eternal Mother. She is the Fulcrum. She is the Union. She is absolute balance and creative potential, the sexless, sex-full, equation for life.

And always and forever, she stands as the bridge across the Abyss. Always and forever she stands as endless spirit in the eternal light facing darkness. She comes to know the nuances of the Abyss. She befriends dark creatures and embraces her lessons. The unknown becoming known is the source of her creativity and the source of her humility.

She draws from the Abyss the essential energies that represent the highest potencies of the human soul. And these potencies she cherishes and these potencies she nurtures.

She knows the void well. Her body is built around it.

"Close your eyes," Riavek says softly. I hear his voice with my inner ear, soothing and gentle, and I wonder if he will leave me when these meditations cease. "Close your eyes," he whispers, "be in peace, and drop into that deep place from which all vision is conceived."

I feel myself dropping down, down, down, moving deeper into the great Abyss until finally the Theater Eternal appears and the velvet curtains part to reveal the inspirational stage.

The setting is a cathedral and I see myself standing—just as I am today—in a long black dress shivering uncertainly. I am standing still at the entrance to a round labyrinth in the middle of a gray slate floor halfway between a huge stone baptismal font and the last row of rows and rows and rows of pews. The altar at the end of the nave is fantastic. My head is bent forward and my hands are praying with the tips of my fingers touching my forehead.

I stand a few steps from the labyrinth's edge, facing the altar, wavering, as if measuring the scene, considering when or if I will step forward and engage.

The cathedral is cold; cold as ice. I feel a chill moving up through my stockinged feet into my ankles and legs, into my solar plexus. My heart shakes. My hands ache.

Between my praying palms, I hold a metal disk, a circular replica of the 13th-century maze I stand confronting. The cold metal is uncomfortable against my closed palms and yet I cling tightly. I refuse to be daunted.

Red and blue shadows dance like ghosts about the floor.

Gray stone. Gray air.

I am chilled from the outside in, vulnerable from the inside out. I feel ice in my lungs and I worry that I will be ill. With frosted breath, I have walked a hundred steps, passed huge bronze doors. It is stone cold, painfully cold, infinitely cold. Yet I have maintained my mission.

I have removed my shoes; left them on the steps of the font. I have anointed my forehead, my cheeks, my throat. I will speak truth. I have been thrice baptized: Eastern, Western and Universal.

Candles flicker in a black iron sconce. I have kindled a votive for each child. *May you know peace, my daughter. May you find love, dear son.* Many candles dance in the half-light, winter light that flows like slow-burning lava through crystal-blue ice-lined stained glass. My hair stands on end—I am cold or ill or out of breath—and my palms, fused together with the power of intention, begin to grow wet as if the medallion is creating a physical reaction of rejection. I feel the metal begin to heat. I feel it sear. I want to drop the medal, but my hands will not obey. My blood races. My body screams with physical pain. My heart wants to cry out. I feel a little tear upon my cheek, but I will not part my hands to brush it off. My friend has died in the morning.

Fear. My friend has died and this seems like the central question: *Why are we born just to die?*

I stand facing my own fear of the unknown, fear of not knowing what the labyrinthine passages hold. Weakness overshadows strength. The order of things—which seemed more certain earlier—becomes confused.

Is the challenge to surrender and move to the next level?

Is the challenge to trust what we know to be true? Because nothing is real, *nothing*, except that which we internalize through our own individual experience.

I stand at the mouth of the labyrinth, hesitating, deliberating. I feel alone, even though I am not. Others have entered the twisting pathway already. I wait.

The labyrinth, viewed from a distance, fills a huge circle that seventy-five people with hands joined together might encompass. A single path winds through in a pattern of four quadrants of concentric circles, weaving in and weaving out in hairpin turns that sometimes take you close to center, sometimes far away. There is only one path, one path with no blocks or tricks—only one path that leads in which is the same path leading out—and still it is impossible to discern who walks before and who walks behind, so great is the labyrinth's complexity.

At the center of the labyrinth is a single rosette, an empty space around which six petals open outward. This is a space in which ten people could join hands, stand or sit, kneel or prostrate themselves in stillness at the heart of endless movement. You could pause at center to touch the divine.

I step forward in silence. I decide to begin, to sacrifice myself willingly to what may become. And as I walk, I begin to remember.

I am a mystical arrow delivered by a mysterious bow. I am moving in a mysterious flow and I must move in awe. *Replace fear with awe. Replace fear with awe.* This comes to me strongly now.

My teacher once said to me, "What should I do if I find I am going down the road in fear?" She did not wait for me to answer. "I should turn around and go the other way, that is what I should do. The other way is the direction of faith. Fear and faith are two different directions on the same road. Either direction you choose will take you to the same destination—because there is but one road and one end—but you can reach the destination in fear or in faith. The choice is yours. Which way do you want to go?"

I gather strength to move in faith.

Over and over, I relearn that I was released to the world protected.

In the beginning of this incarnation, I entered through my parents.

My parents were the bow, and I am the arrow who issued from their embrace.

But before I came from them, I came *to* them. I flew into their union, and, as I round the first turn in the labyrinth, moving in faith, a vision of what was suddenly awakens.

The way I came to my mother's womb—I remember just now—was dark and it was light also. I passed through levels and layers of pain and fear and darkness, legions of monsters with gnashing teeth and shrieking shadowlike phantoms that clawed after my form. I passed through regions of light so brilliant it became a frequency that blasted me to pieces. There was a time there was nothing but shimmering luminescent fog—pure suspension. And there were beings of gold and strange golden flowers, soft, gentle, loving, inhabiting worlds of pure joy and endless beauty.

I walk slowly and I remember the journey as I round a corner close to center. The labyrinth opens, pauses, twists back on itself. I walk the path, remembering, passing through the countless realms.

I pass through regions of becoming as a starseed, twirling like the shadow of a snowflake, lifted by a winter wind that whispers and cajoles me, and, as close as I can come to telling, the breath of the Spirit melodiously sings out: *Love. . .Love. . .Love. . .Love. . .Love. . .Love. . . Love. . .*The language of the angels is *Love.*

As I drifted into form, I was like the rest, indiscernable as a fleck in a blizzard, and yet I carried a seed structure with the recipe for life and the codified graven imprint of two hundred and fifty generations, along with the hopes and dreams and incredulous wonder of pure individual potential.

I swirled through ages and dimensions, spiraling, spiraling, spiraling, until I found myself suddenly pulled into a massive cycloning vortex of centrifugal energy. Down, down, down I sailed, spinning in imposing force and the spiral of movement until the door between the worlds cracked open and into her womb I flew.

It is the egg, the beginning and end of the cycle of being, that reaches out and embraces the sperm. The High Priestess of Becoming chooses one blessed fish of the many thousands who stand at the holy gate begging entrance to the adytum.

The teachers of the Ancient Mysteries have always spoken: "Many are called, but few are chosen."

The spirit of me was there, floating in the cosmic sea, but neither was I egg nor sperm, then both egg and sperm dissolved into one being and the starseed of me entered the inner sanctum as an offering upon the Altar of Life and physically began to multiply in dividing spheres of actual material form.

I became the arrow that shot from the bow.

My father was the arch ascending, the bow's upper end. He was the Sun: constant, eternal, light on the horizon, waking the days with awesome brilliance. He lit the fields, woke the tillers. Movement. Power. Glory. Courage. Fire. Intensity. Force. He was pulsing voltage, searing control. If you could not see him, you had clouds in your eyes.

Dance like an eagle! Fly to the sky! You are limited only by how you choose to develop your skill and your will to persevere. These were his teachings: *The right of flight is yours. Build wings that last.*

Will of the World, my father was the Eternal Father described by ancient Cabalists, moved not by victory, nor by defeat—this was his secret—and he succeeded always. Following his convictions, he worked in timely ways and Heaven and Earth saw fit to conform and obey.

Dedicated, loyal, masterful, and noble, my father was the Sun and the God of the Sun. He laid claim to the sacred oracle and instructed politicians. He sought Liberty or he sought Death. His Law was Society; he retained the right to rebel against injustice. Sun God Apollo, far-shooting Lord of the Silver Bow, my father walked at no man's heel. It is written:

From your throne of truth,
From your dwelling-place at the heart of the world,
You speak to men.
By Zeus's decree no lie comes there,
No shadow to darken the word of truth,
Zeus sealed by an everlasting right
Apollo's honour, that all may trust
With unshaken faith when he speaks.

My father was Apollo reborn in the 20th century. Freedom was his cause. Truth was his method. He would have agreed with Thomas Jefferson who said: "I have sworn upon the altar of God eternal hostility against every form of tyranny over the mind of man."

As my father was the Sun and the God of the Sun, my mother was the Moon and the Moon Goddess also. She was the bow's lower arch, the Eternal Mother of the Cabalists: a watery door in the midst of the endless curves of circling night, spiraling tunnel-like to the deepest, darkest core of vision. She was the doorway to forever. Her reflection enthralled, fascinated, and captivated. She was the protectress of dewy youth, protectress of the heart of inner sight. Opening. Waxing. Waning. Descending.

Sinking down in meditation, she bore the gift of all creation. Channel of universal energies, she dreamed in colors while my father, beside her on the double bed, enacted his nightly dreams in black and white.

My mother awakened in dreams. She lived in wonder. She was Artemis: Lunar Virgin, Mother of Creation, Huntress. She conceived and birthed all form and to her all form returned. She was the goddess of cycles, the doorway to the beginning and end, the first and the last, the alpha and the omega. Her message was: *Imagine.*

Twin sister to Apollo, my mother was the Lady of Wild Things. She was Artemis and Nature was her Law. Thus rings her Homeric hymn:

> *I sing of Artemis*
> *whose shafts are of gold*
> *who cheers on the hounds*
> *the pure maiden*
> *shooter of stags*
> *who delights in archery. . .*
> *Over the shadowy hills and windy peaks*
> *she draws her golden bow*
> *rejoicing in the chase. . .*
> *and when she is satisfied. . .*
> *she hangs up her curved bow and arrows*
> *and heads and leads the dances*
> *gracefully arrayed*
> *while they all raise their heavenly voice. . .*

"Behold! The woman is a great warrior," the followers of Artemis cry, "She has gone forth and captured a soul!" My mother captured the souls of dreams and brought them forth through art. Her hunting grounds were the subconscious landscape. She wielded her arrows in the dark without fear.

This I remember as the path twists from center: I first saw the work of Käthe Kollwitz in my mother's art studio. This reminds me: *Be of stout heart.*

My father was the Sun. My mother was the Moon. The two were one bow, two gracefully extending limbs carved of the same energy.

With praying hands, as I walk the labyrinth, I ask: Who created the archer's tool? Who searched the forest, discovered the tree, cut the branch of lemonwood, yew, or hickory conducive to such perfect curvature, such resilient flexibility? Who knew that Apollo must ascend while Artemis was descending? What brilliant master, what ingenious mistress, did realize that the exaggerated tension of opposites creates such fierce and pleasing flow? And who named the weapon? Who engraved upon its back the words *Freedom, Compassion, Wisdom, Possibility*, for surely this must be the bow's name, as surely as Sun and Moon arise at the eastern horizon and set in the west.

How wise is she who finally sees that the bow, at variance within itself, within itself intensely agrees.

Walking in faith, it is easy to honor your father and your mother. Divine Man springs from Divine Woman. Divine Woman springs from Divine Man. The two intertwine and unite and all posibility is born.

I shot from the womb on the path of the arrow with no string attached to the bow. I carried my own source of propulsion. I tried to walk in faith and if I shivered inside, I usually kept it to myself.

When I walk the path in faith, I walk the way of beauty stepping ever in eternal being.

My friend has died—just hours ago—and I say to her now, speaking with my heart: *Judy, do not be afraid. Travel the path in faith and I will travel with you.*

She is walking the labyrinth with me. I feel her presence with me and I weep. I cannot help myself.

"Judy," I whisper, "the path twists and turns. We are moving toward center, always toward center. To enlightened being. To perfection. To universal harmony. Love has always been with us, love has always been our guide, and so it ever shall be. Love is the greatest freedom because through love our spirit soars. Our spirit—like a graceful angel—soars beyond laws of society, beyond laws of nature. Judy, dear Judy, there is nothing in this world or the next so powerful as to alter the course of love."

I feel her walking with me. I feel her strength. I feel her tenacity, her resilience. She is with me, gaining strength for her journey. I am with her, facing another dimension with open eyes.

The path twists and turns. We cannot see the overall design at the moment we are inside it. We walk in faith. We walk in trust. We make of ourselves an offering, walking in the memory of pure divine being. We arrive at center and remember who we are. Then we walk back out, twisting and turning on the same path by which we came, carrying with us the illuminating force of pure realization.

I remember Judy's last words to me, her last gesture before she departed this realm.

She could not speak, or so I believed. She could not move. Her body was still. She could not raise her head, her hands. She could not even blink. Her eyes were half-open, glazed and staring into the direction of nothingness. And still she was beautiful. She was the apparition of an angel, her cheek soft against the pillow.

The light around her glowed with a mysterious aura. Her room was the opening between worlds. She was surrounded by flowers. She was surrounded by gods and goddesses, by sacred art now ensouled with holy presence. Her spirit stood at the threshold and the angels were calling. Her spirit rose to join the angels, but then something in the world called her back.

I looked upon my friend—she who had cared so much that the world should be at peace, that we should enjoy multicultural realities, that divinity was the birthright of all beings—I looked upon my friend and beheld her comatose state, the voice discarded that would never again preach about how it might be, and I could not contain my own suffering. I stroked her hair. I picked up a pink rose, hanging down its head in a glass of water on the table beside the bed. I said to my sister, "My love, what beautiful fragrance comes from the rose. See how the rose has blessed you." I stroked her beautiful long gray hair, pushing it back from her face and I sprinkled her pillow with the rose petals that voluntarily floated from the stem. It was as if by the testament of the fading rose, the dying woman was blessed by nature. The tears, which I had tried so hard to contain, then began to spill out against my will, but I did not cry out of pain. I did not weep in agony. I cried in suffering, but the suffering was more from the beauty of the moment. I cried with love for my friend. I cried for her beauty. I cried for the love of life, for the understanding of every cycle. For every birth. For every death. For every child that walks upon this Earth.

The tears poured down my face, and with these tears I anointed my sister. With my tears, I painted her body with holy signs and symbols of protection for the journey she would take. "My dear sister," I said, "I have only my tears for holy water and with my tears I anoint you with the sacred symbols of protection for the journey. Call me, call me in your mind, and I will be with you on the path. Call me if you are afraid and I will bring you strength. I will bring you love." I anointed her forehead, and we took all our thoughts into one single thought centered just behind the eyes, and the name of that thought was *Love*.

The sky was dark beyond the window, but the room glowed with a radiant, otherworldly light. There was the city beyond, people going to and from work, tourists crowding the marina, the cable car ringing its bell as it was passing by in front of the apartment, a passing siren. All of this was transpiring all around, but in the midst of all the movement,

I sat with my friend in the rarefied space at the cusp where life and death join hands. I held her beautiful hand.

"Judy," I said, "I am not crying because I am sad. I am crying from happiness. I am so happy because I can see that you are an angel, that you are an angel taking flight. I can see your wings. They are extended and ready. They are open for flight. Your soul is free. You are called to greater life. You are called to greater love."

Her eyelids fluttered a little. Always I knew her soul could hear me. Always I could hear her soul speaking in my heart.

"And Judy," I said, "This is what I can see that I never saw before. I can see that I, too, am an angel. You have taught me this, dear sister. I am your soul's reflection. I, too, have wings. We are sister angels on the path, sister angels flying toward the center, toward the light, toward the heart of being, and upon this path, dear sister, we have never been separate."

Her hand in mine moved just the tiniest bit. A single tear rolled from her half-open eye and settled on her nose. She knew we were both angels. I cried all the more at this small communication. But I knew, somehow, that mine were tears of joy strangely arising in the midst of human suffering.

I cried with love, with pain, with surrender, with peace. I said, "You have wings and I have wings, dear sister, and we can jump off and fly. We can jump off the cliff and together we can fly into the black abyss carried on the wings of love. We can fly! We can *fly!*"

My heart felt like it would break in two; the tears poured over my cheeks. And I laughed a little for the irony and the beauty of life and I know that Judy was laughing with me. I could feel her laughter. I know we were laughing and crying together, and I laughed and cried and stroked her beautiful hair that fanned out upon the pillow.

I sat beside her bed. I prayed and meditated with her. I sounded the tones of my seven-metalled singing bowl, the one made by monks from Tibet, and these tones I played over her body from the top of her head to the tips of her toes and back again to the top of her head. I told her I loved her. I told her she was loved and cared for by the holy mother, by the divine father, by all the angels, that she was flying now, back to the radiant sea from which she had earlier come.

After a long, long time, after many hours, I stood up and bent over and kissed her on the forehead. "I will come again to visit," I said. I walked over and stood by the door, tears still blinding my sight. I said, "I love you, Judy." And, even though I believed her eyes could not see me, I blew her a kiss.

Her eyes could not see me, but her soul saw all.

Suddenly she opened her eyes. She looked deep into my eyes. She came alive and looked piercingly and it was as if the woman I had known suddenly reentered the near-lifeless form. With all the might that was in her, with every ounce of energy she could muster, she spoke ever so slowly, ever so haltingly and these were her words: "I-love-you-Pa-me-la."

Then very, very slowly, as if aided by the angels in the other dimension, she slowly raised up her thin arm—the arm I never believed would move again—very, very slowly, moved her curled, unstraightenable hand to her lips, and blew to me her last kiss.

All that we believe is not possible is possible. Together, my friend, we walk the labyrinth.

Ashes to ashes, dust to dust, they say. We shall scatter your ashes in the ocean, and they shall blow back over the beach and the bluffs, and mingle with the rain. We shall scatter your ashes in the place that you played and lived and loved in the days when you were free and happy.

Sometimes we cannot imagine when we are in that place how much we love it. Sometimes it takes the perspective of having lived much longer before we can remember how happy we were in a certain place at a certain time.

We shall scatter your ashes in the place you lived when you were married. At your last request, we shall throw your ashes over the edge of the cliff to the crashing sea below. The waves shall be breaking in all directions. The ocean shall be in storm. The day shall be blustery and your ashes shall fly back into our faces and land upon our coats and in our hair. We shall be coated in your ashes, and the ground shall be coated with your ashes, and the sea shall carry your ashes to distant lands, to the sacred and ancient temples of the goddess that you love.

And together we shall utter the ancient Celtic Blessing put into poetry by Mary Rogers, the last stanza altered to fit our momentary need:

> *Deep peace of the running wave to you,*
> *of water flowing, rising and falling,*
> *sometimes advancing, sometimes receding. . .*
> *May the stream of your life flow unimpeded!*
> *Deep peace of the running wave to you!*
>
> *Deep peace of the flowing air to you,*
> *which fans your face on a sultry day,*
> *the air which you breathe deeply, rhythmically,*

which imparts to you energy, consciousness, life.
Deep peace of the flowing air to you!

Deep peace of the quiet earth to you,
who, herself unmoving, harbours the movements
and facilitates the life of the ten thousand creatures,
while resting contented, stable, tranquil.
Deep peace of the quiet earth to you!

Deep peace of the shining stars to you,
which stay invisible till darkness falls
and discloses their pure and shining presence
beaming down in compassion on our erring world.
Deep peace of the shining stars to you!

Deep peace of the watching shepherds to you,
of unpretentious folk, who watching and waiting,
spend long hours out on the hillside,
expecting in simplicity some Coming of the Lord.
Deep peace of the watching shepherds to you!

Deep peace of the Child of Peace All-Illumined
who, swift as the wave and pervasive as the air,
quiet as the earth and shining like a star,
breathes into us Peace and Spirit.
Deep peace of the Child of Peace to you!

And your ashes shall fall upon such grasses as have braved the salt and sea and winter storms and our tears shall fall into the rivulets carved by the season and we, by our acts, shall be redeemed.

Ashes, they say, have the power to absolve and to forgive the living. By touching ashes we are burned clean, the way the field is cleared by burning for a new season of growth. We scatter your ashes and we are purified. We are burned clean in spirit, heart, mind, and body. We open and become creative.

The physical body, poured upon the Earth, makes the Earth fertile while the spiritual body soars.

The cathedral is dank and cold. I stop in the labyrinth and glance upward. There is a huge black opening, a huge window—it seems fifteen feet high— framed by cold gray stones in the top of the back wall. This window does not lead to light outside; it opens onto interior darkness. Through the arched opening, you can only see blackness. Not darkness, not shades of gray, but sheer and deep blackness. It is a massive black hole of unmoving energy. There is a small candle perched upon the lower ledge. It is so high up, I think there must be stairs behind it or you could not place a candle there. How would you set a candle there? All at once, against that darkness, the candle's tiny flame seems as bright as it seems diminished.

Like the flash of a comet, we are small flares streaking the night sky.

In geological time, we are not even a comet's tail.

They say if we look at earthly existence in the time frame of a clock that has twenty-four hours on its face rather than twelve, so that what is normally six o'clock would be twelve o'clock noon, and what is normally twelve o'clock would be twelve midnight, the simplest life forms did not even begin until 3:50 in the morning. Then nothing at all happened until almost 9:00 in the evening—seventeen hours later, about six hundred million years ago—when diverse and complex organisms began. Then around 10:30—about a hundred and forty-five million years ago—dinosaurs began to roam the earth and they were on the planet for *a hundred million years.* At 11:59:59:02, just before midnight—that was *a hundred thousand years ago*—Homo sapiens appears. At 11:59:59:09, humans begin to write their story.

We are a flash in the pan, just a twinkle in daddy's eye, and yet, that flash in the pan is everything.

I remember my son's 3rd birthday. It was the first year he realized that his birthday was his special day. We had moved to the beach about three months earlier. We had a wonderful back yard, just perfect for eight rowdy little boys—all new and fascinating acquaintances—to play in. We had a great party. There were birthday hats and hotdogs, balloons, a big chocolate cake saying *Happy Birthday Taylor,* a papier maché piñata filled with candy and plenty of toys. We made a bonfire and sang songs. Taylor opened a pile of presents. We took home movies. All in all, it was about as glorious as any party could ever be.

At nine o'clock that night, I dressed Taylor in his pajamas and tucked him in his cozy little bed. But he said he couldn't sleep. He had to go in his sister's room. All right, then. I arranged a sleeping bag for him on Kätchen's floor right next to her bed where they could talk quietly and hear each other breathing. I left the room. Then suddenly I heard Taylor crying. He was crying and crying for Mama. *Mama! Mama!*

I went back into the room. "What is it, Taylor?" What's the matter?"

I scooped his baby body into my arms and hugged him and rocked him until he became quiet and could get back in his sleeping bag. "Now why were you crying, Taylor?" I asked.

"Mama," he said, "I sinked about da party and it will never come again."

I knew he meant he thought about the party and was sad that it was over. "Oh, *that*," I said and the solution to his sadness seemed very simple, indeed. I said, "Taylor, you get to have a birthday *every* year. Isn't that exciting! We will have so many parties. They will be so wonderful, just like today. We'll have balloons and cake and hotdogs. The boys will come. You'll all play games. Kätchen will be there. You wait and see. A birthday is a wonderful thing."

But he said to me, "Mama, *dis* day will never come again."

Gone. Irretrievable. Over. I understood. Then *I* cried.

I am walking the labyrinth and I remember Taylor's birth. It was so beautiful after the stormy assembly-line fraught-with-confusion and technical difficulties birth I had with Kätchen in the hospital. Taylor was born in a soft and gentle birth home.

A few days after his birth I wrote:

> *In sacred waters you were anointed*
> *They rubbed olive oil into your black hair*
> *when all we knew of you was one small patch*
> *Olive oil in your hair*
> *And you were born bare*
> *reborn naked*
> *consecrated boy*
> *And they blessed me, consecrated me, anointed me*
> *your oil the same as mine*
> *as you came down in time—birthing*
> *The two of us*
> *Anointed the both of us*
> *In sacred waters we were born*
> *as two*
> *consecrated as two, consecrated anew*
> *And then formally divided by the one who made us one*
> *by the one who made us two*
> *Formally divisible*
> *We were formally divided in the moment we were blessed*
> *secrets now confided, secrets now outside us*
> *confessions and pure knowing*
> *in tenderness*

and in holiness
With each caress my soft tears fell
and mingled with the holy waters
mingled with the sacred waters
in which my son was blessed
mingled with the holy oil
the olive oil
Which was your path, our path, to life.

You sleep softly. Your hold your little hands by the side of your face. I carry you to the bedroom. Your arms move in a reflex reaction. You are dreaming. Are you dreaming of your days in the womb? Are you dreaming of the strange and forgotten world from which we have come? You are so close to that world. You are so fresh. So new. Only days old. I wish I could see into your dreams. In your eyes I see glimmers. . .Sleep softly, my son. I kiss you on your soft cheek.

You were born on a Thursday. Thursday's child.

The contractions began at night. I slept. I woke at six in the morning feeling like I was 8 years old and it was the first day of school. Today my child would be born! Today I would meet a person who would be with me, at least in my heart and soul, for the rest of my life.

I stood in the shower washing carefully. Blood—deep and rich, not like the pink-tinted water of last night—flowed down my legs from my vagina and swirled down the drain. I was deep in labor, but I refused to succumb to whimpering. I challenged the labor. I called upon the tightening to come. I screamed at the contractions. I called upon them to strengthen: *Come. Come. Come! Come on. Come on as strong as you can. I can ride the waves. I dare you to come! I dare you. I am fearless. You will see. . .Come! Pain? Hah! Come, pain, come. . .*

I sent challenge after challenge to the throes of nature and my own potential for survival. I would bear my child with the strength of a mother bear.

I washed my hair. Water ran down around my ears. It flowed upon my breasts and caressed the baby within me. It felt like soft, hot rain falling on my body. Soft, hot rain, soothing me, loving me.

At length, I emerged, chose a loose dress that would not show wetness.

I combed my hair. I must be beautiful to meet my baby.

At seven o'clock I called the doctor. The doctor spoke from a half sleep, his voice was tired and sexy, choked with early morning. Perhaps it was me who felt sexy. Fluid and female and primal.

The doctor thought, then asked, *What signs?*

"Bloody show. Close contractions. Sheer excitement." I was pacing. Walking fast, walking hard, restricted only by the length of the telephone cord that tethered me to the wall.

"Get in the car and come now!" he said.

We drove over to the birth home. I made myself a cup of tea. Why *hurry?* I thought. I was a woman, truly in my power. I set down the cup. I leaned against the kitchen counter and breathed heavily. I closed my eyes and I breathed and breathed until I moved into the inside of my own breath. I breathed in. One-two-three. Held my breath. One-two-three. Out. One-two-three. Everything in the world faded. Everything but my own breath. I became my own breath and stayed like this for a long time.

When I opened my eyes, the doctor was standing before me laughing. I had not heard him come in.

I moved into a state of surrealism. People were coming and going. Friends. Family. It was 9:20.

I was on the bed in the lovely room with plants and French doors leading out to the garden. Mourning doves cooed under the fruit trees. The light flowed into the room like warm honey. People were bringing in flowers. My mother arrived with Kätchen—there were soft strains of Bach sonatas playing in the background—and every single thing seemed to be right.

The doctor checked the dilation of my cervix and grinned. He said, "You're eight centimeters." I said, "I don't believe it. Are you sure?" He checked me again. Eight. My husband told me to get a look of disbelief on my face and he snapped my picture. We all laughed.

We were laughing and the doctor said, "Well, I guess I won't be going to the office this morning." And we all laughed some more.

I laid down on my side. I breathed. In. One-Two-Three. Hold. One-Two-Three. Out. One-Two-Three.

Between contractions, I laughed. I continued to chide the contractions: *Come on, I dare you to get stronger. Come on, I dare you. You think I can't handle it? You're wrong. You're wrong. . .*

The golden light shone in the nurse's blond hair. The golden light danced in the doctor's red beard.

My husband and my friend held my hands. We breathed together. We all breathed. We shared the same breath. Life is one. Life is one breath.

10:15. A tiny lip of cervix left. Soon. . .Soon. . .

Mama! Mama! Kätchen called out to me. And she ran to me and she jumped on the big bed and I held her while I labored. We were all sitting there on the big bed and my mother was leaning against the French door crying.

The nurse massaged my vagina with olive oil. She was opening, opening, a passage for the baby. Blankets were warming in the oven. I was pushing. "Aaaaaagh."

"Breathe out!" they said.

Hands were supporting me.

"Push hard!" they said.

I pushed as hard as I could, then I looked up and saw my friend in the doorway. "I'm pushing, Barb!" I called, and my cry was gleeful. She came in and joined us on the bed.

Hands were on me supporting me. "Okay," said the doctor, "Now some gentle pushes. Try pushing between contractions. Push whenever you want. My mother was holding Kätchen. I pushed. I was controlled. "Aaaaaagh! (Breathe out.) Aaaaaagh!"

My vagina was stretching, stretching, stretching. I gritted my teeth. My body was opening, opening like a flower, and the *I* of me had nothing to do with it. *Open!*, I screamed inwardly, still challenging. It was the most intense burning I have ever felt, but I still refused to call it pain.

"*The baby's coming!. . .The baby's coming!*" This was me calling out. I was letting them know that the baby was almost here. My mother yelled, "That's the baby's head!" and the tears were streaming down her face.

I wanted to cry, too. I felt my throat tighten, but there was so much work yet to be done. I pushed. I pushed. I pushed. I stretched. I burned. I burned. Then the head was out. 10:44.

The doctor said, "Here comes your baby. Reach down!"

I sat up and reached down between my legs and took a firm hold of my child. I reached beneath the baby's arms—heard a small cry— and pulled my child from my womb onto my belly. I pulled my child right up out of my womb. *Ohmigod! Ohmigod!* The baby was wet and purple and its face was squashed like an old, old man. I held the baby on my stomach and felt the velvet skin. Gently, I rubbed the baby's back. Gently, I rubbed the velvet skin. I rubbed the vernix into the wrinkles on my face because the midwives had told me vernix was the best skin cream in the world. I held the baby close.

"Is it a boy or a girl?" I asked.

"Feel and see," the doctor said. Everyone waited.

I had a little surge of egotistical anxiety. Suppose I could not tell?

I reached down around the baby's bottom and slid my hand between the little legs. "It's a *boy!*" I announced. And all the world echoed, "It's a boy. It's a boy. It's a *boy.*"

All the world's heart was dancing.

I lay for a long, long while with my babe upon my belly.

CHRISTOPHER TAYLOR

Born: 10:44 in the morning
Weight: 8 pounds, 7 ounces
Length: 20 and a half inches
Temperature: 97.5 degrees
Condition: Born in the Golden Light of Love

We are a fleck of light shooting briefly through the night sky—nothing—and yet our fleeting moment is everything.

I was thinking about this as I sewed the minister's stole for my ordination. I was sewing strips of rich purple brocade onto rich warm cream-colored satin. I was stitching the sacred piece of ritual clothing, the one I would wear to officiate at weddings, funerals, baptisms, the one in which I would be ordained, the *outward sign* of my ordination, and I thought of how unimportant the whole thing is, and yet how completely important it all is right at the same time.

I experienced, as I sewed, something that felt like a past life memory. I remember hemming priests' vestments, but the vestments were not for me. Women were forbidden. We were forbidden because God gave to man a *son* and, because male priests bear a *natural resemblance* to the son, it is *fitting* that only *male priests* should perform the son's role at the mass. This logic comprises the official position and the official statement of the Catholic Church.

It was called "revolutionary" by historians—it was called the "Second Reformation"—when the Anglican Church began to ordain women priests in 1993.

The Second Reformation of the Western Tradition is about *allowing* women, at last, to become celebrants. But it is much more than that also. The Second Reformation is about moving, as theologian Mary Daly would say, beyond God the *Father*. It is about recognizing that divinity is contained in feminine forms. It is about the recognition of the mother as sacred, recognizing that the Mother Earth is sacred. It is about ecology and human rights and self-esteem. It is about changing the stories, composing new myths, recreating the mythological underpinnings that inform and direct the course of our lives.

The Second Reformation is a stage, like a psychological stage in the development of a child. The *womanly* has been degraded by Western religion and it has become our task—as free-thinking women and men—to reconceptualize ourselves as a reflection of the divine and to remember and celebrate the divine within ourselves. We must accomplish our mission before we will be able to realize—on a full planetary scale—that divinity is contained in all, in every man, woman and child, in every blade of grass. As we begin to recognize the divinity in all, we will move forward in divine partnership with every force and form in the world.

I sew onto my stole a Venusian cross, a cross with a hole in the upper arm; an Egyptian ankh to represent birth and life, the cross of the body of the female, the womb from which we all emit, the womb to which we all return. I sew on the ankh to remind me of the female body, *my* body, the body that surrounds the Abyss. I contain the void. This I remember and this is my power.

Beautiful purple brocade. Beautiful eggshell brocade. Fab- ulous golden lace. I sew on garnets to remind me of my womanhood, to remind me of my womanblood, that I am a woman, that I have made love, that I have given birth, that my breasts have filled with milk, that I have loved deeply, that I have cradled to my heart the dying, that I have bathed this body in the ashes of the dead.

The cathedral is cold. It is empty. It is dark. The labyrinth seems endless. I pray. I walk. Sometimes I move toward the altar, sometimes I move away.

The hungry soul coming for solace, may be left unsolaced still. One who walks the path in the soul's dark night may stay in the dark night ever. We create realities by which we are denied. And yet, we have choice: We can focus our attention on the depths of the abyss, or we can focus attention on the miniscule flame.

Like Divine Fools, we can dance in faith at the Edge of the World. We can dance in our ideals. We can skip into the black Abyss crying *Love, Soul, Earth, Water, Sky, Father, Mother, Seasons!*

We can take the sacred vow. We can speak the ceremonial oath. We can pray! We can chant! We can raise our voice in song! We can celebrate in silent beauty; enact the power of creation to invent worlds never before known.

Love. Love Divine. Blessings of Love upon you.

I step into the center of the labyrinth and there stands my friend Sister Lani. She is praying. She is smiling. She is blazing like the holy mother. She has given me her poem which I carry in my heart:

Love
Love is

Love is all
Love is all there
Love is all there really
Love is all there really is
Love is all there really
Love is all there
Love is all
Love is
Love.

A teenage boy comes into the circle, pauses briefly at the side, laughs a little, too timid to occupy space. Quickly he moves out. I love this boy. I love this boy intensely.

I walk to the center. I let go. I release. I hear Judy's voice ringing like the voice of an angel: *Celebrate Life! Celebrate Life!* I move into the labyrinth's eye. I step into the center of the maze and the light streams down upon me. I open my hands to receive the light, exposing the small bronze labyrinth I have carried all this way. It sparks with uncanny radiance. Holy of holies. Power of initiation. I close my eyes and feel—I feel this time and place so deeply—and when I open my eyes, the center of the labyrinth is full of people, and they are standing and kneeling, some with eyes closed, some with eyes open, some with tears streaming, some smiling gently. I stand, awestruck, recognizing some, not recognizing others, realizing how we have all walked the path as one.

Union. I am joined with the infinite. Past and future spiral into this moment at the center of the rose. Cold and hot intertwine. Known and unknown merge. Woman and man conjoin. I see myself chanting in a temple with the master of masters from across the sea. His beard is undulating upon his chest. His brown hands are calloused and folded upon his knees. We breathe together and we chant together, and together we call the divine, and all is of one essence, and the name of that essence is Love. Love is the center of all. All is reborn in Love.

And the voices of a billion women rise up and sing *Love*. And the voices of a billion men rise up to join them. Nothing else matters, not gods and goddesses. Not Apollo and Artemis. Not woman. Not man. There is one bow. There is one essence. No division. No separation.

Love is the bow. Love is the arrow. Love is the target. Love is the message. Love is the prophesy.

And Judy stands there, glowing like an angel. She stands at the labyrinth's heart, radiating in the center of all that is and she whispers for all wise pilgrims to hear: *Celebrate Life! Celebrate Life!*

I remember the words of my teacher: *Call into yourself the highest, most loving and instructive powers in the universe and the path of your soul will be revealed.*

I call the sisters to join me and instantly they are there: Lai-ila, Meritaton, Alilat, Electra, Hypatia, Bitten-By-The-Wolf, Diana, and a thousand others I know and know not.

Lai-ila places her beautiful long hands in prayer position, bows to me, and says, "Welcome. I honor the sacred within you." Meritaton crosses her loving heart with her fingers outstretched like wings, bows, and says, "Lady of the White Dove, come and join our dance."

And then there is dancing and I see a form dancing, moving like a golden wave, graceful as a willow, light as a silver flickering flame. She opens like a lotus—the sacred open channel, conductress of the spark of life—and to her I am drawn as a pilgrim is drawn to inner light. Then her face opens to me and her face is my face and I know her as She Who Has Always Been and I hear her name whispered *Silver Reed.*

We dance and we dance as if we are dancing in the stars and the sisters call out the words and sounds and phrases in all the sacred languages and the tomes and chants vibrate dusts into spiraling vortices and swirling spheres.

Love. Truth. Beauty. Wisdom. Freedom. Soul. Life. Healing.

Particles charge with force and current leaps.

Indescribable aurora.

We are laughing, dancing out beginnings. Lai-ila opens her hands and cries out, "Life is sacred!" Her words soar in the void and clouds of dust are summoned and swirl into action.

Meritaton shakes her sistrum and all vapors iridize.

Alilat sings, "Live in Love! Live in Love!"

Electra wraps her fingers through those of Alilat, the two raise their arms in triumph, and Electra calls "Joy, Sister! Joy! Through Love we know the World's Heart!"

Bitten-By-The-Wolf chants in strange and beautiful tongues and all of creation assumes rich coloration.

Hypatia cries, "Dance upon the ashes of the dead and gain strength for living!"

Diana calls, "After the forest burns, the doe gives birth to twins!"

Hypatia calls, "Life springs eternal!"

All respond, "As does thy Spirit!"

Silver Reed calls out, "What, Sister Pamela, do you have to teach us? What are the words of your song?"

I look down at the little bronze labyrinth in my hands. It glimmers and shines in the halflight of the church. And suddenly I am back in my room.

I open my eyes and there is my little candle flickering upon the makeshift altar. I pause for a minute, feeling very reflective, very senti-mental, very attached to the little life I have created.

Before me are shelves of books and writings from the decade I worked on my doctorate and from my first decade as a university educator.

There are books and writings from my recent studies: the *Upanishads*, the *Bhagavad Gita*, the *Zend Avesta*, the *Tao Te Ching*, the *Book of the Hopi*, the *Koran*, the *Bible*, the *Zohar*, the *Sepher Yezirah*, a big collection of books on the cabala, books about all the goddesses. There are books about the religions of indigenous peoples, and books about medicine and healing that overlap all the stages through which I have passed. There must be at least fifty volumes on childbirth, including one I authored myself.

There are novels, too: *Steppenwolf* and *Siddhartha*, *Death Comes for the Archbishop*, *Zorba the Greek*, *To the Lighthouse*, *Animal Dreams*.

There are rows and rows of journals that I have kept for twenty years and a crystal ball containing two pillars of black tourmaline.

There is the *Tarot of the Spirit* which I created with my mother.

There are many kiln-fired spirit dolls—some pure white porcelain, some ruddy terra cotta—that I sculpted over the years as I sat in my art studio meditating and contemplating the melodious strains of the Indian and Japanese flute. Every fingerprint in the clay, now forever etched by fire, bears a prayer: *May I live my life in alignment with the perfect movements of heaven and earth.*

There are flowers—yellow mums, white roses, pink orchids—and pictures of my children.

"Do you remember," says Riavek, "when Taylor was 5 years old and the three of you were sitting at the dinner table eating pizza, and Taylor announced that he would never die?"

"Yes." I was a single mom then, and I remember how hard it was to get home from work before the day care center closed. Those were dif-ficult times—especially when I was taking commuter flights back and forth from San Francisco to Los Angeles. . .

"Do you remember," he asks, "how Kätchen argued with him. How she informed him that everybody has to die? Even *Taylor*. . ."

"Yes." Remembering that makes me sad.

"Remember, too, how, when he was 13, his room became a shrine to the dead? He played music exalting death and he papered his walls with posters of musicians and actors, all of whom had died so very young?"

"Yes."

"Do you remember that you were like that when you were 13? You, too, had already found the hole in your soul and you were trying, just like Taylor, to make sense of it all."

I smile and shake my head. I can see myself in Taylor. I can see myself in Kätchen, too.

What is our quest if it is not to understand the meaning of birth and death, rebirth and *love?*

"Taylor will be okay," says Riavek, "You have shown him what it means to care."

The feeling of emptiness creates a desire to know fullness. The desire to know fullness leads to a life of spiritual seeking. Those who follow the spiritual path, who move into a life of intense spiritual devotion, come to realize that love is the essence, love is the power.

Love is patient. Love is kind. Love is expansive and forgiving. Love rejoices in truth, in freedom, in exploration. Love bears all things, believes all things, hopes all things, endures all things. As it says in the *Bible,* "Love never fails; but if there are gifts of prophecy, they will be done away; if there are tongues, they will cease; if there is knowledge, it will be done away. For we know in part, and we prophesy in part; but when the perfect comes, the partial will be done away."

The perfect is love. Love is the redeemer, the sanctifier, the creator. When one comes into the power of love, one's heart opens to the heavens, to the Earth, to every single creature and every sprouting seed. One's heart floods with compassion for all and the reigning desire is to serve the beloved.

I have a vision: the world is coming to an end. *Soon!* Things that have been shall cease to be. The old shall die. The old shall fade away. Shall fall away distortion, discord, division. Shall fall away separation. Clashes of will.

We shall grow from every challenge. We shall properly attune. We shall activate our compassion, our conscience, our highest forms of service, and we shall become dedicated, loyal, and noble.

We shall move into a deep understanding of creative principle. We shall imagine a world that has never been—a world in alignment with the harmonious movements of Heaven and Earth—and we shall move through the portal toward perfection.

We shall move through the portal into new forms of being, bringing every impulse, emotion, thought, word and deed into alignment with our deepest soul. We shall unite the world under love's healing banner, the banner of the radiant heart.

We shall not compromise; we shall seek the perfect balance of intellectual pursuit and loving understanding. We shall break the screen of oppression and emerge clean, clear, pure and deserving.

We shall move in grace in the beautiful dance. We shall honor those who dance together and those who dance alone. And every path of spirit shall be recognized as the *right* way.

We celebrate the coming of the All-Illumined Child of Peace! I bow to you, dear sister! I bow to you, dear brother! *You are the one whom we have so long awaited!*

Radiant and united, with freedom, compassion and wisdom as our guides, the six billion that we are—male, female, black, brown, white, yellow, gold, pink, olive, and red—join hands and walk into new possibility. We imagine a world where all of life is sacred and every single being is divine.

We walk as one and hold the deep knowledge in our hearts: whatever we create *becomes.*

We shall be of one heart and in the process, we shall be like the willow: ridicule shall pass like a breeze between our branches.

I get out a sheet of paper to more clearly record my thoughts. I scrawl out the "Code" under which I shall be ordained.

Knowing how my views change as lessons are revealed, however, I decide not to carve the precious words in stone.

♥ Code of the Radiant Heart ♥

I honor the wonder of life and believe that life is sacred.

I honor the individual's direct experience and interpretation
of the sacred.

I honor deep contemplation of the meaning of personal and
collective life, and believe that such reflection is essential to
attaining a balanced individual and social state of being.

I honor considered and conscientious understanding,
thought, speech, and action.

I honor and celebrate diversity in lifestyle and perception.

I honor perspectives that unify and integrate.

I honor empathy and kindness.

I honor non-violent approaches to conflict resolution.

I honor the simple, natural, creative, and responsible life
which does not harm or endanger others or the Earth's
resources.

I honor the equality of all.

♥

IN THE SPIRIT OF FREEDOM, COMPASSION, WISDOM, AND POSSIBILITY.

Signed, *Sister Pamela*

ᘒ

Riavek speaks, "Your spirit goes back to the beginning. Your heart goes back to the beginning. Your mind goes back to the beginning. You are the body of nature embracing the soul's deep mystery. Feel the life-force quivering. You are ready, Sister Pamela.

"The message of your spirit is freedom. The message of your heart is love. Your mind calls you to wisdom. Your body whispers *awaken*. Awaken to the sacrament of life.

"Awaken. Awaken at last. Step into the soul's deep mystery, the mystery of electrifying beauty, step into the soul's deep mystery and occupy eternal being.

"The legacy of passion's flame eternally afire is yours. You are the cosmic sea giving birth to all creation. Tremble amidst the awesome forces. Amidst the winds of swirling change, center yourself in pure being. You have reached the far land for which you were destined and that sacred country is the still and precious garden at the center of your soul.

"Know this garden, tend it, and there celebrate the holiest of holy sacraments for you are the guardian of forever, the Priestess of the Eternal, and that, my dear, is your strength.

"The garden of the soul is a universe. The universe continually expands and contracts. The universe endlessly spins and the heart of the spinning is stillness. Stillness lives in the labyrinth's eye. At the calm, quiet center, the gardener plants a seed. The seed sprouts and blooms and the gardener cries out, gasping in awe, for the wonder of the incomprehensible potential and the majesty that is life."

CHAPTER 13

SILVER REED
ETERNAL REALITY

The White Room, The Future.

Nine returns to itself. Nine times two is eighteen. One and eight is nine. Nine times three is twenty-seven. Two and seven is nine.

Nine sisters. Nine days.

On day nine, I light the white candle, and I begin to see that every single thing at last returns to itself.

I drop down in meditation and immediately I see her—Silver Reed. She is in the round white room, the place I saw in the beginning, a vision of absolute loveliness, filmy and translucent. She speaks, not directly to me, but like a partially-disinterested tourguide, to any and all who might care to pay attention.

"When you are visiting a place for a while, when you stay long enough to begin to get inside the reality of the natives, when you begin to see as they see and hear as they hear, as you begin to understand their social conditioning, as you begin to take in through the same kind of filter system they have, a filter system of common understanding, common perceptions, created by the communication of a shared belief in what is real and the limits and possibilities of that reality, when you begin to stand inside the natives' reality and view the issues, actions and outcomes from the natives' vantage point to the extent that you want to defend the natives, you want to explain what they are doing and why, there arises this passionate desire and even the accompanying tendency to want to 'go native.'

"It was not without some sadness that I finally returned home."

"It is interesting how one can attach to struggle. Conflict and polarization produce energy and energy is excitement. As I lived Earth reality, walking in it as a native living on the inside—and in the back of my mind thinking all the time I was there to introduce the *radiant light*—I realized how seductive and even productive discordance can be.

"For example, I could tell you about what was called the Age of Electro-Wars. This was a time in the Earth World's history when war technology and even the definition of war dramatically shifted—when the natives had created the potential for instantaneous electronic hard communication between nearly three billion points on the planet and many points beyond. 'Hard-communiqués' were data-bits sent by electronic means from a certain point to any number of designated receivers.

"I specify the definition of electronic hard communication because, at the same time, another form of instantaneous communication had developed which was referred to as 'telecommunis.' Telecommunis was developed by individuals and groups of individuals who had realized the potential of instantaneous information transfer by thought. No electronic devices were required to activate what came to be known as the Soft Web.

"The Hard Web and the Soft Web were about equally reliable—as misunderstandings and communication breakdowns could happen in either area.

"Interestingly, however, it was not the Hard Web and the Soft Web that came into ultimate battle with each other because, in order to fight, there must exist certain shared perceptions as to what is important enough to fight about—I am not saying there was no overlap between these two groups, but the nuances comprise another story—but rather both began their own form of internal warfare.

"The Hard Web began a battle of sweet temptation. The idea was to use 'The System' to entreat 'hard-webbers' through enticing offers to engage in the electronic transfer of funds and resources which would ultimately result in global shifts in wealth and power. As the game escalated, electronic viruses were introduced into The System which could create and destroy recording systems and even whole branches of The System, itself. Some of these viruses could be transferred to humans using The System which resulted in new waves of physical and mental disorders, previously unknown in the history of the Earth World. Internationally, care programs sprang up to aid the afflicted and from every angle the ethics of The System were questioned.

"I do not want to give the impression, however, that the motivation for developing The System was entirely diabolical, because it certainly was not. Much of The System was developed by people with good intentions, imaginative people, the culture's youth, those whose world guaranteed them nothing, and who were forced by the sheer numbers of humans combined with the shrinking resources on the planet to create for themselves methods both to guarantee survival and to enhance the circumstances of that survival. The culture's youth perceived infinite potential in the worldwide market.

"Some of them believed—with all their hearts—that The System could be used to educate people to realize their fullest potential as citizens of the universe.

"That is where I was in that lifetime—a lifetime I will not describe at this moment. I was sitting at my work station, half-human, half-machine, watching the screens and sending out hard-communiqués internationally. These communiqués comprised a body of spiritual teachings I hoped would affect the philosophy and values of the people. I was fighting also what I perceived as the soft webbers' invasion of thought space. I was in the overlap group—completely open to telecommunis when I wanted to be, but objecting to the impulse some people were engaging in to try to control people without their knowledge or consent. The object there, of course, was also the control of resources. That was another form of thievery on the telecom- muni-highway as far as I was concerned.

"For some reason, when I think of this now, it makes me laugh. I don't know, though, what is so funny about it. I remember it seemed tragic at the time.

"There were people gathered around my bed when I died—my nervous system had been affected by a virus in the Hard Web. We did not understand then the full implications of external electrical current interacting with human forcefields.

"I suppose what makes me laugh is how hard I tried. I was young and idealistic—not only when I was on Earth as an insider, but when I first left home before I crossed the River. It took me over six thousand years in Earth time of engagement on the Earth Plane to realize that people enjoy struggle. Even *I* came to revel in struggle, though I would not have admitted it at any time over the course of those six millenia. First of all, I did not fully realize how struggle creates energy, since I had come to see with the perspective of a native. Secondly, it would not have been fashionable to admit such an addiction to creating energetic force from the inside perspective of the culture.

"Energy is passion.

"For example, the struggle for material security and gain produces extraordinary excitement in the human, but, the struggle eventually ends by creating imprisonment within the very wealth that is acquired. Eventually such wealth is allowed to dissipate or it is formally cast aside—no longer seeming meaningful—to be replaced by an equally engaging struggle of spirit.

"The spiritual struggle begins with an individual revelation that sheds light on life's 'true' meaning. The revelation creates a founding principle for the development of spiritual community. The community develops structure which takes on a life of its own. It is believed by insiders that the structure exists to ensure the good of all. The structure is a springboard for spiritual studies, but, it also becomes a control mechanism that curtails individual freedom. Ultimately, the individual, feeling confined, rebels against the structure. Seeking the path of spiritual freedom, the individual turns attention to a deep struggle of the heart.

"The heart opens to feel, and with that opening comes the stirrings of all emotion. The heart opens to experience all sensitivities, and the individual is moved into awareness. All of life becomes filled with poignancy. The rose, whose petals are torn away by crashing waves in the roaring sea, entreats the poet to weep. All of life becomes grit for the pearl. The individual moves into the deep dark chasm of the self and discovers empty spaces, spaces that seem to lead through a hole in the soul into some great universal abyss. It is then that the individual realizes the only way out is to rethink the situation—to come out of the depths—and the struggle of heart is abandoned in favor of a struggle of mind.

"An idea comes. A light turns on, dries the tears and illuminates the darkness. The light increases in intensity as the idea takes form and is nurtured. The individual is rescued from the emotional abyss of the heart by thinking things through, by thoughtfully and consciously reflecting and coming to terms with ways to correct whatever is amiss. Chaos becomes orderly. Layer upon layer of thought is painstakingly developed to create a network over the abyss which the individual uses like a ladder to move into new possibilities on the material plane.

"At last the intellectual struggle can be abandoned to be replaced by a struggle to recreate material conditions to reflect the new exalted thought pattern. A new material struggle begins. The material struggle moves through its cycles, eventually giving way to a new spiritual struggle and the whole cycle begins again.

"There are lessons at each moment in the turning, of course, and all of these lessons are entirely important. Through engaging in the spiritual struggle, the entity begins to understand the meaning of *freedom*. The emotional struggle creates a deep sense of *compassion*. The mental struggle ultimately evolves a state of *wisdom*. The material struggle evokes a sense of *possibility*."

"The perception, the meaning of each of these qualities, of course, remains entirely subjective."

"So, then, looking back, I have to laugh at my own intensity. If you can see the humor in it, it can be really funny.

"In that Webberian lifetime—my name was Copper, by the way—before I became afflicted by that blasted Pathoteletronitis (PTT)—and could no longer input data physically or mentally, I was sitting at my work station, lost in the deep dark entrails of that labyrinthine network sending out, on both the Hard and Soft Webs, the ultimate realization at which I had arrived. The ultimate lesson of Earth School, I implored (to anyone who would tap in) is about understanding the meanings of *Freedom, Compassion, Wisdom,* and *Possibility.* When we understand this, I pleaded, we can actualize our full potential as free agents who, in perfect alignment with the most evolved love and truth, create perfect possibility in an idyllic universe.

"Can you see the irony of that scenario?

"I thought I had missioned to Earth to affect the philosophy and values on the planet, I thought I had chosen to emanate with that mission freely and clearly, but what I did not realize when I left home to go to Earth was that I was not on the planet to teach, but to learn.

"In fact, everyone on the Earth Plane is sent there to learn his or her subjective lessons, the ones that will affect the ultimate course of eternal universal ways.

"It bears repeating that the experience is entirely subjective and each participant is in the exact part of the cycle that is required for his or her own specific education at an absolute and particular highly-determined moment in time."

"The Earth World is a small and intricate classroom, elaborately equipped and designed for an infinite number of experiments."

"Having exquisitely enjoyed all the cycles many times over—though I did not often think I *enjoyed* it at the *time*—I left, finished, but with my heart broken open, celebrating the exquisite poetry of Earthly forces and forms. I left as acculturated as anyone of you might have become who emerged on the planet and throughout each heart cycle, found yourself 'going more and more *native.'*"

"There is something to be said for being willing to engage in the struggle."

"When my heart broke—and it happened when I fell in love—I realized I had one."

"Before closing, I will communicate just a bit about who and where I am and where I am going.

"Silver Reed is not my name, of course, but rather a code-name. The reed is a hollow transmitter. Silver is a euphemism for the ultimate power of conduction. Rhyavect, which in my lifetimes as Pamela and also as Copper—as my memory was awakening—I misunderstood and misspelled as 'Riavek,' to the detriment of the understanding of the Webberians (a story I choose not to go into at this time), is the stream of connection that electrifies and illuminates universal transmission.

"You will remember that in going to the Earth World, I crossed the River of Forgetfulness so that I would be able to experience the Earth World from the inside. My full memory of my origins and my destiny did not return until I had long since left behind the twisted body of Copper, collapsed and turned inward with that dread neurological PTT.

"I did not realize until then (as you must already have guessed) that 'Riavek' and I were two aspects of the same being.

"I am, as I was and as I ever shall be, the essence of creative principle.

"Pamela almost understood the nature of this essence, which, as you must know by now, was her own essence and also yours, when she one day realized that 'Riavek' was the Metatron and asked him if she could change his name to Metatron in her book Priestess.

"At the very suggestion, he doubled over laughing. He thought it was hysterical and said she could call him anything she wished. Her reasoning, at the time, was her sudden revelation that the one she called 'Riavek' was the beginning, the end, between, with, before and after, there and back again, eternal stability and change, the boundary and the threshold—thus Meta—and the instrument or tool of all this as well, thus tron.

"'Riavek' appeared like an angel in her Earthly-conditioned thought patterns, and one day it came to her in a flash of insight that she had been dealing with the Angel Metatron all along, the one who was pure illuminati, the one who had delivered the mystical cabala to the people, the one from whom all knowledge emitted, the one to whom all knowledge returned.

"When I embodied Pamela, I saw through the veil, but dimly.

"The thing that I/she had trouble conceptualizing was that I am everywhere and nowhere, and from her standpoint, in a very specific latter 20th-century, Earth-based context, filled with energized polarities, this was difficult for her to comprehend—since she had completely and passionately been 'native' for five thousand years in body, mind, heart and spirit."

"She did, one time in March of 1993, formulate the question though: *How could I be everywhere and nowhere when I am sitting right here in California scribbling in my journal?*"

"I am sure you know what I mean."

"By now you understand that I am the transmitter, the receiver and that which is transmitted and received. In short, the creative principle, your own individual essence.

"I can tell you that you are free, you are loving, you are wise and you are infinite, but I know that, whatever you learn, you will learn in your own way in your own time.

"One small afterthought. . .*There is a tiny little bud on the end of a branch on the tree in the middle of the garden; be still and know; the most exquisite blossom that ever was stands ready to open and flower.*

Open your eyes to see: She blooms with time. She blooms with love. Life is sacred and just as life guards you, you are Life's blessed guardian.

PART III

THE MINISTRY

CHAPTER 14

THE ORDINATION

Pennsylvania, Late 20th Century

At take off I feel the exuberant joy of life coursing through my veins. Blood surges; the heart shrieks. Pinned against the seat by the centrifugal force of forward movement, I feel the rattle of life shake creation into motion. Five. Four. Three. Two. One. Up. Yes!

I am dancing in circles with the wings of eagles flying on my arms. Praying. Spinning. Yes! The thrill of being.

An hour into air, we emerge from the land of purling burnt sienna into a red land of angular forms that stretch as far as anybody can see. Peter, who has joined me for the journey, is exhilarated. I touch his hand. Black snakes—a hundred miles of monstrous sidewinders—cut deep black crevices in red stone. A miracle. An absolute miracle.

Then the monstrous serpentine rivers suddenly seem like tiny babes as they converge in the form of one great titan mother, zig-zagging languidly through the center of the ancient ocean floor.

Dry brown dirt becomes dry tan sand. Colossal monuments appear in our view: Gigantic rock formations—spirit-callers—rise from the ground, rise from a desert of tumbleweeds and puffs of thin gray sage, calling through the sky's stillness: *Arise my friend and greet the new day!*

I place my offering on nature's altar:

> *To all gods and goddesses*
> *known and unknown*
> *dead and gone and yet to be*
> *I offer this day as a sacrifice*

—me—
I willfully leap into death, life
eternity and mystery.

The land changes, becomes brown sand.

In the distance, the Great Rock rises, sails like a ship upon the spirit sea. All who know the power worship the power. Those who have eyes to see know they are in the spirits' desert home; the call of wildness lights up the mundane.

You can feel the energy radiate through the vast terrain. Waves course over the land, into the air. Monolithic vibrations shake the fuselage. Earth pulses. Morning's early rays gently kiss the warming topsoil. All the world awakens. The miracle of the sleeping land unfolds as Dawn begins her daily fare. This world is ancient, older than time.

Drawn am I to the energy of the earth's center, the soul of me flies, skims, merges with warm cracked summer clay.

No, I am not her caretaker. . .She is mine.

A layer of cloud coverage separates my vision from the lands below.

Dotted clouds stretch infinitely. I am on the other side of Georgia's canvas.

Down at Abiquiu, the red hills roll in shadow. Horses—Old Rhone, Nellie, Star Step Tommy, Ginger, Maybelle, Fire Tail, Peanuts, Bob, and Miracle, spirit mares and stallions of the wild range—graze endlessly, eternally, idly, nuzzling each others' soft muzzles, snorting gently, lustily shoving each other from clump to clump of the last of the sweetest spring grasses.

Jack Frost etches stenciled designs on the bottom edge of the little portal through which I witness the magnificence of creation. It is freezing cold up here—on the outside—but we passengers stay fairly warm insulated in the hermetically sealed flying chamber.

They play a movie for entertainment. You can rent a headset to hear for three dollars.

You can make a phone call from up here to anywhere on the planet.

Ground: Thirty-seven thousand feet below: Parched, broken; heat waves rising, ghost lake mirages, spinning dust devils, pocket reflections of the sea before time; our winged shadow, our overpowering roar, is a wisp of reality passing in a flash like a summertime insect, soaring, then more than quickly gone.

How wonderful to drink of life and linger. As Stephan Hoeller says: the problem is not lack of experience. Even the most bored, lackadaisical person has more experiences than she can handle. The problem is not lack of experience, but *too much* experience—and no way to organize or find meaning in the continuous sensory onslaught.

Oh, but my soul is exuberant. I am *alive.* I am *alive* and living with a *flourish!*

Going to my ordination, I am filled with anticipation. Of what? I don't know.

My teacher said, *At your ordination I will lay my hands on your head and my teacher in the other dimension will lay hands on my head at the same moment, and my teacher's teacher will lay hands on my teacher's head, and my teacher's teacher's teacher will lay on hands, and so on and so forth, back and back and back in time and space, and the spark of cosmic fire will flow through the hands of all the teachers, all the way back to the first teacher, the greatest teacher, and this spark, my dear, the sacred spark of the spiritual torch, will be transferred to you. The spark will be transferred to you and the spark of your ministry will be ignited. You will receive the power to enact your calling. It is up to you, then, to fan the flame.*

It was a roundabout way I met my teacher, a friend of a friend kind of thing. People had been asking me to officiate at weddings and so on, so I thought I might pick up some sort of certification. As I was looking around, I became connected with an actual seminary—something I would never have imaged for myself.

When I called the teacher, who was wintering in Florida, she said, "I'm so sorry, my dear, but we had to close the seminary five years ago, so I'm afraid I can't help you."

We talked for awhile about other things, and I was thinking in the back of my mind, *This is silly anyway, I already have several advanced degrees—including a doctorate. The last thing I need is another degree.*

Suddenly she paused and said, "Hold on a minute. Wait." The line went dead. Just as suddenly she came back on and said, "I'm being guided by *God* to open the seminary for you." She said, "I have to fly back to Pennsylvania to get the course work out of storage."

That was that. For four years, I studied—under her tutelage by mail—Comparative World Religions I & II—Taoism, Confucianism, Buddhism, Hinduism, Zoroastrianism, Judaism, Christianity, Islam, Earth-Based Religions—Principles of Metaphysics I & II, Great World Teachers, Ministerial Counseling, Techniques of Meditation and Prayer, Techniques of Inner Self Healing, Color, Music, The Western Mystery Tradition, The Human Virtues, The Philosophy of Yoga, and The Cabala.

I studied many roads to spiritual consciousness and I saw that all roads lead to the center of the same extraordinary labyrinth.

Every spiritual map creates a meaningful context for living.

When my daughter was 10, her father took her to a Christian Sunday School, thinking she needed some religious education. The teacher, *a very nice man*, said to her, "Jesus is the way." Kätchen thought that over and replied, "Yes, I know Jesus is the way. Buddha is the way also." The nice man frowned, thinking about how to handle it. Finally he said, "I'm sorry about this, hon, but you're wrong. Jesus is the *only* way."

Kätchen came home crying and said, "Mama, do I have to go back to that Sunday School?" I said, "I've got an idea. Why don't you go back as a spy."

I am going back to Philadelphia to be *ordained*—to receive the consecrated "order" of *Spirit*.

I entered the seminary for my own growth. The last thing I want to engage in is anything that is potentially politically devisive. Love is the only true protection, they say—and I am a woman of love. All other forms of protection, they say, lead to acts of war.

I was conceived in Philadelphia. That is where my parents were living when my father was finishing graduate school. Philadelphia is the place my soul flew in.

I wonder now, fleetingly, if I am returning to Philadelphia to be *reconceived.*

Phila—love of. *Delphia*—womb.

Philadelphia: the Cradle of Liberty, City of Brotherly Love, Independence Hall, Thomas Jefferson, the Masonic Temple with rooms to ritualistically celebrate the Oriental, Egyptian, Greek, and Roman Mysteries, General William S. Schuyler's Masonic Apron with Isis as Liberty holding the torch at the top. This apron was a gift to Schuyler from General George Washington; Schuyler was a member of his staff.

Philadelphia: freedom of speech, freedom of the press, freedom of religion, founding ground of the three pillars of American government—executive, legislative, and judicial—mirroring the Three Pillars of the Cabala.

Philadelphia: Benjamin Franklin in a toga, an incredible amount of street violence. I can almost hear Abigail Adams calling, *John, dear, please don't forget the ladies.*

Peter and I walked all over town.

We saw Thomas Eakins' "The Crucifixion" at the Philadelphia Museum of Art. Frightening. I wonder if I carry my great uncle's iconoclastic gene.

We saw the *Tarot of the Spirit* in the window of a bookshop on South Street. What a strange experience that was!

My dad always talked about the pursuit of happiness. Nobody said you were guaranteed happiness, he always said. The Declaration of Independence attempts to provide a social structure to give all Americans certain "inalienable rights," the rights for all to life, liberty and the pursuit of happiness, and within that structure, you have to search for happiness all by yourself.

It seems like when we find our own *nature,* we begin to discover our happiness. It seems like nature is the *key.*

Peter and I rented a car, crossed the Poconos and entered, at last, the Endless Mountains. We arrived at the Wyalusing Rocks on the Susquehanna River just in time to meet up with a caravan led by my teacher headed for a pow-wow of the Eastern Delaware Nations.

At the pow-wow, we met the Grandmother and the newly appointed Chief. The Chief told us he had much work to do, but he was young and his shoulders were broad. I respected this tremendously.

Then, as we went from booth to booth, sampling herbs and teas in the sweltering heat—I was drinking iced tea made from raspberry leaves because it was my time of the month and I was bleeding— we overheard many heated conversations.

"What is important to the tribes," one man said, "is the traditional and spiritual nature. There is no place for politics in traditions and spiritual life."   "Yeah," his friend answered, "That's what I was thinking, but I have never heard anybody say it."

"If these people who just want power want to go that way, just let them go and join the American president and the rest of those crazy people."

It was a hundred degrees. I bought a flute from Greg from New Mexico.

An Eastern Delaware tradition says that once in a lifetime, when a boy is young and strong, but old enough to begin to take responsibility, he goes out alone on a quest to find his song. When he hears his song, he knows who he is and he begins to comprehend his destiny.

That night, a song came to me and I played it over and over on the flute Greg made. It was beautiful and harmonious, but the words didn't come out until a long time later:

> *Life is just a dream in the making*
> *dream in the waking*
> *dance by a stream*
> *Life is but a song in the meadow*
>
> *deer in the meadow*
> *deer by the stream*
> *dance in the dream*
> *dance by the stream*
> *waken the dream. . .*

The night before the ordination, I can hardly sleep.

We walked out at sunset on the Wyalusing Rocks and stood on the cliff hundreds of feet above the Susquehanna River.

We walked the riverland, buzzing with birds, frogs, snakes, crickets, hummingbirds, rabbits, butterflies, locusts, ducks, swans, all manner of nature's wonderful creatures.

In the Victorian Inn, in the lovely, lacy room—I find I can hardly sleep.

My body trills with excitement.

I am ready.

We—there are six Ordinees, six for whom the seminary has been opened by the time I graduate: Deborah, Barbara Rose, Shane, Tracy, Rosemarie and me; all *women*—sit in front of the many witnesses, all our friends and family, in our long white dresses.

My womanblood is upon me. It is pouring out of me beneath my long white dress. I feel so powerful. I feel as powerful and as vulnerable as I have ever felt in my life. It is as if I am acting for my grandmothers and for theirs, for my granddaughters and my grandsons. I am the ancestress of the future and I am forging a life.

Our teacher stands up before the people. She says, "Most Holy and Glorious Spirit, Infinite and Eternal, Source and Life of all things visible and invisible, Thee we worship, Thee we venerate, Thee we adore. To Thee be praise, honor and glory, now and ever and unto ages of ages."

Then the people sing: *Heal in remembrance. . .Love in remembrance.*

Our teacher speaks: "Let us lift our hearts and minds to contemplation of things Eternal. The Contemplation of Spiritual Faith. We contemplate in adoration the One Spirit, Infinite, Eternal and Sublime, the Life Intelligence and Bliss of the Boundless Universe, who creates, maintains, and resolves all things visible and invisible. . .We contemplate in Reverence the profound mysteries of the Universe and the changeless reality of Cosmic Law, whereby all worlds are governed; the rotation of the heavenly spheres and the cyclic courses of the suns and planets, whereby destiny is unrolled and fate decreed; the rhythmic pulsation of life and the two-fold round of incarnate and excarnate existence, whereby humankind, through successive embodiments progresses toward perfection. We contemplate in Exaltation. . .Wisdom . . .Spiritual Power. . .Divine Truth. . .the way of attainment, the mystical union with Divine Being and Life Everlasting. . ."

She says, "Let us pray. . .," and all of us bow our heads reverently. As she speaks aloud, each of us silently meditates:

> From the point of Light within the mind of God
> > Let Light stream forth into our minds
> > Let Light descend on Earth.
>
> From the point of Love within the Heart of God
> > Let Love stream forth into our hearts.
> > May Love inhabit the Earth.
>
> From the center where the Will of God is known
> > Let purpose guide our little wills
> > The purpose which spiritual seekers know and serve.
>
> From the center which we call the race of humanity
> > Let the Plan of Love and Light work out.
> > And may we understand the Divine Plan.
>
> Let Light and Love and Power restore the Plan on Earth.
>
> Infinite and Eternal Being, who hast interwoven the visible and invisible worlds in mysterious union, grant that we may esteem as priceless treasure the inspiration flowing from Spiritual Realms. Teach us to know more fully that our thoughts, emotions, words, and acts create inevitable consequences, and that whatsoever we sow, that we shall surely reap,

to the end that we may guide our lives aright and grow in spirit. To the honor and glory of Thee.

Infinite and Eternal Spirit, who art manifested as True Being, Awareness, and Bliss, unveil our spiritual vision and unfold in us the faculty of discernment, that we may clearly distinguish what is permanent and abiding from what is transitory, what is real from what is unreal to the end that we may turn from vain and worthless things to those of enduring worth. Amen.

We listen to kind words. We break bread together, sharing of the same loaf. Together we sing. I cannot hear the words.
All the time I am shaking.

The stole which I have made is laid upon the altar with the stoles of all the other Ordinees. It is deep purple and rich cream. I can see the little red garnets I sewed on with gold metallic thread glowing all along the edge, sparkling jewels in the morning sunlight. Those are the drops of my womanblood. I can feel myself bleeding.
I am a woman who bleeds.
I am wearing a long white dress.
I am ready to be ordained.

I hear: ". . .Peace is my gift to the pure in heart. . ."
I hear: "Salaam, Salaam Aleikum. . .May the Grace of God, the Love of the Christs. . .be with you. . .be with you. . ."
Love of the *Christs!*

And now it is time. Now it is *time.*
She is speaking. She is saying, ". . .gathered at this time. . .Ordain the candidate for the Ministry. . ."
I am shaking. I am shivering.
We are asked to rise and step forward.
I am shaking and I hope I will not fall. I stand. I step forward. We are standing in a semi-circle facing our teacher, standing in a semi-circle with our backs to all the people. We do not make eye contact with each other. We stare deeply into our teacher's eyes. I am aware that I am standing up very, very straight. My white hair hangs down about my shoulders. My long, white dress hangs in folds to the ground.
I say to myself *Breathe. . .Breathe. . .*
I feel I am not breathing. I feel I might faint. *Breathe. . .*
My teacher addresses the people generally:

"Has this candidate been deemed worthy and is she willing to assume the spiritual responsibility necessary to hold this Ministry?"

Answer: "She is."

"Has this candidate been strictly examined and approved?"

Answer: "She has."

"Then let the Ceremony of Ordination begin." She turns to each of us. I am perspiring. I can feel a drip between my shoulder blades. I do not know if it is becoming as hot as it was yesterday afternoon at the pow-wow, or if it is just me. She is speaking to me: "Dost Thou solemnly declare on Thy honor that Thou has been led to apply for Ordination, not by any unworthy motive but solely by an impelling desire to help others?"

Answer: "I do."

"Art Thou willing to take the Vow of Ordination?"

Answer: "I am."

"Then, repeat after me: I, Pamela, of my own free will and accord—"

"*I, Pamela, of my own free will and accord—*"

"In the presence of the Infinite Divine Life and Angelic Forces in Spirit realms—"

"*In the presence of the Infinite Divine Life and Angelic Forces in Spirit realms—*"

"And of the witnesses here assembled, do solemnly and sincerely promise—"

"*And of the witnesses here assembled, do solemnly and sincerely promise—*"

"And vow that—"

"*And vow that—*"

I am repeating the vow, but I begin to repeat it blindly. I cannot hear what she is saying. I am speaking but I cannot hear myself speak. My awareness seems to move into another dimension. I seem to move into an altered state of consciousness. I cannot hear, and yet I answer. I am saying something about serving, something about offering myself in service.

Then my teacher says something about investing me with "all the rights and privileges. . ." Something about "in the Name of the Infinite, the Ineffable, and the Supreme. . ."

My teacher places her hands upon me, moistens her thumb with Holy and Blessed Oil. She makes a sign upon my forehead with this oil. She says I am anointed with Holy Oil and she says I am signed, which means I am receiving the power of Spirit, and that I will go forth in an abundance of the power of Spirit and Love and Light.

Then, she anoints the top of my head with Holy Blessed Water, symbolic, she says, of the outpouring of Truth. *May I think Truth. May I speak Truth. May I live Truth.*

Breathe. . .Breathe. . .It seems so long. I am weaving. I am swaying. *Breathe. . .Breathe. . .Do not pass out. . .Do not pass out. . .*

Then two people—two *women*—position themselves behind me, at either shoulder, to make three points of a triangle—the first point right before me is my teacher—and they place their hands upon my head and shoulders. My teacher speaks the words, *loud:* "RECEIVE THE POWER OF THE SPIRIT."

Suddenly, it is as if an electric current is turned on inside of me. It courses through my body. Coursing. Pulsing. Coursing. Pulsing. Electric. Charged. Exuberant. Incredible. No words. Wonderful. Blissful. Powerful. Outrageous. Outrageous.

It moves through my body like soft lightning, soft lightning—later they say my energy is soft lightning, they call me Soft Lightning—and the soft lightning pours out of my eyes and my eyes are crying, and the tears are flooding down my face but I am not sad. The tears are flowing, and they are tears of power, tears of current, tears of the ineffable flooding through my form.

The experience is awesome. It is awesome. Thrilling. Awesome. Indescribable. No words.

I am standing there awestruck. The teacher is blessing me. Her teacher lays on hands and all the teachers from all the dimensions lay their hands upon me, and the current flows. Riavek. Silver Reed. All the Sisters. They are with me and in me. The Metatron lays on hands. The attending Angels lay on hands. The Holy Ones. The Infinite Spirits. It is awesome. It is awesome. More people come, lay on hands. The energy increases. I am awestruck. The tears flow freely. I have never experienced anything that comes close to this in my life.

Then the current is broken.

"Let us pray: Infinite and Eternal Being, who through the Angelic forces has called this newly Ordained Minister into Thy Service of the Holy Ministry, send forth the power upon her in her execution of her Ministerial Office. Imbue her with an abundance of Thy boundless wisdom. Invest her with an influx of Spiritual power and inspire her to be a Light in Thy Service, a worthy guide for humanity. Amen."

My teacher picks up my stole from the altar—the stole I have so carefully sewn—and says to me: "Take Thou this stole, then, the symbol of authority and of the power of the Ministerial Office, and wear it as a living channel of the ever-flowing streams of Celestial Love."

She places the stole over my head and adjusts it so it hangs down beautifully over the folds of my dress.

I know then that I am Ordained.

Someone comes up behind me and lovingly adjusts my hair over the back of my stole. I feel the essence of love flowing from whoever it is who has stepped in to help me.

My teacher places in my arms a bouquet of flowers, pink and white carnations, and says, "I present Thee with these flowers as a symbol of the beauty of Holiness which Thou are henceforth to exemplify in ample measure before humanity."

She takes from the altar a silver Venusian cross with a purple amethyst in the top—*an ankh!*—and places it around my neck. "This cross," she says, "which I place on Thee, is the Venusian Cross. It symbolizes the circle of God over humanity."

I know: *The ankh is the circle of the womb, of life, of death, of blood, of the infinite Mother from which we all emit, of the infinite Mother to which we all return. The ankh! She is ordaining me with the ankh!*

I know I am in the right place. I know this is the right time.

"As I have ordained Thee in the Holy Apostolic Church, you are now unquestionably invested with genuine Apostolic Succession along ten historic lines. You possess valid orders whose ecclesiastical authority is, from every point of view, unassailably and absolutely sound. I now extend my hand in the welcome of fellowship and Love, and receive you into the body of the Ministry, which Thou will ever find willing to aid Thee in the performance of Thy spiritual tasks.

"And now a story," and my teacher begins.

She says, "Manly Hall, with whom I studied, told the story of the Indigo Cape, and this story I relate to you.

"There was an old master, a hermit who lived in a cave. In his 82nd year, he thought he must find someone to carry on his work. Seven years passed, and a youth who was lost, wandered into the cave. The old hermit believed the youth had been sent to him to apprentice, to carry on his work. He asked the youth if he was lost. The youth said yes, and they spent the next three years in a conversation talking about what it means to be lost.

"The old man wore a Cape which he never removed. It was the sign of his learning, his power, his understanding, and his authority.

"In his 93rd year, he felt he could no longer bear the weight of the Cape.

"He went for a walk, asking the Great Spirit to remove him from his body, as he was too old and he could no longer go on. He could no longer bear the weight of the Cape.

"When he came back to the cave, he found the young man fast asleep in his chair. He took off the Cape and covered him with it, transferring, in that act, all of his power to the youth. The mantle of power, understanding, learning, and authority was now released from the old hermit into the body of the young man.

"Again, the old hermit walked outside, preparing now to leave this life. He walked only a few yards when he felt a weight descend upon him. It became heavier and heavier.

"Then the trees and rocks began to fade. Everything around him began to disappear.

"He felt himself floating up and he realized a new Cape had been placed about his shoulders.

"This Cape was a much deeper indigo than the one he had relinquished. He opened out the cape like beautiful wings and the whole inside was full with fabulous solar systems.

"The Cape relinquished, Manly Hall says, is never traded for a lighter load."

Our teacher then turns to each of us individually and announces to us the task of our Ministry. Mine, she says, is to move into the White Cape. *You must let go the Cape you have worn,* she says. *It is time for you to take on greater responsibilities. You will adorn the White Cape. You will gather together the ancient family. You will learn from them and they will learn from you and you will guide them to the perennial wisdom. You will instruct them in timeless ways. You will teach the Ageless Wisdom and you will become a teacher of masters.*

I accept my task. I feel the White Cape descend. I feel the nature of whiteness within me. White is emptiness, the breath of spirits on the wind, bleached bones, the ashes of the dead.

I accept my task. I have much work to do, but, though my shoulders may not be as broad as the Chief's, I have *life* and my will is strong. I am ready. I will go forward.

"Let us pray. May this newly Ordained Minister be blessed in all her ways. May she rise and embrace the task before her. May she go forth in radiant energy. May she walk in the Light of Beauty. May she walk in Wisdom. May she walk in the way of Love. Now and Forever. Amen."

I am almost positive I can hear Riavek laughing mirthfully by the flowing stream. I know I hear the frogs and they are singing like a choir. Wondrous praises to the Sacred in us all. *Wondrous praises to the Sacred in us all.*

CHAPTER 15

THE SACRED CIRCLE

Creating Our Own.

After the ordination, Riavek no longer appeared to me on a daily basis. I was told I would receive the spark of Cosmic Fire and it would be up to me to fan the flames—and that is exactly what happened.

As I reflect now upon the events leading up to the ordination, I cannot help but feel that my story is about inspiration, that the Cosmic Fire is *inspiration*.

To *inspire:* to breathe in; to *spiral* in; to stimulate; to motivate; to guide; to dance a sacred rhythm through Life's twisting labyrinth.

Throughout the meditations, so much of my life was put into perspective. Now, daily, my life has become so marvelously radiant, so deliciously colorful, so exquisitely meaningful, that I desire—deeply— to help others find their inspiration.

We can learn to unlock the great bronze doors that seem to enclose us in particular coordinates of space, time, matter and belief. We can be *free*.

My work, I have learned, is to find a way to inspire existence, to awaken the inner sense of spiritual freedom, no matter what the external circumstances may be.

My work is to illuminate *soul*, the indelible, inerodable, personal connection with the turning and pulse of the universe; to encourage expression of the singular song, the special gift that each of us carries.

My work is to free the deepest internal truth, to create a burrow beneath the layers of education and socialization in the place where the soul resides, and then to begin to take that truth into a wise interface with the external world.

And my work is to help discover and create possibility—and considered plans of action—where it seems none exist.

My ministry—the Ministry of the Radiant Heart—is about activating imagination, taking the bare and empty skeleton of Life and layering it with the unparalleled riches of individual meaning.

As we find our own path, the way we live changes. Soul radiates outward and the soul of the world is moved.

To hear the song of our soul, we must be still and listen.
Then, when we hear our song, we must will ourselves to sing.

"Be still and listen. . ."
As I walk upon the blufftops, orange poppies shoot their pods of seeds out everywhere. I can hear them snapping, then I hear words so soft they feel like the child of a voice. *It is the summer wind, Skipper's tail against the sagebrush, the soft swish of pampas grass. . .*
*Be still and listen. . .*The words are so soft I can barely hear.
I think the question: *To what shall I listen?*
And I quickly hear the whispered response, breathing gently like a spirit's sigh: "Listen, my daughter, to *emptiness. . .*"

Be still and listen. Be still and listen. Be still and you shall journey in the labyrinth of the soul. You shall spiral into center and there you will hear your song.

We journey toward the heart of all and as we reach the labyrinth's center, we begin to hear the one song, we begin to dance the one dance, breathe one breath. . .know one love. . .
At center, we dance together, dance out universal love. We share our melody, our poetry, our steps. We learn to sing in Fire. We learn to dance on Water.
Then, we learn to hold the mane as we ride out singing, bareback, on the Wind.

The purpose of our journey is to learn to ride back home.

Love is the point of departure. Love is the point of return. Love is the goal and the goal is the source. The circle of the world is joined by Love.

The purpose of our journey is to learn that we *are* the love we sought without. We are children of the Universe, standing in love with the world at our feet.

We *are* the Universe: One Verse. One Song. One Turn. The rhythm of the Heavens. The music of Earth.

May love be with me!
May love resound in stillness!
May love blow through my heart
like winds through the willow.
May love flow through my heart
like the scent of sage in spring.
May love warm my heart
like the Sun's golden rays.
May love illumine me
like silver light from the Moon.
May love, like a fire,
burn a path before me.
May love, like the sea,
baptize me with pure intention.
May love be with me!
May love resound in stillness!

Can you feel the endless rhythm? Can you feel the pulsing vibration?

Our hearts throb together with the cadence of Love. Our breath sighs out the lilting meter. Our blood courses like music through our veins.

The power of Love is in me and with you.

The power of Love billows. A thousand blackbirds call greetings to a raindrop. Love! A bright red squash blossom opens on the vine. Love!

Love is the prophesy. Love is the message. There is a new prophet coming and she is called *Love*.

Love is the power of reception, the power of understanding, the unmitigated glory of the open heart.

Those who become receptive to Love's power shall prophesy. In their vulnerability, they shall become strong.

And there will be many: They shall number in the *billions*.

Our words will come. Our time will come. All we have to do is listen. Be still and wait.

We are learning the great secret. The great secret is the balanced and harmonious establishment of material energy. We are guided by spirit. We are guided by heart. We are guided by body. We are guided by mind. Spirit, heart, body, and mind converge in the sacred. In sacred realms we begin. To sacred realms we return.

We move in universal flow. We give up in order to gain, surrender in order to win, bend like the willow in order to be strong.

Take refuge in Love, my Sister!
Take refuge in Love, my Brother!

We shall reside in the heart of all as all the world creaks and spins. In the center of the world, we meet, and radiance streams from us.

At the center of the world, we sing, we dance, we join hands and celebrate. We celebrate the holy sacrament of Life.

My Ancient Family, I can feel you in my heart.
My Ancient Brothers, I have missed you!
My Ancient Sisters, we reunite at last!

CHAPTER 16

THE JOURNEY BEGINS

The Tools.

To minister is to serve, and now, dear one, with some excitement and some trepidation, I share with you a meditation to guide you into the spiral labyrinth that has the power to reveal the nature of your soul.

I am excited because I have experienced the awesome potential of the journey. I am a little worried also, because, as Hypatia has shown us, the path may entail frightful moments.

We must be strong. We must enter the labyrinth willingly and know, in our hearts, that every lesson illuminates. Every experience leads us closer to center.

I invite you now to join me in eternal time and space. I invite you to join me in pure inspiration.

Know that inspiration is spontaneous, but it may also require discipline and perseverence. It may take practice to open up the deepest channels. Do not give up until you reach the center. Keep on, keep on, and you will be rewarded with your own deep tale, the story only you can tell.

Know that if you are frightened, you can retreat to ordinary time and space simply by saying, "One, Two, Three, I'm Out!" You hold this power in the strength of your mind.

Know, too, how precious you are. Another like you has never been. Another like you shall never be. You are the treasured blossom blooming on the Tree of Life at the Garden's center. Be still and know that you open in Love.

THE JOURNEY

Be still.

Sit comfortably.

Breathe. Breathe. Close your eyes. Relax.

Take long deep breaths and begin to relax. Begin to relax your whole body.

Relax your body. Relax your mind. Relax your heart. Relax your spirit. Breathe deeply. Slowly.

Relax. Relax. Relax.

Let your breath come deeply. . .rhythmically. . .

Deep and soft. . .deep and soft. . .

Imagine a beautiful color, a color that feels inspirational, a color that feels creative, a color that makes you feel like creating. . .Imagine this beautiful color pouring over you like soft and gentle rain. Imagine this color pouring over you, flowing into your body, your mind, your heart, your spirit, flowing into you, flowing through you, like the soft and wondrous love of the universal energies.

Imagine this color, like gentle rain, moving through every pore of your body, into every cell, relaxing, relaxing, relaxing.

Imagine this beautiful color flooding gently into the region of your heart. . .relaxing. . .relaxing. . .relaxing. . .

Imagine that your heart becomes very peaceful. . .very peaceful, slow and open. . .tranquil. . .serene. . .

Imagine beautiful color flowing outward from the region of your heart. . .relaxing your chest. . .your lungs. . .your back. . .your solar plexus. . .

You can feel the relaxing energy of color moving into your spine. . .relaxing your spine from the top to the bottom. . .Your entire spine relaxes.

Breathe. Breathe deeply. Feel your heart relaxing. . .relaxing. . .relaxing. . .

Your shoulders relax. . .deeply relax. . .and it is as if a great weight is lifted from you.

Your arms relax. Color moves through your upper arms. Your elbows. Your lower armswrists. . .hands. . .your palms. . .all of your fingers.

You may feel warm. . .That is well. . .

Your neck relaxes. Your head relaxes. Color flows into your head. Color flows into your head and your head relaxes. Your head relaxes inside and out. . .

Your whole face relaxes. Your jaw relaxes. . .opens slightly. . .Your cheeks relax. . .your temples. . .your forehead. . .your eyes. . .

Your eyelids become heavy and relaxed. . .heavy and relaxed.

You become so relaxed, so relaxed, so relaxed. . .

Breathe. . .breathe. . .

Your scalp relaxes and even your ears relax. Your ears relax and every normal sound in your environment just takes you deeper. . .deeper. . .into a deep, deep state of relaxation.

Your whole upper body is relaxed and the beautiful color of relaxation begins to spread downward relaxing you. . .relaxing you. . .

All of the small muscles of your abdomen relax. . .your hips relax. . . your lower back relaxes. . .

You are so relaxed, so relaxed, and the feeling of relaxation begins to move down your legs, into your thighs. . .your knees . . .your ankles. . .

Your ankles relax, deeply relax. Your feet relax. . .the tops of your feet. . .the soles of your feet. . .every toe. . .

You are so very, very relaxed. You are so very relaxed. . .very relaxed . . .

Every fiber of your being is relaxed and filled with the wonderful color of inspiration.

You are totally relaxed. . .beautifully relaxed. . .

Float in the loving energy of relaxation and enjoy this moment. Relax and enjoy. . .Relax and enjoy. . .

When you are ready, let yourself go deeper into relaxation, deeper into relaxation.

Imagine yourself going deeper and deeper as you count from five to one.

Five. Go deeper.

Four. Go deeper.

Three. Deeper still. Deeper still.

Two. You are very, very deeply relaxed.

One.

Imagine that you drop down, down, down into the landscape of your deepest soul. Imagine that you travel deep into the deepest regions of your deepest soul.

Imagine that, as you journey, you are guided by the highest, purest, most loving powers of the universe. You are lovingly guided, lovingly guided, and so it has always been. So it shall ever be.

You are lovingly guided into the deepest realms where the deepest revelations are disclosed.

Take a moment to experience the guidance that is with you. You have been ever guided and so it shall always be. Feel the guidance. Know you are loved. Feel the love and know you are loved.

You will be shown something important, something very important about the path of your soul through time. You will be gifted with a revelation that illuminates your nature, who you are and why. You will be gifted with a revelation about the nature of your soul.

This revelation may come in the form of a vision. It may come as a voice, a sound, a color, a feeling. . .Trust your experience. . .Even the way you receive your own experience illuminates the nature of your soul.

Receive. Receive now. Trust your experience. Stay with your experience. Let it open. Let it inspire. Let it become more and more clear. . .more and more clear. . .

When you have found what you came to discover, give thanks for the loving guidance you have received.

Then begin the journey back from the soul's deep interior.

Begin to come back up. . .back up. . .returning. . .returning. . .

One. Your body is bathed in beautiful color, beautiful light.

Two. Returning. . .Returning. . .Your mind is bathed in beautiful color, beautiful light. . .

Three. Your heart is bathed in color and light, and your spirit is radiant.

Four. Your spirit is completely illuminated. Allow yourself to return fully to waking consciousness, bringing with you knowledge of the nature of your soul.

Five.

Open your eyes. Open your eyes remembering. Remember what you have learned. . .

As you open your eyes, dear one, your eternal soul greets the world!

How wonderful to see you again, my Ancient Sister!
How joyously I greet you, my Ancient Brother!
I bow to you, my friend, and I say to you with all my heart:

May every blessing of the universe
be with you on your journey.
May you walk the path in Freedom.
May you find your way in Love.

APPENDICES

WOMEN IN WESTERN RELIGION TIME LINE

B.C.E (timeline axis marked: 0, 1000, 2000, 3000, 4000, 5000, 6000, 7000, 8000, 9000, 10000, 11000, 12000, 13000, 14000, 15000, 16000, 17000, 18000, 19000, 20000, 21000, 22000, 23000, 24000)

CAVE AGE
Mysteries: unknown; *Symbols* cave paintings, female figures (Willendorf, Austria, c. 25000; Laussel, France, c. 20000).

STONE AGE
Catal Huyuk, Anatolia, and 3000 other sites where the Great Mother was revered; *Mysteries*: regeneration, maternity; *Symbols*: fish, bird, snake, deer, bear, tree, circle, spiral, female figure; *Temples*: above ground, painted with frescoes.

COPPER AGE
CIRCA 3500: **Avebury, England;** *Mysteries*: fertility and life cycle (pre-Celtic); *Symbols*: sun, moon bisexual snake/dragon goddess, pubic triangle; *Temples*: standing stone circles—henges.

UNDERGROUND SANCTUARIES AND MAZES
CIRCA 2200: **Ireland and France; CIRCA 3400: Egypt** (Dynasties begin); *Mysteries*: birth, death, resurrection; *Symbols*: personal gods and goddesses; *Temples*: pyramids. *Special Note*: Amenhotep IV (Akenaton) (1375-1350), teaches that divinity is contained in heat and light, symbolized by the sun; **CIRCA 3500-2500: Malta: goddess worship; CIRCA**

MYSTERY CULTS
CIRCA 1000-600: **Hebrew Mysteries:** Canaan, Ashera ("She Who Issues from the Womb") is worshiped. *Special Note*: King David suggests the ultimate power of Jehovah, a personal male god, circa 1000; writes psalms, the 104th Psalm is adapted from the writings of Akenaton. King Soloman, David's son, erects pillars to Ashera and writes the Song of Songs.

PATRIARCHAL POWER INCREASES
639-609: **Deuteranomic Reforms of King Josiah;** goddess-oriented temples and asheras are destroyed; **509-27: Roman Republic** dictates that women must marry before 18 and bear children for the Republic (legally enforced; women begin to rebel 100 years before the end of the Republic); **427-347: Plato** argues for women's equality; **356-323: Alexander the Great** spreads Greek culture into Asia Minor, Egypt, and India;

3500-500: **Ancient Near East;** *Mysteries*: birth, death, spiritual birth. *Symbols*: Inanna, Ishtar, Astarte (in Sumeria and Babylonia); *Temples*: ziggurats; **CIRCA 600: Crete;** *Mysteries*: maternity, procreation; *Symbols*: goddesses, serpent, bird, fish, tree; *Temples*: enclosures, pillars.

CIRCA 1000: **Zoroastrian (pre-Mithraic) Mysteries** begin.

Zoroaster (also called Zarathustra) begins teachings of the Zend Avesta.

600-400: **Greece: Eleusianian Mysteries:** *Mysteries*: separation, transition, reintegration; birth, death, rebirth; *Symbols*: turning of seasons, story of Demeter and Persephone, growth of complex symbology; *Temples*: pillars and chambers, female oracles; **47 B.C.E Library and Temple of Jupiter Serapis** in Alexandria burned by Julius Ceasar, documentation of ancient mystery schools survives.

PATRIARCHAL POWER UPHELD THROUGH DOCTRINE

?-67 C.E.: Apostle Paul admonishes students of the Greek Mysteries.

Late 200s: Library and Temple at Alexandria stormed under edict of Emperor Aurelian.

161 C.E.: Cabalism takes hold, Simeon ben Jochai sentenced to death by Lusius Verus, co-regent of Marcus Aurelius Antonius.

Special Note: Ain Soph as the conception of the divine becomes the heart of mystical cabalism which, in turn, becomes the cornerstone of Rosicrucianism and Freemasonry.

312: Roman Emperor Constantine is converted to Christianity.

4th century: Christian canon established. *Special Note:* Genesis becomes the official creation story, woman is subjected to man, the symbology shifts to male birth, death, and resurrection. Men are referred to as kings, chiefs, and family heads (see Genesis); women are stereotyped as evil, foolish, contentious, cunning, fond of self-adornment, led by impulses and easily led into idolatry.

391: Library and Temple of Jupiter Serapis stormed by Christians under the edict of the Roman Emperor Theodosius; the serapheum collection is destroyed.

415: Hypatia, Alexandrian mathematician, eloquent speaker on the Christianization of the pagan mysteries is torn from her chariot and killed.

PATRIARCHAL POWER UPHELD THROUGH VIOLENCE

Special Note: Exodus 22:18, "You shall not allow a sorceress to live." Deuteronomy 18:10-12, "There shall not be found among you anyone who makes his son or his daughter pass through the fire, one who uses divination, one who practices witchcraft, or one who interprets omens, or a sorcerer, or one who casts a spell, or a medium or a spiritist, or one who calls up the dead. For whoever does these things is detestable to the Lord; and because of these detestable things the Lord your God will drive them out before you."

500: Under Frank law, a witch's right to practice is recognized; **643:** Under Frank law, an edict against burning witches is declared; **634:** Stones at Avebury desecrated; **1000:** Crusades begin; **1144-1250:** 80 cathedrals and 500 churches of near-Cathedral size are built in France, all dedicated to the Holy Mother; **1225-1274:** Thomas Aquinas derides the female gender; **1252:** Pope Innocent IV issues an edict against heretics; **1257:** Torture of witches is officially sanctioned by Pope Innocent IV (remained legal in the Church until abolished in 1816 by Pope Pius VII); **1325:** Pope John issues a bill stating it is heresy to state that Jesus and the apostles owned no property; inquisitors become extremely wealthy; **1486:** *Malleus Maleficarum* is written by Dominican monks, Kramer and Sprenger (the printing press had just been in-

vented by Johann Gutenberg and one of the first books to be printed was the *Gutenberg Bible* in Mainz sometime before 1456; **1300-1736:** Up to 9,000,000 "witches" were executed; **Circa 1610:** Rosicrusianism and Freemasonry arise; **1776:** American Revolution, led by Masons; **1789-1799:** French Revolution, Masonic roots; **1792:** *Vindication of the Rights of Women* is written by Mary Wollstonecraft, published in England; **Late 1800s:** There is a feminist movement, women enter colleges and universities, openly practice as spiritualists, work toward suffrage; **1877:** Madame H. P. Blavatsky (born 1831) publishes *Isis Unveiled*; **20th century:** Women return to roots as wise women, ministers and priestesses; **1920:** American women granted voting privileges; **1993:** Anglican Church ordains women as priests.

LIFE IS JUST A DREAM
IN THE MAKING...

Life is just a dream in the mak-ing, dream in the wak-ing,

dance by a stream, dance in a dream. Life is but a

song in the mea-dow, deer in the mea-dow, deer by the stream

Dance in the dream, dance by the stream, wak-en the stream.

Music by Pamela Eakins. Transcribed by Taylor Haisch.

NOTES AND ACKNOWLEDGMENTS

CHAPTER 1. THE MOSQUE

Special Acknowledgments: The description of orgasm is excerpted from the volume edited by Susie Bright and Joani Blank (see Daphne Slade, p. 73; Daphne is not the student of whom I speak). The discussion of Islam is based on Huston Smith's teachings. *Mercy Oceans* was given to me by the "master of masters."

Bright, Susie and Joani Blank, eds. *Herotica 2*. New York: Plume, 1992.

Mevlana Sheikh Abdulla Ed-Dagistani En-Naqshbandi. *Mercy Oceans*. Konya, Turkey: Offset Printers, 1980.

Smith, Huston. *The Religions of Man*. New York: Harper & Row, 1958.

CHAPTER 5. LAI-ILA

Special Acknowledgments: While I was recording this story, my friend, Dr. Constance M. Piesinger, a Near Eastern archaeologist who has worked in Mesopotamia, was working on a dig in Oman. I sent her the tale of Lai-ila and asked her if she felt it was plausible given what we know about ancient Sumer. She felt it was entirely plausible and I felt encouraged to continue with the creation of *Priestess*. "Your breasts, my Bride, my Sister. . ." was inspired by the "Song of Songs" in the Bible which, some scholars have concluded, dates from ancient Sumerian times. For more information about ancient Sumer, see the following books:

Bauman, Hans. *In the Land of Ur*, translated by Stella Hum- phries. New York: Pantheon Books, 1969.

Kramer, Samuel Noah. *Cradle of Civilization*. New York: Time, Inc., 1967.

Mellaart, James. *Earliest Civilizations of the Near East*. New York: McGraw-Hill, 1965.

Oppenheim, A. Leo. *Ancient Mesopotamia: Portrait of a Dead Civilization*. Chicago: University of Chicago Press, 1964.

Perera, Sylvia Brinton. *Descent to the Goddess: A Way of Initiation for Women*. Toronto: Inner City, 1981.

Wolkstein, Diane and Samuel Noah Kramer. *Inanna, Queen of Heaven and Earth: Her Stories and Hymns from Sumer*. New York: HarperCollins, 1983.

Woolley, C. Leonard. *The Sumerians*. New York: AMS Press (1929), 1970.

CHAPTER 6. MERITATON

For more information about ancient Egypt, refer to the following books:

Breasted, James Henry. *A History of Egypt*. New York: Charles Scribner's Sons, 1909.

Davidovits, Joseph and Margie Morris. *The Pyramids: An Enigma Solved*. New York: Hippocrene Books, 1988.

Edwards, I. E. S. *Tutankhamun: His Tomb and its Treasures*. New York: The Metropolitan Museum of Art and Alfred A. Knopf, 1976.

Greener, Leslie. *The Discovery of Egypt*. New York: Viking, 1966.

Hoving, Thomas. *Tutankhamun: The Untold Story*. New York: Simon and Schuster, 1978.

Murray, Margaret A. *The Splendour that was Egypt*. New York: St. Martin's, 1963.

Pritchard, James B. *Ancient Near Eastern Texts Relating to the Old Testament*, translated by John A. Wilson. Princeton University Press, 1969.

Weber, Eugen. *The Western Tradition*. Toronto, London: D.C. Heath (1956, 1959, 1965), 1972.

CHAPTER 7. ALILAT

Note: Allat is the feminine form of Allah. Facts about the life of the Queen of Sheba are from the Bible. Other interesting references are as follows:

Heaton, E. W. *Everyday Life in Old Testament Times*. New York: Charles Scribner's Sons, 1956.

Keller, Werner. *The Bible as History*. New York: William Morrow, 1956, revised 1964.

Morton, H. V. *Women of the Bible*. New York: Dodd, Mead, 1941.

CHAPTER 8. ELECTRA

Special Acknowledgments: "Aisha, the cosmic order. . ." is adapted from *The Zend Avesta of Zarathustra*, trans. from *The Zend* by Edmond S. Bordeaux (Costa Rica: International Biogenic Society, 1973).

The following resources were extremely helpful in clarifying details of daily life in ancient Delphi and surrounding areas:

Baldson, J. P. V. D. *Roman Women: Their History and Habits*. New York: John Day Company, 1963.

Bouquet, A. C. *Everyday Life in New Testament Times*. New York: Charles Scribner's Sons, 1953.

Carcopino, Jérôme. *Daily Life in Ancient Rome: The People and the City at the Height of the Empire*. New Haven and London: Yale University Press (1940), 1969.

Hamilton, Edith. *The Echo of Greece*. New York: W. W. Norton, 1957.

Hawkes, Jacquetta. *Dawn of the Gods*. New York: Random House, 1968.

Kitto, H. D. F. *The Greeks*. Chicago: Aldine Publishing, 1951.

Mireaux, Emile. *Daily Life in the Time of Homer*, translated by Iris Sells. Toronto: Macmillan, 1969.

Quennell, Marjorie and C. H. B. Quennell. *Everyday Things in Ancient Greece*. New York: G. P. Putnam's Sons, revised 1954.

Robinson, C. E. *Everyday Life in Ancient Greece*. Oxford: Clarendon Press, 1933.

Spretnak, Charlene. *Lost Goddesses of Early Greece*. Boston: Beacon Press, 1978, 1992.

Zend Avesta of Zarathustra, translated by Edmond S. Bordeaux. Costa Rica: International Biogenic Society, 1973.

CHAPTER 9. HYPATIA

Special Acknowledgments: Thank you, James Wanless, for encouragement in a difficult moment as I was writing Hypatia's story. I thank Peter Brown for information about the Bishop Sinesius and the colorful contrast between the Greek and Christian teachings. I thank Eugen Weber for the ancient Sumerian prayer: "May the god who is unknown. . ." (pp. 31–32) which I adapted for Hypatia. Eugen Weber found this prayer in "Penitential Psalms, " tr. Robert F. Harper, in *Assyrian and Babylonian Literature*, ed. R.F. Harper (New York, 1901). I thank John G. Jackson for compiling references comparing the various sun gods. Thanks to Louise Paré, for sending me information relating Hypatia's death to March 12.

Socrates' dialogue concerning his vision is from Plato's description. See Charles Eliot, *The Apology, Phaedo and Crito of Plato*.

Years after I wrote this story, a book called *Hypatia of Alexandria* was released in which the author, Maria Dzielska, attempts to create a scholarly reconstruction of Hypatia's life. Unfortunately, however, only a few letters from her student Sinesius and two extremely brief contemporaneous descriptions of Hypatia survive as a testament to her values and teachings. Other writings exalting the legend of Hypatia appear from time to time throughout the next fifteen centuries. A few discrepancies emerge between Ms. Dzielska's conclusions and my own writing. These are Hypatia's and Theon's dates of birth and Theon's date of death. Sadly, unless more information about Hypatia is discovered, we will never be able to determine these dates via historical "fact." Further, whether or not Hypatia was initiated in the mystery tradition cannot be historically verified.

Borror, Donald J. *Dictionary of Word Roots and Combining Forms*. Palo Alto, CA: National Press Books, 1960.

Bouquet, A. C. *Everyday Life in New Testament Times*. New York: Charles Scribner's Sons, 1953.

Brown, Peter. *The World of Late Antiquity: AD 150-750*. New York: Harcourt Brace Jovanovich, 1971.

Dzielska, Maria. *Hypatia of Alexandria*, translated by F. Lyra. Cambridge: Harvard University Press, 1995.

Eliot, Charles W. ed. *The Harvard Classics: The Apology, Phaedo and Crito of Plato*, translated by Benjamin Jowett. New York: P. F. Collier (1909), 1937.

Greer, Thomas H. *A Brief History of Western Man*. New York: Harcourt Brace Jovanovich (1968), 1972.

Hadas, Moses. *Gibbon's The Decline and Fall of the Roman Empire*. New York: Capricorn Books (1962), 1969.

Hall, Manley P. *The Secret Teachings of All Ages*. Los Angeles: Philosophical Research Society (1929), 1988.

Hamilton, Edith. *Mythology*. New York: New American Library, 1940.

Jackson, John G. *Pagan Origins of the Christ Myth*. Austin, TX: American Athiest Press, 1988.

Kingsley, Charles. *Hypatia*. Blauvelt, NY: Freedeeds Library (1852), 1987.

Meadows, Denis. *A Short History of the Catholic Church*. New York: Devin-Adair, 1959.

Neumann, Erich. *The Great Mother*. Princeton, NJ: Princeton University Press (1955), 1963.

Taylor, Thomas. *The Eleusinian and Bacchic Mysteries*. San Diego: Wizards Bookshelf (1875), 1987.

Weber, Eugen. *The Western Tradition*. Toronto & Lexington, MA: D.C. Heath (1956, 1959, 1965), 1972.

CHAPTER 10. BITTEN-BY-THE-WOLF

Special Acknowledgments: The Saxon poem about Wergulu (p. 168) is excerpted from Paul Huson's *Mastering Herbalism* p. 267.

Barstow, Anne Llewellyn. *Witchcraze*. San Francisco: Harper Collins, 1994.

Blavatsky, H. P. *Isis Unveiled*. Los Angeles: The Theosophy Company (1877), 1982.

Davis, R. H. C. *A History of Medieval Europe*. London, New York, Toronto: Longmans, Green, 1957.

Ewen, C. L'Estrange. *Witchcraft and Demonianism*. London: Heath Cranton, 1933.

Greer, Thomas H. *A Brief History of Western Man*. New York: Harcourt Brace Jovanovich (1968), 1972.

Grieves, Mrs. M. *A Modern Herbal, volumes 1 and 2*. New York: Dover (1931), 1971.

Holmes, George. *The Oxford Illustrated History of Medieval Europe*. Oxford: Oxford University Press, 1988.

Holmes, Ronald. *Witchcraft in History*. Secaucus, NJ: Citadel Press, 1974.

Huson, Paul. *Mastering Herbalism*. New York: Stein and Day, 1974.

MacNulty, W. Kirk. *Freemasonry*. London: Thames and Hudson, 1991.

Previté-Orton. *The Shorter Cambridge Medieval History, volumes 1 and 2*. Cambridge: Cambridge University Press, 1952.

Stephenson, Carl, revised by Bruce Lyon. *Mediaeval History*. New York: Harper & Row (1935), 1962.

Waite, Arthur Edward. *A New Encyclopedia of Freemasonry*. New York: Weathervane Books, 1970.

Walker, Barbara G. *The Woman's Encyclopedia of Myths and Secrets*. San Francisco: HarperCollins, 1983.

CHAPTER 11. DIANA BROSSEAU

Special Acknowledgments: The numbers of witches killed are from historian Anne Llewellyn Barstow (see chapter 10). Stories of the "Witch of Newbury" and Mary Spencer are excerpted from Barbara Walker's *The Woman's Encyclopedia of Myths and Secrets* (chapter 10). The description of King Francis' entry into Paris is adapted from the National Geographic Society's book on the Renaissance. Divinatory meanings for *Les Sortes* are based on the Fifteenth Century *Visconti Sforza Tarocchi Deck*. Thanks to Stuart Kaplan for providing interpretations. For this chapter, I consulted all the books listed for chapter 10 in addition to the following books:

Elton, G. R. *Reformation Europe: 1517–1559*. New York: Harper & Row, 1963.

Kaplan, Stuart R. *The Encyclopedia of Tarot, volume 1*. Stamford, CT.: U.S. Games, 1978.

Kramer, Heinrich and James Sprenger. *The Malleus Maleficarum*. New York: Dover (1486?), 1971.

Masonic Museum, Philadelphia, private communication.
National Geographic Society. *The Renaissance*. Washington, D.C.: National Geographic Book Service, 1970.

Pierpont Morgan Visconti Sforza Tarocchi Deck. Stamford, CT: U.S. Games, 1975, 1984.

Rice, Eugene F. Jr. *The Foundations of Early Modern Europe: 1460-1559*. New York: W. W. Norton, 1970.

Russell, Jeffrey B. *A History of Witchcraft*. London: Thames and Hudson, 1980.

CHAPTER 12. PAMELA

Special Acknowledgments: The poem of Apollo, "From your throne of truth. . ." (on p. 226) is excerpted from Edith Hamilton's *Mythology* (p. 30). Artemis' Homeric hymn, "I sing of Artemis. . .," (on p. 227) originally composed by Hesiod, is excerpted from Nor Hall's *The Moon and the Virgin* (p. 114). The last verse of the poem by Mary Rogers (from *Earth Prayers from Around the World*, edited by Elizabeth Roberts and Elias Amidon, San Francisco: HarperSanFrancisco, 1991) has been altered from the original "Son of Peace" to "All-Illumined Child of Peace" (see *Earth Prayers from Around the World*, pp. 172-173). Information about geologic time is from the museum at Dinosaur National Monument in Utah.

Bhagavadgita. Gorakhpur, India: Gita Press, N.D.

Blazer, Lani. *Love is. . .*©1995. Inquiries: Pacific Center, Box 3191, Half Moon Bay, CA, 94019.

Cather, Willa. *Death Comes for the Archbishop*. New York: Vintage (1927), 1971.

Cowen, Painton. *Rose Windows*. San Francisco: Chronicle Books, 1979.

Daly, Mary. *Beyond God the Father*. Boston: Beacon Press, 1973.

Eakins, Pamela. *Tarot of the Spirit*. York Beach, ME: Samuel Weiser, 1992.

Evelyn-White, Hugh G., translator. *Hesiod, The Homeric Hymns and Homerica*. London: William Heinemann, 1967.

Hall, Nor. *The Moon and the Virgin*. New York: HarperCollins, 1980.

Hamilton, Edith. *Mythology*, New York: New American Library, 1940.

Hesse, Hermann. *Siddhartha*. New York: New Directions, 1951.

———. *Steppenwolf*. New York: Bantam (1929), 1974.

Kazantzakis, Nikos. *Zorba the Greek*. New York: Ballantine, 1952.

Kingsolver, Barbara. *Animal Dreams*. New York: HarperCollins, 1990.

The Koran. J. M. Rodwell, translator. New York: Dutton (1909), 1968.

Lao Tzu. *Tao Te Ching*, New York: Concord Grove Press, 1983.

The Open Bible. New York: Thomas Nelson, 1979.

Prabhavananda, Swami and Frederick Manchester. *The Upanishads*. New York: New American Library, 1948.

Rogers, Mary. "Deep Peace of the Running Wave to You" from Elizabeth Roberts and Elias Amidon, eds. *Earth Prayers from Around the World*. San Francisco: HarperSanFrancisco, 1991.

The Sepher Yezirah, translated by Isidor Ralisch. Gillette, NJ: Heptangle, 1987.

Waters, Frank. *Book of the Hopi*. New York: Penguin, 1963.

Woolf, Virginia. *To the Lighthouse*. New York: Harcourt Brace, 1927.

Zend Avesta of Zarathustra, translated by Edmond S. Bordeaux. Costa Rica: International Biogenic Society, 1973.

Zohar, translated by Daniel Chanan Matt. New York: Paulist Press, 1983.

CHAPTER 14. THE ORDINATION

Special Acknowledgments: The wonderful teacher of whom I speak throughout *Priestess* is the Archbishop Roberta S. Herzog. Thank you, Roberta, for your endless loving kindness.

CHAPTER 16. THE JOURNEY BEGINS

Special Acknowledgments: Thank you to Josie Hadley with whom I studied during the writing of this chapter.

For information about audio tapes for the "Spirit Jouney," write to Pacific Center, P.O. Box 3191, Half Moon Bay, CA 94019, USA.

Hadley, Josie and Carol Staudacher. *Hypnosis for Change*, 2nd ed. Oakland, CA: New Harbiner, 1989, 1993.

BIBLIOGRAPHY

Baldson, J. P. V. D. *Roman Women: Their History and Habits*. New York: John Day Company, 1963.

Barstow, Anne Llewellyn. *Witchcraze*. San Francisco: Harper Collins, 1994.

Bauman, Hans. *In the Land of Ur*, translated by Stella Humphries. New York: Pantheon Books, 1969.

Bhagavadgita. Gorakhpur, India: Gita Press, N.D.

Blavatsky, H. P. *Isis Unveiled. Los Angeles*: The Theosophy Company (1877), 1982.

Blazer, Lani. *Love is. . .*©1995. Inquiries: Pacific Center, Box 3191, Half Moon Bay, CA, 94019.

Borror, Donald J. *Dictionary of Word Roots and Combining Forms*. Palo Alto, CA: National Press Books, 1960.

Bouquet, A. C. *Everyday Life in New Testament Times*. New York: Charles Scribner's Sons, 1953.

Breasted, James Henry. *A History of Egypt*. New York: Charles Scribner's Sons, 1909.

Bright, Susie and Joani Blank, eds. *Herotica* 2. New York: Plume, 1992.

Brown, Peter. *The World of Late Antiquity: AD 150-750*. New York: Harcourt Brace Jovanovich, 1971.

Carcopino, Jérôme. *Daily Life in Ancient Rome: The People and the City at the Height of the Empire*. New Haven and London: Yale University Press (1940), 1969.

Cather, Willa. *Death Comes for the Archbishop*. New York: Vintage (1927), 1971.

Cowen, Painton. *Rose Windows*. San Francisco: Chronicle Books, 1979.

Daly, Mary. *Beyond God the Father*. Boston: Beacon Press, 1973.

Davidovits, Joseph and Margie Morris. *The Pyramids: An Enigma Solved*. New York: Hippocrene Books, 1988.

Davis, R. H. C. *A History of Medieval Europe*. London, New York, Toronto: Longmans, Green, 1957.

Dzielska, Maria. *Hypatia of Alexandria*, translated by F. Lyra. Cambridge: Harvard University Press, 1995.

Eakins, Pamela. *Tarot of the Spirit*. York Beach, ME: Samuel Weiser, 1992.

Edwards, I. E. S. *Tutankhamun: His Tomb and its Treasures*. New York: The Metropolitan Museum of Art and Alfred A. Knopf, 1976.

Eliot, Charles W. ed. *The Harvard Classics: The Apology, Phaedo and Crito of Plato*, translated by Benjamin Jowett. New York: P. F. Collier (1909), 1937.

Elton, G. R. *Reformation Europe: 1517–1559*. New York: Harper & Row, 1963.

Evelyn-White, Hugh G., translator. *Hesiod, The Homeric Hymns and Homerica*. London: William Heinemann, 1967.

Ewen, C. L'Estrange. *Witchcraft and Demonianism*. London: Heath Cranton, 1933.

Greener, Leslie. *The Discovery of Egypt*. New York: Viking, 1966.

Greer, Thomas H. *A Brief History of Western Man*. New York: Harcourt Brace Jovanovich (1968), 1972.

Grieves, Mrs. M. *A Modern Herbal, volumes 1 and 2*. New York: Dover (1931), 1971.

Hadas, Moses. *Gibbon's The Decline and Fall of the Roman Empire*. New York: Capricorn Books (1962), 1969.

Hadley, Josie and Carol Staudacher. *Hypnosis for Change, 2nd ed.* Oakland, CA: New Harbiner, 1989, 1993.

Hall, Nor. *The Moon and the Virgin.* New York: HarperCollins, 1980.

Hall, Manley P. *The Secret Teachings of All Ages.* Los Angeles: Philosophical Research Society (1929), 1988.

Hamilton, Edith. *Mythology.* New York: New American Library, 1940.

———. *The Echo of Greece.* New York: W. W. Norton, 1957.

Hawkes, Jacquetta. *Dawn of the Gods.* New York: Random House, 1968.

Heaton, E. W. *Everyday Life in Old Testament Times.* New York: Charles Scribner's Sons, 1956.

Hesse, Hermann. *Siddhartha.* New York: New Directions, 1951.

———. *Steppenwolf.* New York: Bantam (1929), 1974.

Holmes, George. *The Oxford Illustrated History of Medieval Europe.* Oxford: Oxford University Press, 1988.

Holmes, Ronald. *Witchcraft in History.* Secaucus, NJ: Citadel Press, 1974.

Hoving, Thomas. *Tutankhamun: The Untold Story.* New York: Simon and Schuster, 1978.

Huson, Paul. *Mastering Herbalism.* New York: Stein and Day, 1974.

Jackson, John G. *Pagan Origins of the Christ Myth.* Austin, TX: American Athiest Press, 1988.

Kaplan, Stuart R. *The Encyclopedia of Tarot, volume 1.* Stamford, CT.: U.S. Games, 1978.

Kazantzakis, Nikos. *Zorba the Greek.* New York: Ballantine, 1952.

Keller, Werner. *The Bible as History.* New York: William Morrow, 1956, revised 1964.

Kingsley, Charles. *Hypatia*. Blauvelt, NY: Freedeeds Library (1852), 1987.

Kingsolver, Barbara. *Animal Dreams*. New York: HarperCollins, 1990.

Kitto, H. D. F. *The Greeks*. Chicago: Aldine Publishing, 1951.

The Koran. J. M. Rodwell, translator. New York: Dutton (1909), 1968.

Kramer, Heinrich and James Sprenger. *The Malleus Maleficarum*. New York: Dover (1486?), 1971.

Kramer, Samuel Noah. *Cradle of Civilization*. New York: Time, Inc., 1967.

Lao Tzu. *Tao Te Ching*, New York: Concord Grove Press, 1983.

MacNulty, W. Kirk. *Freemasonry*. London: Thames and Hudson, 1991.

Meadows, Denis. *A Short History of the Catholic Church*. New York: Devin-Adair, 1959.

Mellaart, James. *Earliest Civilizations of the Near East*. New York: McGraw-Hill, 1965.

Mevlana Sheikh Abdulla Ed-Dagistani En-Naqshbandi. *Mercy Oceans*. Konya, Turkey: Offset Printers, 1980.

Mireaux, Emile. *Daily Life in the Time of Homer*, translated by Iris Sells. Toronto: Macmillan, 1969.

Morton, H. V. *Women of the Bible*. New York: Dodd, Mead, 1941.

Murray, Margaret A. *The Splendour that was Egypt*. New York: St. Martin's, 1963.

National Geographic Society. *The Renaissance*. Washington, D.C.: National Geographic Book Service, 1970.

Neumann, Erich. *The Great Mother*. Princeton, NJ: Princeton University Press (1955), 1963.

The Open Bible. New York: Thomas Nelson, 1979.

￼penheim, A. Leo. *Ancient Mesopotamia, Portrait of a Dead Civiliza-*
￼n. Chicago: University of Chicago Press, 1964.

Perera, Sylvia Brinton. *Descent to the Goddess: A Way of Initiation for*
Women. Toronto: Inner City, 1981.

Pierpont Morgan *Visconti Sforza Tarocchi Deck.* Stamford, CT: U.S.
Games, 1975, 1984.

Prabhavananda, Swami and Frederick Manchester. *The Upanishads.*
New York: New American Library, 1948.

Previté-Orton. *The Shorter Cambridge Medieval History, volumes 1 and*
2. Cambridge: Cambridge University Press, 1952.

Pritchard, James B. *Ancient Near Eastern Texts Relating to the Old Testa-*
ment, translated by John A. Wilson. Princeton University Press, 1969.

Quennell, Marjorie and C. H. B. Quennell. *Everyday Things in Ancient*
Greece. New York: G. P. Putnam's Sons, revised 1954.

Rice, Eugene F. Jr. *The Foundations of Early Modern Europe: 1460–1559.*
New York: W. W. Norton, 1970.

Robinson, C. E. *Everyday Life in Ancient Greece.* Oxford: Clarendon
Press, 1933.

Rogers, Mary. "Deep Peace of the Running Wave to You" from Elizabeth Roberts and Elias Amidon, eds. *Earth Prayers from Around the*
World. San Francisco: HarperSanFrancisco, 1991.

Russell, Jeffrey B. *A History of Witchcraft.* London: Thames and Hudson, 1980.

The Sepher Yezirah, translated by Isidor Ralisch. Gillette, NJ: Heptangle, 1987.

Smith, Huston. *The Religions of Man.* New York: Harper & Row, 1958.

Spretnak, Charlene. *Lost Goddesses of Early Greece.* Boston: Beacon
Press, 1978, 1992.

Stephenson, Carl, revised by Bruce Lyon. *Mediaeval History.* New
York: Harper & Row (1935), 1962.

Taylor, Thomas. *The Eleusinian and Bacchic Mysteries.* San Diego: Wizards Bookshelf (1875), 1987.

Waite, Arthur Edward. *A New Encyclopedia of Freemasonry.* New York: Weathervane Books, 1970.

Walker, Barbara G. *The Woman's Encyclopedia of Myths and Secrets.* San Francisco: HarperCollins, 1983.

Waters, Frank. *Book of the Hopi.* New York: Penguin, 1963.

Weber, Eugen. *The Western Tradition.* Toronto & Lexington, MA: D.C. Heath (1956, 1959, 1965), 1972.

Wolkstein, Diane and Samuel Noah Kramer. *Inanna, Queen of Heaven and Earth: Her Stories and Hymns from Sumer.* New York: HarperCollins, 1983.

Woolf, Virginia. *To the Lighthouse.* New York: Harcourt Brace, 1927.

Woolley, C. Leonard. *The Sumerians.* New York: AMS Press (1929), 1970.

Zend Avesta of Zarathustra, translated by Edmond S. Bordeaux. Costa Rica: International Biogenic Society, 1973.

Zohar, translated by Daniel Chanan Matt. New York: Paulist Press, 1983.

Peter Perkins

Pamela Eakins, Ph.D., counselor, teacher, and minister, received her doctorate from the University of Colorado at Boulder in 1980, then spent the following decade conducting research at Sanford University. She has taught at the University of Colorado, Stanford University, and the California Institute of Integral Studies. Dr. Eakins was ordained in 1993. For information about audio tapes and courses in spirituality and the ageless wisdom tradition, kindly write to Pacific Center, Box 3191, Half Moon Bay, CA, 94019, U.S.A.